As It Happened Yesterday (Krynki, Poland)

Translation of
Vi Nekhtn Geshen

Author: Yosl Cohen

Originally published in New York 1953

JewishGen
מרכז עולמי לגנאלוגיה יהודית
The Global Home for Jewish Genealogy

A Publication of JewishGen, Inc.
Edmond J. Safra Plaza, 36 Battery Place, New York, NY 10280
646.494.5972 | info@JewishGen.org | www.jewishgen.org

MUSEUM OF
JEWISH HERITAGE
A LIVING MEMORIAL
TO THE HOLOCAUST

As It Happened Yesterday (Krynki, Poland)
Translation of *Vi Nekhtn Geshen*

Author: Yosl Cohen
Project Coordinator: Susan Kingsley Pasquariella
Translated by: Beate Schützmann-Krebs
Cover Design: Nina Schwartz, Impulse Graphics
Layout: Jonathan Wind
Original Book Cover and Drawings by Note Kozlovski

Printed in the United States of America by Lightning Source, Inc.

Library of Congress Control Number (LCCN): 2023931945

ISBN: 978-1-954176-73-7 (hard cover: 332 pages, alk. paper)

About JewishGen.org

JewishGen, an affiliate of the Museum of Jewish Heritage - A Living Memorial to the Holocaust, serves as the global home for Jewish genealogy.

Featuring unparalleled access to 30+ million records, it offers unique search tools, along with opportunities for researchers to connect with others who share similar interests. Award winning resources such as the Family Finder, Discussion Groups, and ViewMate, are relied upon by thousands each day.

In addition, JewishGen's extensive informational, educational and historical offerings, such as the Jewish Communities Database, Yizkor Book translations, InfoFiles, Family Tree of the Jewish People, and KehilaLinks, provide critical insights, first-hand accounts, and context about Jewish communal and familial life throughout the world.

Offered as a free resource, JewishGen.org has facilitated thousands of family connections and success stories, and is currently engaged in an intensive expansion effort that will bring many more records, tools, and resources to its collections.

Please visit https://www.jewishgen.org/ to learn more.

Executive Director: Avraham Groll

About the JewishGen Yizkor Book Project

Yizkor Books (Memorial Books) were traditionally written to memorialize the names of departed family and martyrs

during holiday services in the synagogue (a practice that still exists in many synagogues today).

Over the centuries, as a result of countless persecutions and horrific atrocities committed against the Jews, Yizkor Books (Sefer Zikaron in Hebrew) were expanded to include more historical information, such as biographical sketches of famous personalities and descriptions of daily town life.

Following the Holocaust, the idea of remembrance and learning took on an urgent and crucial importance. Survivors of the Holocaust sought out other surviving residents of their former towns to memorialize and document the names and way of life of those who were ruthlessly murdered by the Nazis. These remembrances were documented in Yizkor Books, hundreds of which were published in the first decades after the Holocaust.

Most of these books were published privately, or through landsmanshaftn (social organizations comprised of members originating from the same European town or region) that still existed, and were often distributed free of charge. Sadly, the languages used to document these crucial histories and links to our past, Yiddish and Hebrew, are no longer commonly understood by a significant percentage of Jews today. As a result, JewishGen has undertaken the sacred responsibility of translating these books into English so that the culture and way of life of these communities will be preserved and transmitted to future generations.

In 1986, a group of farsighted JewishGenners started a project to pool their efforts together in groups based upon their ancestors from each town and donate money to get

the Yizkor books of their ancestral towns translated into English. As the translated material became available, it was made accessible for free at www.JewishGen.org/Yizkor. Hardcover copies can be purchased by visiting https://www.jewishgen.org/Yizkor/ybip.html (see below).

It is our hope that the translation of these books into English (and other languages) will assist the countless Jewish family researchers who are so desperately seeking to forge a connection with their heritage.

Director of JewishGen Yizkor Book Project: Lance Ackerfeld

About JewishGen Press

JewishGen Press (formerly the Yizkor Books-in-Print Project) is the publishing division of JewishGen.org, and provides a venue for the publication of non-fiction books pertaining to Jewish genealogy, history, culture, and heritage.

In addition to the Yizkor Book category, publications in the Other Non-Fiction category include Shoah memoirs and research, genealogical research, collections of genealogical and historical materials, biographies, diaries and letters, studies of Jewish experience and cultural life in the past, academic theses, and other books of interest to the Jewish community.

Please visit https://www.jewishgen.org/Yizkor/ybip.html to learn more.

Director of JewishGen Press: Joel Alpert
Managing Editor - Jessica Feinstein
Publications Manager - Susan Rosin

Notes to the Reader

The original book can be seen online at the Yiddish Book Center website:

https://www.yiddishbookcenter.org/collections/yiddish-books/spb-nybc200158/cohen-yosl-koslowsky-nota-vi-nekhtn-geshen

A list of all books available from JewishGen Press along with prices is available at:
https://www.jewishgen.org/Yizkor/ybip.html

Translator's Foreword to
"As It Happened Yesterday"

Yosl Cohen, who was born in 1897 into that small shtetl belonging to Russian Lithuania, not far from Bialystok, describes in "Vi nekhtn geshen" not only his childhood and the turbulent Jewish shtetl life, but also the truly exploding revolutionary movement that turned Krynki into the first workers' republic; and he does so with a ruthless frankness and fascinating sensitivity.

We learn details about religious, family and cultural daily life in the shtetl; we read in detail about the practice of leather tanning in Krynki and about the history of streets and neighborhoods. We learn the characteristic "Krinker dialect", and hear how the special "nicknames" of the families were formed. We take part in typical children's games in the courtyards and together with them we avoid the biting pigs in the marketplace.

We learn about the fierce disputes between Misnagdem and Chassids and receive the holy Shabbat together with Yosl Cohen and his family.

We see how a small town suddenly rises up, goes off the rails and becomes a center of the growing revolutionary, anti-capitalist and anti-czarist movement. It is the children who meet secretly in the forest and take a sacred oath to sacrifice their lives for their ideal; for a free, self-determined, just world for all.

We experience a time of upheaval and the germination of a great hope - the dream of building a new existence in America.

We accompany very young, naïve people who, with their commitment, become "heroes" in a way, but at the same

time bloody "perpetrators"; we see how the internal struggle escalates, especially between the anarchists and the social-democratic Bundists, splitting the movement; and we witness the great tragedy of the terrible anti-Jewish pogroms that sweep the country.

In order to clarify and deepen the political-social background, I have supplemented the translation of this book with many appendices. I went in search of traces within the Yiddish-language historical press and literature and included newspaper and book clippings, but also poems by the author.

My complete work, together with many translated poems from the author and photos from Krynki and surroundings is downloadable for free at this link:
https://www.jewishbialystok.pl/Krynki-Memorial-Book-Vi-Nekhtn-Geshen-translated-into-English-and-German,5407,8450

I invite you to join me on an extremely interesting, incredibly exciting, but also sad journey into Krynki's past!

Beate Schützmann-Krebs
March 2023
Germany

Dedication of the translator

I dedicate the translation of this book to my friend **Susan Kingsley Pasquariella** and to "The Jewish Place in Bialystok" www.jewishbialystok.pl

May the translation of this book serve the eternal memory of Jewish life in the shtetl Krynki; may it bear witness to those who lived there and used a language which, with its warmth and melody, carries light into our hearts.

May we remember its sound and the yearning that is vibrating in it to find a real homeland. May we be reminded of the ideals, hopes and aspirations of those people to create a new, more righteous world.

My transcription of Yiddish ("Romanization") is done according to the international YIVO standard.

https://en.wikipedia.org/wiki/Yiddish_orthography

In reverence and respect for the people who spoke and wrote the "old" Yiddish as their mother tongue, I refrain as far as possible from adapting the names into German or English. For these reasons, I also refrain from adapting the Ashkenazic pronounced Hebraisms.

My heartfelt thanks to JewishGen for making this translation possible as a printed book.

Beate Schützmann-Krebs

Geopolitical Information

Krynki, Poland is located at 53°16' N 23°47' E and 136 miles ENE of Warszaw

	Town	District	Province	Country
Before WWI	Krynki	Grodno	Grodno	Russian Empire
Between the wars	Krynki	Grodno	Białystok	Poland
After WWII (c. 1950):	Krynki			Poland
Today (c. 2000):	Krynki			Poland

Alternate Names for the Town:

Krynki [Pol, Rus], Krinek [Yid], Krienek, Krinki, Krinok

Nearby Jewish Communities:

Odelsk, Belarus 9 miles N

Kolonia Izaaka, Belarus 9 miles N

Vyalikaya Byerastavitsa, Belarus 11 miles ESE

Gródek 12 miles SSW

Indura, Belarus 13 miles NNE

Sokółka 16 miles NW

Michałowo 18 miles SSW

Jałówka 18 miles SSE

Kuźnica 18 miles NNW

Supraśl 18 miles W

Svislach, Belarus 21 miles SE

Mstibovo, Belarus 22 miles ESE

Lunna, Belarus 24 miles ENE

Wasilków 24 miles WSW

Sidra 25 miles NW

Zabłudów 25 miles SW

Volpa, Belarus 25 miles ENE

Ros, Belarus 26 miles E

Golobudy, Belarus 26 miles SE

Janów Sokolski 27 miles WNW

Narew 27 miles SSW

Nowy Dwór 27 miles NNW

Białystok 28 miles WSW

Vawkavysk, Belarus 29 miles ESE

Hrodna, Belarus 29 miles N

Skidel, Belarus 29 miles NE

Narewka 30 miles S

Jewish Population: 3,542 (in 1900)

Map of Poland showing the location of **Krynki**

יאסל קאהן

אריוסגענעבן פון

א גרופע טרייד יוניאן פירער

ניו-יארק

1953

Author's Acknowledgment and Dedication

An acknowledgement to the creators from the "book committee":

Yosef Breslov, Louis Galak and Yosef Dorfman, whose dedication has made possible the edition of this book.

*

Special thanks to:

David Dubinski (Dubinsky), Yakob Potofski, Louis Holender (Hollander), Izidor Nagler (Isadore Nagler), Louis Stalberg, Gedalye Rubin, Israel Horovits, Henri Grinberg (Greenberg), Benjamin Kaplan, Louis Nelson, Sasha Zimerman, Chaim Beker, Natanyel Minkof, Henri Shvarts, Louis Blak and Filip (Philip) Lubliner, for their friendship and help with the book.

This book - In memory of my uncles, aunts and cousins:

Dvoyre (Deborah) Sofer, Yisroel (Israel) Moyshe Sofer and his family.

Meyshke Pruzhanski and his family.

Khaye Sore (Sara) Pruzhanski and her two daughters- Fanye and Sheynke.

Yente Levin, her husband Yankel and their families.

Khayim Pruzhanski and his son Fayv(e)l, his daughter Khane and their families.

Yente and Osher Halpern and their families.

All of them perished at the hands of Hitler's murderers, may the names and the memory of our enemies disappear!

All Krinker holy and noble people who were destroyed by those murderers in the concentration camps,
in the Krinker ghetto and in the limekilns (crematoria).

This dedication shall be like an eternal light for their souls!

Cover Photo Credits

Front cover:

Background: *Krynki Impression,* ©2016 by Tomek Wisniewski.

Yosl Cohen, age 10, before leaving for America, 1908. From the original book.

Khayim-Osher Pruzhanski, Yosl's maternal grandfather, c.1905. From the original book.

19th century Kiddush cups from the family of Aba Yudel Krinker. Photo courtesy of Susan Pasquariella.

Back Cover:

Mashe Cohen née Pruzhanski, Yosl's mother, age 25, c.1905.

Krinker revolutionaries in the courtyard of Grodno Prison, 1905. From the original book. On the right is the hero, Nyomke Fridman (Nyomke, Hershl the "Kretsikns"); on the left, behind bars, is Leybke Noskes (Louis Sheyn).

Table of Contents

First Part

Grandma Rive

Second Part

Father's Family

Third Part

The Shtetl

As It Happened Yesterday
(Krynki, Poland)

53°16' / 23°47'

Translation of
Vi Nekhtn Geshen

Author: Yosl Cohen

Published in New York, 1953

Acknowledgments

Project Coordinator:

Susan Kingsley Pasquariella

Translator:

Beate Schützmann-Krebs

**Our sincere appreciation to Susan Kingsley Pasquariella and Beate Schützmann-Krebs,
for their permission to put this material on the JewishGen web site.**

This is a translation from: *Vi Nekhtn Geshen*;
As It Happened Yesterday, Author: Yosl Cohen,
Published by "A Group of Trade Union Leaders", New York 1953

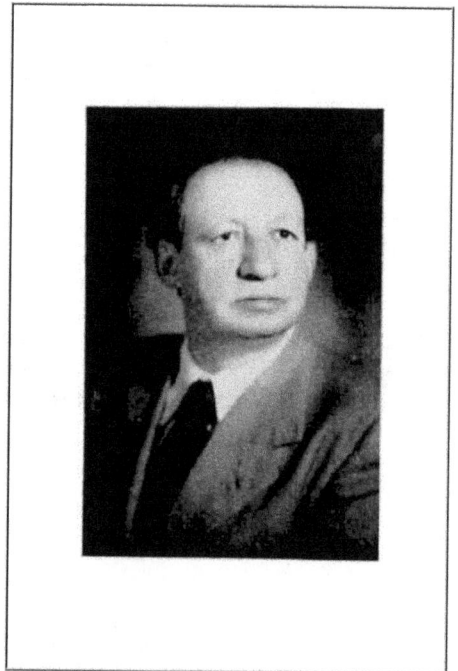

[Page 6]

<u>First Part</u>

Grandmother Rive

[Page 7]

My Grandma Rive

My Grandma Rive had the gestures and charisma of an aristocrat, only unfortunately, she had no principality to go with it.[1]

She came from Poland but a sad fate cast her as a young Jewess into a Lithuanian shtetl located in a valley between Bialystok and Grodno.

This shtetl Krynki, which connected itself with the outside world by ox and horse carts, resembled in all its characteristics all the other towns that were in the "Tkhum" (the Jewish residential area) of Tsarist Russia: There was the shul (synagogue), the Bote-Medroshim[2] and quite a few Hasidic shtiblekh (prayer rooms or houses) of Lithuanian Rabbis[3]; also a leather factory, which was among the second most important in all of Russia.

And there was a youth that was drawn to the wide world, dreaming of shaking off all the old habits and customs of their grandfathers and fathers to create a world of freedom, brotherhood and justice.

But the shtetl additionally housed its fools and quacks. And to tell the truth, it was precisely these characters who shaped life in the Jewish residential area and drove it dynamically. They provided variety and strove to create constant curiosity and expectation.

Well, actually such a small town full of "Misnagdim"[4] condemned everything that looked like noise and tumult as sacrilege against the Holy of Holies. But the cliques of schoolchildren had fun chasing through the streets and tormenting those miserable unfortunates who came to the town from Poland for income reasons.

That they had to laboriously move forward with the ox was still the least punishment compared to the torment inflicted on them by the adults, in the form of silent scorn and derision, but by the children, in a quite open manner, when they saw the Jews coming with their long caftans, the little "goles"(exile) hats and their strangely drawn-out, singing language.

The merchants, who even came all the way from Warsaw to buy leather, survived a few days of agony with misery, only to return to their families - far away from the Lithuanian rascals. It remained bitter only for those who had to settle down, either for financial reasons or as a result of a marital union with someone from the town.

And this very misfortune came upon girls from distant and foreign lands, who were destined to marry a lad from Krynki and had to move to their husbands to live the life of a kosher Jewess.

[Page 8]

They had children who were brought up to be Misnagdim and later probably also belonged to that crowd of school children who caused suffering to those Jews who so strangely lengthened the vowels "i"[5] and "o"[6].

It was precisely to this shtetl that Grandma Rive was banished - and thus torn away from her Jewish-Polish environment. And she was not spared from the attitude of the townspeople and for quite some time became the target of all kinds of mockery.

It was not only her language but also the strange contrast between the appearance of her and Grandpa Khayim-Osher that provided enough material for the small-town wisecrackers and mockers. She was tall and thin and behind closed doors they called her "Big Shabbat"[7]. In contrast, Grandpa was small in stature and had been nicknamed "Short Friday"[8].

But it was not that Grandma was annoyed that the townspeople were having fun at her expense; no, from the beginning it only aroused her defiance and stubbornness to maintain her otherness now more than ever.

She clung stubbornly to her Yiddish-Polish dialect and even many years later, as is still clear in my memory, she used to repeat her "nuu, vuus zoogstii" with special fervor[9] even longer and stronger and, on Friday, she entertained me with a piece of her potato "kigl".[10]

Which areas in Poland she actually came from, I could not find out to this day. After all, I left the shtetl when I was still very young. I never asked my mother, peace be upon her, about Grandma Rive's origin and so her place of birth is actually not registered anywhere.

Her appearance, not only in terms of the physical aspect, was certainly very strange for a Jewish woman at that time. She had a self-confident appearance and her own perceptions of things and events. And she did not give in so quickly.

As long as she was convinced she was in the right, it was hard to persuade her. If she was defiant she had to go through with what she thought was right, come hell or high water, even if it meant taking a risk with herself and her family.

My strange Grandma Rive!

[Page 9]

I was perhaps six years old when I listened to Grandpa Khayim-Osher telling the story of the shidekh, the marriage match between him and Grandma.

My Grandpa, a Slonimer Hasid, had married off his daughter, and as is the custom among the Hasids, they celebrated the "Sheve-Brokhes"[11] with large feasts. At long wooden tables the Hasids from the Slonimer Shtibl[12] sat, drank and conversed with stories and miracles of the Rabbi.

The Rabbis of other dynasties had been "excluded", and people gave themselves up to hours of continuous debate and joyful enthusiasm.

As for Grandpa's family, they were all Hasids of the Slonim dynasty and influential people, the richest in the city, and now they begged Grandpa urgently, to tell the story of the "shidekh" with his "Polish" wife.

Thereupon, such a whimsical story unfolded that everyone listened to Grandpa's sincere narration with open eyes, quiet as a mouse, while the grandmother's figure shone in its majesty in ever greater light. It spread, grew in height over the guests, and soon encompassed the shtetl and the whole surrounding area.

Grandpa's father, Yosl, had come to Krynki at that time from the village of Tsherezbug[13], which the town Jews mistakenly called "Tsherebukh".

He, a Jewish merchant, traded in wood and manufactures, and for this he traveled throughout the great "Tkhum Hamoyshev"[14], to Volhynia, to Rasin and Poland.

In a Polish town he befriended an innkeeper, moved in with him, and virtually became a member of the family there. The innkeeper owned a house, and in it there were children - but above all five grown-up daughters.

Yosl "Tsherebukh" was a passionate man, and one Shabbat, after the cholent meal, and after several sips of brandy, both Jews - Yosl Tsherebukh and Moyshe the Schenker (the Innkeeper) - decided to crown their friendship with a marital union.

"I," said Yosl, "have a lad at home who sits and learns diligently. An upright and honest man he is, and no financial problems he knows. So let us become relatives!"

Thus they gave each other the holy handshake[15] and after the havdole[16] they concluded the tnoim[17]. The day of the wedding was agreed upon, which, according to custom, was to take place in the bride's little town.

[Page 10]

When the holiday approached, Yosl returned from his journey and summoned Khayim-Osher to inform him that he was hereby a happy bridegroom. And to his near ones he informed that they may prepare themselves for the wedding.

Already several weeks before the wedding, the carriages with the groom and his closest relatives rolled out of Krynki. The roads were bad, and it was necessary to prepare for a lot of time that the journey would take until the arrival in the Polish town.

On the wedding day, they prepared for the (new) relatives in the bride's house. But from the "Litvakes"[18] there was not the slightest sign. They had lost their way. Night fell, but nothing was heard or seen of the "Litvakes". The bride's house was in a catastrophic mood. It was not until late at night that the message finally came, "They have arrived!"

The Poles ran out to receive the groom's family.

The bride was burning with curiosity: what does her intended one look like? Is he tall? Is he handsome? Is he a Jewish lad who resembles the son of the big landowner who always comes to the tavern with yellow boots and a whip in his hand?

Rive was a personality! A tall one, a confident one with brown hair and expressive eyes. Surely, she thought, he takes after Yosl, his strong, tall and broad-shouldered father with the thick blond beard.

Her curiosity drove her. Secretly, she sent one of her sisters downstairs to look through the window into the parlor where the men were staying and see what her groom looked like. It remains a mystery how her sister found out who among the many strange men was the groom, in any case, she told her sister that he was a personality.

But when the groom came and put the veil over her face, she saw him - and she felt sick. And when everyone was preparing to go to the "khupe", the wedding canopy, the bride refused to go. She would not budge. There was an uproar; they harassed her.

But she persisted:

"Naain, naain, for such a little creature I will not go!"[19].

Not even the moral sermons moved her. She remained stubborn. Her father's Rabbi threatened her with all the punishments of hell. Her mother fainted, her father screamed and raved, her sisters cried, and the "Litvakes" stood there quite perplexed and awkward.

"Why won't you go to the Khupe?" the Rabbi asked her. "A Jewish daughter must not shame a Jewish lad. It was finally decided to have a shidekh, by a holy handshake!"

[Page 11]

Bitter and difficult is the fate of a Jewish daughter.

"Rabbi," she said, "how can I marry such a little creature? The children will look like him!"

Thus the Rabbi pronounced a blessing on her:

"Your children and your children's children will not look like him!" So she gave in. This blessing had broken her stubbornness. But her dream was over. She went to the khupe and after "Sheve-Brokhes", she drove away together with the foreign Jews- away from her parents, sisters, brothers, friends, relatives and comrades; away from the carefree youth, from father's house, and from his psalm-singing on Shabbat evening.

She lost herself in the unknown, strange somewhere, among Jews with strange rituals and a strange, harsh language. There she went with the special blessing of the Rabbi, away to that "little creature"

Would the blessing come true?

[Page 12]

My Grandma Rive

Translator's footnotes:

1.   somewhat freely translated
2.   Plural of בית-מדרש = A Bes-(Ha)medresh is primarily a house for studying the Talmud, but it is also used as a synagogue (shul).
3.   רביים = rebeyem, also rabeim, Plural of "rebe", Hasidic Rabbis.
4.   מתנגדים = Misnagdim: Plural of misnaged, Lithuanian Hasidic opponents, pious Jews who are more rationalist in orientation and do not believe in a mystical miracle Rabbi; sometimes used as a synonym for "Litvaks", Lithuanians.
5.   חיריק = Khirek or Hiriq= a Hebrew punctuation mark, pronounced ee or i, see https://www.ivritalk.com/hebrew-vowel-signs-explained
6.   חולם = Kholem or Hulam= a Hebrew punctuation mark, pronounced o, see https://www.ivritalk.com/hebrew-vowel-signs-explained. Vowel signs can also be used for Yiddish Hebraisms, but may differ slightly in meaning
7.   שבת-הגדול = the "great Sabbath before Passover"
8.   = "Short Friday" = Friday evening, or a few minutes before sunset, the Sabbath begins, and certain activities may not be performed then according to Jewish religious law, the Halakha. Work is stopped earlier, and since many arrangements must also be made, the day appears shorter.
9.   Now, what are you thinking about? Not only did she stretch the vowels, but, in keeping with her dialect, she also interchanged the "u" with the "i".
10.   potato-kugel, see https://www.thespruceeats.com/classic-potato-kugel-2122379
11.   שבע - ברכות = the "7 blessings", the gathering of the guests in the house of the newlyweds on the Friday evening after the wedding.
12.   Slonimer shtibl= Prayer house of the Hasids of the Slonimer dynasty.
13.   Tsherezbug, „через (реку) Буг"= across the river Bug.
14.   תחום-המושב = permitted residential area for Jews in tsarist Russia.
15.   תקיעת-כּף = Word of honor, sacred promise by handshake.
16.   הבדלה = havdole, havdala, ceremony at the end of the Sabbath.
17.   תנאים =, Tnoim, written contract before marriage.
18.   litvakes= Lithuanian Jews, who often had the reputation of being particularly rationalistic and skeptical, in addition to their excellent Talmudic scholarship. The term is also commonly used as a synonym for opponents of the Hasids ("Misnagdim"). In fact, there were heated arguments and even hostile clashes between the two groups.
19.   "No, no…"

[Page 13]

A Stranger in the Shtetl

Grandma Rive not only brought the Rabbi's "brokhe" (blessing) , but also her Yiddish-Polish dialect with her to the shtetl. Never before had she embraced the strange flavor of her language as she did there, after her arrival in the valley of the little Lithuanian town.

Because there it had an important meaning for her. With the help of her long-drawn dialect, she was able to maintain a connection with her (former) household: her father, her mother, her brothers, her sisters, with her old home, and not least, with all her dreams.

Her Yiddish-Polish language only aroused in her more resistance to the new town, to the Jews there, and to the "little creature" who had become her husband. The more people were amused by her linguistic expression, the more doggedly she clung to it. She took particular pleasure in using her dialect in front of the townspeople.

On purpose she came to the butcher's store just when it was crowded with other customers, and in her serene but very drawn-out way of speaking, she used to order the "find flaisch" (pound of meat) or ask for a "ling" (lung).

The women then winked at each other, laughed silently to themselves, and looked at her like a savage who, God forbid, had been dragged from far away places.

The winking and laughing, however, only made her prouder. She looked the women straight in the eye and, with a tossed "gitn tung" (good day), she then strutted through the streets, basket in hand, toward her house feeling very pleased with herself for being "different"; after all, she was the only one who had attracted special attention.

And Grandma wanted to be "different" with all her might! She wanted to make everyone feel, and know, that she stood out from others and went her special way.

She loved to grab attention in her surroundings and impress everyone, be it with her confident figure or even with her different language.

Everything that happened outside, she tolerated. But in her house she shaped every little corner and took all activities there into her hands.

Grandpa was only the "little one." He was not really of substance to her, but only a something that had been grafted onto her through the Rabbi's blessing. And that very blessing created in her a martyr complex.

[Page 14]

She believed,that it was her destiny to suffer for the sake of the "brokhe". The blessing lived in her and gave her hopes for later, both in the form of children and grandchildren, and for a happy afterlife[1] that would be granted to her: namely, for the mitsve[2] to tolerate such a man, such a shtetl with such Jews, and on top of that to have been chased away and cast out into homelessness, away from her parents and neighbors.

Rive now lived only for the brokhe. With great anxiety she watched her first child grow up. What would happen if the brokhe did not come true and her boy, Perets, took after his father? So time passed, and one day she saw that the boy was already taller than his father. The brokhe had indeed come true!

All of a sudden, Rive felt that she had taken root. Everything now belonged to her: the shtetl, its people and also its language!

After all, it was the language of her son - and the blessing was revealed through him; because of him, hopes and dreams were revived. Her son did not speak like her; to him his mother's different way of speaking sounded rude and weird, and when she called him with "kimm ahier!"[3], it seemed strange to him.

However, if she now spoke like her son, it would create a close relationship. But if not, she thought, he would, after all, become very much like his father; for the boy was simply more familiar with his father's mannerisms and his way of speaking.

Thus, Rive began to listen more closely to the sound of the Yiddish-Lithuanian dialect. She tried to communicate better with her son - and with her other children who were born year after year.

She began to alienate herself from her dialect, with all its elongations, and to reject it. She got used to saying "meat" and "come here." But on those days, when she was stricken with loneliness and sorrow, she would stretch out on the bed, dressed as she was, and stare at the ceiling remembering, in Yiddish-Polish dialect, her youth in the shtetl with her parents and all those close to her.

And so there were times when she wept bitterly, with longing and the pain of life, over her fate; the terrible estrangement from all who had been near and familiar to her and had caressed her.

The duties of life and the bustle of children soothed her longing a little.

Then, all at once, she realized that it was imperative that she keep a watchful eye on all things, even the smallest, for otherwise everything would crumble like dust.

[Page 15]

Rive realized that she could not rely on her husband. The financial support that her father-in-law, Yosl "Tsherebukh" had granted the young couple for 5 years had already been exhausted. However, three new little souls had already been added in exchange.

Khayim-Osher simply did not know how to face the duties of daily life. He did not know what occupation he could pursue to provide a living for all the family members.

His father Yosl had grown older and did not want to travel around. He limited his business to the surrounding area.

In his hands was the entire trade of "dub". This was an article made from tree bark, which after a drying process was crushed and sold to the leather manufacturers.

This shredded bark called "dub" was very important for the processing of leather, especially for the "wet" tanning techniques[4]. Yosl also took the "Korobke"[5] of the shtetl under his wing.

As Yosl grew even older, one of the younger sons, Yisroel-Toivye (Tuvia) took over the business. Yisroel-Toivye was completely different from his older brother, Khayim-Osher, both in appearance and in his approach to life in business matters.

Yosl Tsherebukh began to rely completely on his younger son, while he himself was engaged in "Toyves-Haklal"[6]. Yosl strongly engaged in city affairs and, with his own money, built a Bes-Hamedresh, which became known as "Kavkazer Bes-Hamedresh". The name was given to this "House of Prayer" because of the area, or rather, district of the city, which was called "Kavkaz" (Caucasus).

Once upon a time, the "strong boys" of the shtetl had lived there, a gang known as "Akhim"[7], "the brothers".

In his Bes-Hamedresh, Yosl assumed the function of a "Gabbai"[8]. He was engaged in charity, and when travelers stopped for a rest in Krynki, they knew only too well that when they arrived at the "Kavkazer Bes-Hamedresh," everything would be taken care of: a night's lodging and a meal for the guests.

As long as Yosl lived, he took care of Khayim-Osher and his household. Khayim-Osher, meanwhile, sat in his father's Bes-Hamedresh and studied.

During that time, the Yeshive[9] was also housed in the Bes-Hamedresh, and Khayim-Osher studied[10] there along with the Talmud students.

[Page 16]

It seems that Khayim Osher's family never really lived comfortably and contentedly.

Khayim Osher was a Jew who did not care about all worldly-material things. A desire for wealth seemed foreign and absurd to him, and so he looked with disdain upon his younger brother Yisroel-Toivye and his commitment to material pleasures.

He had his own philosophy of life. Like all very pious people, he regarded the earthly world as a kind of antechamber through which a person had to pass in order to reach the afterlife. The true profession of a Jewish person, he used to say, was to accumulate as many mitsves as possible in order to earn a (happy) existence in the world to come.

As a result of his attitude to life, money meant nothing to him; in fact he did not know what it was exactly.

I still remember how, in his old age, he took the greatest pleasure in warming himself in winter by the stove of his son-in-law Dodye, the baker.

His whole attitude toward life becomes even clearer when I relate the following:[11]

The wealthiest people of the town, all factory owners and merchants, belonged to his family. Nokhem-Anshel Kinishinski, the biggest leather manufacturer of Krynki, was his "cousin" (on his wife's side). The latter, that is, Nokhem-Anshel's wife Roshke, was Khayim-Osher's biological sister's child (niece)[12].

Grandma Rive was not only very angry about her poverty, but also about the fact that her husband was so indifferent to worldly life and did not feel the need to provide his family with at least the bare necessities.

She constantly compared him with his rich relatives to make him realize even more what a good-for-nothing he was.

"Now just look at Nokhem-Anshel!" she criticized him bitterly, "of the same family he is, of the same blood and flesh! But he's an influential, distinguished man - and you can't even manage to support your family!"

But Khayim-Osher never got upset about it. He did not get excited, but tried to make her understand in his soothing way how null and void[13] human "tkifes" were.[14]

Then, when she had calmed down a bit and unloaded all her grievances, Khayim-Osher used to calmly explain to her:

"What is the value of man's wealth? What happened yesterday is already over, so what difference does it make now?

Well, a person may have eaten something better yesterday, but then it is already gone - eaten up! And in relation to today? Well, it does not matter, Nokhem-Anshel eats just a piece of meat and I eat only dry bread, however, we both are alive!

But tomorrow? You see, this is important: what tomorrow is, none of us knows, I don't and he doesn't either! The future is in God's hands!

[Page 17]

And so we must ask Him and place our hopes for the future in Him!"

When his father Yosl was alive, Khayim-Osher never demanded anything from him, nor did he mind that his younger brother, Yisroel-Toivye, had brought all of his father's business enterprises under his supervision and control.

In my grandmother, however, it blazed like fire. She used to make demands of her father-in-law, but Yosl rejected them. He did not want to put the management of his business in Khayim-Osher's hands. However, he promised her that Khayim-Osher would never do anything wrong in the next 120 years.

And besides, he would receive his share of the inheritance.

However, Khayim-Osher was not destined to become an heir. His father died suddenly of a stroke while praying. And the sole heir of the legacy became Yisroel-Toivye.

Translator's footnotes:

1. עולם-הבא= Literally, "the world to come," the world beyond, where the pious will be rewarded after death.
2. מצווה= This term, "mitsve" does not occur here in the original text, but since there is a reference to it later, I use it here for better comprehensibility. A mitsve is a commandment according to Jewish religion, a good deed.
3. kim ahier: Her dialect instead of "kum aher", come here.
4. "wet leatherworks": The wet leather passed through two rollers whose pressure could be regulated. This pressed residual moisture out of the leather.
5. „korobke"= „Kosher Tax", see https://en.wikipedia.org/wiki/Kosher_tax
6. טובת-הכלל= toyves-haklal, literally "the good in the whole," social benefit, collective interest, charity.
7. אחים= Akhim (Okhim)=Brothers

8. גבאי = "Gab(b)ai", the Hebrew term for a responsible secretary, among others, in the congregation or synagogue, also "treasurer", in Yiddish "gabe". In terms of activity similar to the "Shames", the synagogue servant.

9. ישיבֿה = Yeshive, Talmud school, Jewish college for Jewish young men (="bokherim").

10. ler(e)nen= This word has a double meaning in Yiddish, it can mean "learn" but also "teach".

11. no literal translation

12. "shvesterkind"= actually the English translation is "cousin", but here the niece is meant. We will encounter this phenomenon more often in the book.

13. הבֿל-הבֿלים = literally "breaths of breaths", "nothingness of nothingnesses", a term denoting something void, impermanent, this Hebrew term is the subject of the third part (Ketuvim) of the "Tanakh", in the book of "Kohelet" (Koh 1,2).

14. תקיפֿות = Stubbornness, cockiness, the desire to force, determination, authority.

[Page 18]

Grandpa becomes a Shames

Yosl Tsherebukh's sudden death left all his children orphaned. His inheritance remained exclusively in the hands of Yisroel Toivye.

Besides Grandpa Khayim Osher and Yisroel-Toivye, Yosl had had a son and a daughter.

His daughter Shoshke's husband was a leather manufacturer and, for various reasons, had to flee to America.

One of the sons, Borekh Mair (Meyer), traveled to Wolin, married there, and was not heard from again until, some twenty years later, he came to Krynki to earn a dowry for his daughter.

Khayim Osher did not resent the fact that the complete inheritance had passed to his brother; he never fought for his own claims and was never angry with him. But Grandma could not accept this and found no peace. She dragged Yisroel Toivye to the Rabbi and used to litigate against him constantly.

And there was not a single thing that Grandma Rive did not finish.

But what she ultimately achieved was to sow discord in Yisroel Toivye's entire family. In connection with the inheritance, she also made sure that the inheritors took the surname "Tsherebukh" as a legacy. But pronouncing and associating this surname used to mean scorn and enmity. This name became a synonym of wickedness. Now forever the descendants of Yisroel Toivye remained the "Tsherebukhs".

After Yosl Tsherebukh's death, the need became even greater. Grandpa Khayim Osher became a "Gemore teacher"[1]. All "Khosn-Bokherim"[2] learned with him.

However, to all appearances, he did not derive any income from it. He himself only dealt with the subject matter.

And so Grandma had to go out herself to collect the school fees, which brought her very little. In the end she persuaded Grandpa to give up his teaching job and look for a new livelihood.

Well, the naive Grandpa Khayim-Osher, what could be suitable for him?

He was not suited to, and did not have the right attitude towards, regular work. He had no idea at all of what people called "khayune"[3].

Grandma made heaven and earth move. In addition to providing a permanent livelihood, there was also the dowry for the daughters to think about.

[Page 19]

The oldest boy, Perets, was sent to an apprenticeship as a "Toker" (turner). And until the end of his life, his work was associated with his name: The townspeople called him: "Perets, the Toker".

The only thing that came to mind for Grandpa was to become an employee of the Jewish community. And since his father had built the "Kavkaz" Bes-Hamedresh, Grandma Rive came to the conclusion that Grandpa was entitled to the position of a Shames, a synagogue servant, in this Bes-Hamedresh.

They went to Yisroel Toivye, the community gathered and Grandpa became, "with Mazel" (luck), the Shames in the Bes-Hamedresh that his father had built. This probably remained all the inheritance he received.

The larger the family and the older the children became, the more Grandma took control of the family members into her hands.

Grandpa did not wrestle with her for leadership and influence. In general, he did not concern himself with what happened in the house, because it was not there that his center of life was, but only in the Bes-Hamedresh.

Grandpa's words were not followed anyway, because he never insisted on their abidance. Rive had begun to run everything with a sure and strong hand. She introduced a strict discipline and none of the children ever dared to contradict her.

She not only dealt with their education, but also regulated their lifestyle and behavior.

She chose the professional activities for the children and likewise determined their spouses.

Inside, her children may not have loved her. Well, she herself did not receive love and attention from her own life either. Her influence was limited to a few family members. In the shtetl, however, she remained a stranger. For the "Litvakes", the Lithuanians, she remained a "stranger from the boondocks", and they punished her by calling all of her children, except for Perets, whom they gave the surname "the Toker", after their father's name and not hers.

So they added the name of the father to the first name of each of their children. Such as: Mashe Khayim Osher's, Yisroel Khayim Osher's, Yente Khayim Osher's.

She hated the rich and distinguished relatives, but at the same time tried to betroth her children to the rich and powerful. Because through the marital connections of the children, she herself hoped for a more elevated status within society.

[Page 20]

She could not stand the rich and powerful, and would not tolerate Grandpa going to them now and then as a guest for a meal. She herself also never wanted to come to them for family celebrations or feasts, and usually punished Grandpa for it when he visited the rich Nokhem Anshel for "honey cake and schnapps".

He used to keep his guest visit a secret from her. But Rive noticed immediately if he had been there. For Nokhem Anshel's wife Roshke, it was a custom to invite Grandpa on the days before parties for "honey cake and schnapps". Then, when he came home a little tipsy, Grandma already knew where he had been and not only scolded him, but also inflicted suffering on him.

It was easy to deceive my Grandpa. He could not understand at all how one person could deceive and cheat another. He simply believed everything.

For him, life in this world had only one purpose: to do good deeds and behave like a decent Jew.

He did not need to recite lies and tell fibs. His life was oriented in such a way that he did not feel the need to deceive anyone or obtain anything by trickery.

His credulity was a nuisance for Rive. She thought he was a good-for-nothing and controlled him with a hawk's eye. However, even she could not prevent him from being seduced or deceived.

For her, it was considered an act of stupidity and clumsiness to be invited by the rich relatives.

But just as he had a lot of problems because of her, it was also the other way around. He also caused her heartache because of his diminished sense of reality.

His relatives knew him only too well, and a few times tried to exploit him for their own benefit.

Khayim Osher felt very sorry for Rive. He wanted to win her over with something in view of her difficult life, but he did not know how and with what.

Grandma Rive, with all her stubbornness, also had a tendency to faint. When she realized that she was absolutely no match against certain odds, she used to suffer a fainting fit.

Often, this was a hysterical reaction, but a few times it was also done to attract attention.

The fainting fits she played on the children, namely when a child refused something in relation to her instructions and wishes.

[Page 21]

However, she never used to manipulate Khayim Osher with this trait. But once, after an evil prank was played on him, she actually fainted.

From the entire inheritance, there were quite a few benches left on the eastern side of the "Kavkazer" Bes-Medresh. To my grandmother, these were very precious and she swore that no one would take these benches away from her as long as she lived.

However, the influential Yisroel Toivye had it in for the benches. It is not clear why he wanted these benches so badly from Grandpa. Presumably, he was not comfortable with Grandpa's family claiming the east side of the Bes-Hamedresh, which their father Yosl "Tsherebukh" had built.

For Grandma, however, those benches actually meant "her life." With a bit of haughtiness, she used to take her place on the east side of the women's section, surrounded by her daughters and daughters-in-law: Then she looked down with pride from the Ezres-Hanoshim[4] to her sons-in-law on the east side of the Bes-Hamedresh.

Her sons were Slonimer Hasids.

Yisroel Toivye himself did not use to pray in the Bes-Hamedresh. He owned the benches on the east side of all the Bote- Medroshim, including in the cold shul[5]. To pray, however, he went to the Slonimer Shtibl.

Grandpa Khayim Osher was also a Slonimer Hasid, and never used his bench in the Bes-Hamedresh. He was primarily the Shames there and took every opportunity to sneak into the Slonimer Shtibl. The benches were used only by his sons-in-law, and by his daughters-in-law and daughters.

Grandma used to take very pronounced possession of her place on the east side. It gave her security and underlined her prestige and importance.

Yisroel Toivye tried several times to "grab" these benches.

But Grandma fought him stubbornly. For a while he let go of his ambition to get hold of the benches. But he did not give up his desire. He had set his mind to it and was a man who finished everything he set out to do.

Besides, it did not suit him at all that a stranger from Poland could win the fight and make a fool of him. Once he came running into the Bes-Hamedresh quite innocently. Supposedly he just wanted to see how my Grandpa was doing. He invited him to his place as a guest, and when Grandpa was already a little tipsy after a few sips of liquor, he took the opportunity to talk to him about the benches.

[Page 22]

"Khayim-Osher, what are the benches good for, what do you need them for? Let's make a contract and sign them over to me!"

Grandpa admitted that he actually didn't need them. "But," he said, "what will Rive say?"

But Yisroel-Toivye waved it off, "For her I have a present, namely Mother's fur coat!"

Just at that time, Grandma was sitting on the porch and saw Grandpa, who was in good spirits, coming with a fur coat in his hand. When she saw the coat with the shabby, shed fur that had been lying around in Yisroel Toivye's attic, she knew right away that he had swindled something (from Grandpa).

But when she learned that it was the benches that Grandpa had signed over to Yisroel Toivye, she didn't scream out, but just waved her hands and fell unconscious to the floor.

Translator's footnotes:

1. גמרא= Gemore, Part of the Talmud that explains the Mishna and is written mainly in Aramaic.
2. חתן-בחורים= Khosn-Bokherim, young, marriageable men.
3. חיונה= Khayune, Livelihood, in this case, it surely means "earning a living".
4. עזרת-הנשים= Women's section in the synagogue or Bes-Medresh
5. According to consultation with the historian Mrs. Cecylia Bach-Szczawińska in Krynki, it is in all likelihood the "Great Synagogue", which was difficult to heat due to its enormous size of 7500 m^3 and was therefore called "the cold synagogue".

[Page 23]

Incompatible Marriage Matches

Grandma Rive had a difficult fate. She had been thrown out far away, and in such distant places that she could not visit her parents, brothers and sisters even once. She was all alone now among strangers, with a man who had no meaning for her and remained unfamiliar to her. She did not have a single close person, not even distant relatives around her.

But the more Rive was plagued by loneliness, the more pronounced her hostility became towards her husband's family. She passed on her hatred of the "Tsherebukhes" to her children, and all the other descendants of her husband's family could not escape her contempt either.

With the "Tsherebukhes," Rive used to have only extremely rare contact. She also did not have much to do with the children of her husband's sister, Shoshke. She used to mockingly call their eldest son "Yisroel the Great". And by that she didn't mean his tall stature, but labeled him a big fool.

Whenever she wanted to show him that he was not clever or that he had done something stupid, she called him "Yisroel the Great".

Yisroel himself - whereby there were about ten Yisroels in the family - did not like Grandma very much either. He was also rarely in Krynki, for he married a girl from Grodno, and a great personality at that.

Grandma felt sorry for her and used to say all the time that something must not have been right, that such a personality became the wife of this "Yisroel the Great."

Whenever Yisroel came to Krynki, he would give Grandma's house a wide berth. He was friends only with the "Tsherebukhes", that is, Yisroel Toivye's children.

The only one of her husband's family whom Grandma treated with respect was Yosl Pontes. Yosl was a locksmith, a very gullible man. His brother, an extremely devoted and hardworking student, traded the rabbinate chair in Kaunas for a trading company.

Another brother lived in Grodno. When Grandma went there, she always stayed with the Gendlers'. She was especially fond of Gendler's wife, who was descended from "Rashbam"[1] - and the family name was indeed "Rashbam's". She could not praise the relatives in Grodno highly enough; she especially liked going there and appreciated spending time with this family.

[Page 24]

By the way, Gendler's eldest daughter, Peshe, was the wife of the author Ahron Karlin.

Grandma forged the marital bonds for her children; and she used to exempt the sons-in-law from military service herself. The only one who resisted exemption was my Dad. For he had given her a wrong age. Instead of being called up at the age of 21, he had already committed himself to military service at 19.

In fact, his father, after an experience with his son, who had died, had indicated that he was a few years older. In general, his father was of the opinion that his sons should do their military service when they were still very young. For he calculated that if they were not drafted until they were 21, they would return as "old boys."

My father also had a reason for not telling his grandmother his real age. He really liked to make a show of himself.

He liked to adorn himself with the "uniform". Even when he had already completed his military service, he joined the municipal fire brigade, the "Pozharner Komande", and used to dress up with special pleasure in the fire department clothes, which consisted of a uniform jacket with shiny brass buttons, plus a brass-colored hat with two cap visors (which we called "Kozirokn" in our country) and a wide leather belt with a brass buckle on which was carved an eagle, the emblem of the Russian Empire.

When father put on these clothes and put the axe in his belt like a sword, his face beamed with joy.

The marital unions that Rive forged were not all successful. Because of her unshakable self-confidence, she got her children into trouble. She put all her eggs in one basket, and with unyielding stubbornness she insisted on carrying through all her plans, even with regard to the chosen ones for her children.

She married her eldest son, Perets, to a girl from the nearby town of Sokolka. It was supposed to be a very wealthy match, but something got out of hand, and all that remained of the "lap of luxury" was the "lap".

My uncle Perets did not love his wife. She was a good and well-behaved woman, but she said a lot of stupid things. Unfortunately, she was punished by the fact that she knew exactly what her husband's family thought of her - that is, nothing. Grandma thought she was "meshugge", and this opinion was transmitted to all her children and even to the grandchildren.

[Page 25]

Perets was a smart man and the only one with whom Grandma used to consult. When her other children had something on their minds but did not want to bother their mother, they would come to him with their personal problems.

Perets was an ardent Slonimer Hasid, and turning to Hasidic philosophy provided him with a substitute for all the life he had not really lived. By the old Slonimer Rabbi, and later by his son Shmulik, he was considered one of the very respected Hasids. And often he risked his life to protect the Rabbi against the misnagdic gangs of children, who threw lumps of garbage and old rags at the Rabbi and the Hasids when the Rabbi came to Krynki, for "praven tishn"[2].

When the Rabbi used to come, it meant "danger to life and limb" for the Hasids. The widespread scorn and derision of their parents regarding Hasidic Rabbis further encouraged the school children. My grandfather, that is, my father's father, was a dogged "Misnaged" and hated the Hasids.

He counted them among the "idolaters." And this view prevailed among almost all the Misnagdim of the Shtetl.

Often there were even physical assaults. The Hasids used to resist, and as a result, brawls would break out.

Uncle Perets would then usually stand directly in front of the Rabbi and protect him with his body so that all the lumps would hit him.

These assaults always happened on Shabbat afternoon, when the Rabbi had gone to the festively set table in the circle of the Hasids. Whenever the Hasidic people were about to divide the "Shirayim"[3] among themselves, they were pelted with lumps of garbage and rags.

There were times when a Hasidic guard would block the entrance to the "misnagdic" gang of students, however, at that time this had even worse effects.

The gang usually broke the windows and threw stones at the Hasids. Many people were injured at that time.

And it must be understood that the Slonim Hasids were not of the type of the Polish Hasids. They were rather matter-of-fact, sober people. They lacked the euphoria and flaming passion of the Polish Hasids. Only one of them, Shmuel-Khonen, was a hothead and perhaps had the spark of a Polish Hasid in him - which caused the Slonimer Hasids to consider his behavior even a little exaggerated.

[Page 26]

Uncle Perets was also a "moderate" Hasid, but compared to the others, he was full of fiery passion. If he risked his life for the Rabbi, it was a holiday for him. It gave him the opportunity to increase his notice and prestige, and so he usually waited with impatience for the Rabbi's visit to Krynki.

However, the Rabbi rarely came to Krynki in view of the attacks of the schoolchildren's cliques, although many rich Hasidic people, and indeed large leather factory owners, resided there.

Grandma married her daughter to a rich butcher from Glusk, near Bobruisk. She exempted him from military service and arranged for his settlement in the shtetl. However, he was not a decent man. He did not spend any of his wealth. Moreover, he shamed his entire family. He often got drunk and caused scandals, so my Grandma made efforts to drive him out of town. She finally forced him to take his wife and child and return to his home, Glusk. She actually wanted her daughter to divorce him, but the latter apparently loved her husband very much, and Grandma eventually became disappointed in her and gave up.

She also never went to visit her daughter. Only when she was much older did she allow herself to be persuaded and went to see her. But even when she came back, she rarely talked about her.

Her other children had correspondence with Malke, but Grandma never wrote to her. She silently lamented and wept over her daughter's fate.

Grandma married her second daughter to a Bialystok baker. His father had been a writer, a "soyfer", and his surname was indeed "Soyfer", whereby he called himself "Sofer".[4]

Her son-in-law, Dodye, a curious man and quite a scoffer, liked to hear and tell good jokes and took great pleasure in laughing his head off at people and their foibles. He loved to twist people's names with particular skill.

He was also quite a cynic and had little faith in people. He let himself go all the time, only on Shabbat he would put on different clothes.

With him, everything was messy and nothing was where it belonged. He was a very good baker, but his sloppiness prevented him from becoming wealthy. He could have truly bathed in wealth, but he never kept balance sheets or an account.

[Page 27]

He sold his bread both in the house and at the market, where his wife, Dvoyre, stood in her "butke" (a small wooden stall). Peasants came to his house to buy bread and drink tea. They could also buy liquor from him and cigarettes, which he offered rolled up in a banderole.

He used to put his earnings in a drawer on the table, which was always open for all to see. As soon as he turned away, any sinful person could quickly reach into the drawer and take out money.

He had a son, Yisroel-Moyshe, who was only a year older than me, but actually looked about five years older. Yisroel-Moyshe was a little spoiled.

His parents guarded him like the apple of their eye, for he was the only remaining one of three children. His mother had had him under difficult circumstances. At that time, unfortunately, she had to serve a sentence because of her good nature.

Because of an incident with her father-in-law, there was a court hearing at that time. She gave false testimony for him, but the prosecutor was able to prove that she had sworn untruthfully, and so she was sentenced to three years in prison.

She then gave birth to Yisroel-Moyshe in Grodno prison. His grandfather and grandmother raised the child until his mother was released.

Of all the cousins, I was friends only with Yisroel-Moyshe. We both used to save pocket money that we had previously taken from his father's table drawer. With the money, we would buy cider, toys and various sweets.

Yisroel-Moyshe, after all, was practically bathed in money. He learned early to drink spirits, and since he was quite liberal with his money, different young good-for-nothings constantly gathered around him.

Uncle Dodye did not like Grandma. He couldn't stand her always trying to meddle in his affairs. She, in turn, didn't like him much either.

My Grandma never allowed any of her children to escape her control; even after their marriage she wanted to keep them under her wing.

This is what she did with her daughter Malke, whom she sent away only when she could no longer bear the disgrace caused by her son-in-law, Sender.

[Page 28]

She did the same with her second daughter, Dvoyre. When the latter married, she did not allow her to leave the shtetl.

She exempted the son-in-law from military service - but he could never free himself from his "kile" (inguinal hernia). All his life, he carried this stigma, so that everyone knew why he had been exempted from military service.

Translator's footnotes:

     1.   רשב״ם= Hebrew abbreviation for Rabbi Shmuel Ben Meir, famous commentator on the Tanakh and Talmud in the 12th century.
     2.   praven tishn= The communal sitting of the Hasids around their Rabbi at the long table covered with food at celebrations and Shabbat.
https://en.wikipedia.org/wiki/Tish_(Hasidic_celebration)?fbclid=IwAR08MFJHSjDpNFp5gv7YiYKFvhlS36b2WfaY6sLXqmcvn87T8hlX3WyC0pg
     3.   שיריים= shirayim, Remains of a dish that the Rabbi tasted and which the Hasidic people believe to be a remedy and divide among themselves.
     4.   סופר= Yiddish "Soyfer", Hebrew "Sofer", scribe, writer.

[Page 29]

Dodye the Baker

Grandma Rive had a big heart full of love for all her children. But again and again, something tended to get out of hand, and so it happened that love became one big nagging and scolding. She simply could not watch calmly when things around her did not go according to her sense of orderly processes. And then, just when she was struggling to eradicate these "ailments," new and even bigger ones promptly came along.

She was someone who wanted to keep all the strings firmly in her hands, because after all, she thought, only she could bring everything into orderly structures. But this firm conviction of hers led permanently to quarrels and malice.

Just the sight of her son-in-law Dodye running his business put her in a panic. Nor could she bear to see her daughter Dvoyre toiling from early morning until late at night in her little wooden shack where she sold bread.

Dvoyre was just like her Dad, naive and good-natured, and could not say no. She accepted every job with devotion. At dawn, all by herself, she dragged a cart with bread to her bread stall, the "budke".

(Let me tell you now) about Palyuk the Mute, a goy with flaming red hair, who was probably raised by Pavel. He hauled water and chopped the wood needed for the oven in the bakery.

This Palyuk was often seized by fits of laughter that could last for hours without stopping. All of a sudden, the laughter would burst out of him, and he would roll and writhe with laughter, which would turn into exhausted sobs. Together with the crickets, whose song sounded incessantly from the baker's oven, a strange symphony was created.

But whenever Palyuk got a laughing fit, there was no one to bring Dvoyre the bread or small meals. Dodye preferred to stretch out on the stove, which was flat as a board, and slumber. Palyuk's laughter merely announced to him that someone else had to bring Dvoyre the cart with the bread.

However, the only son in the house, Yisroel Moyshe, was very lazy and always found an excuse to avoid activities that might help his father or mother.

[Page 30]

Dodye was an extremely hot-tempered man, and when anger seized him, he threw anything he could get his hands on. He had split more than one head in the meantime with a piece of wood, which he used to throw down from the stove immediately at whoever dared to anger him.

And since there were more than enough pieces of wood on the stove to dry, he always had one at hand.

If Yisroel did not want to obey while Dodye was lying on the stove, the pieces of wood would immediately pelt down. Yisroel Moyshe, however, was already trained to duck quickly, and the result was that the log would hit a valuable object in the house or a person standing to one side.

So it happened one day that my younger brother, Mair (Meyer), was hit by a piece of wood that split his head, but I can tell you[1] that he is now a famous surgeon in Newark!

Poor Aunt Dvoyre suffered additionally from worms in her stomach! We called them "geytsen". In general, she was always suffering from something and in pain. But she had no time to take care of it, because she was constantly " harnessed tightly to the plow" and was toiling away. Although everyone needed little to live on, often the proceeds were not enough, and the money that went in, immediately ran out again.

Grandmother was very distressed to watch Dvoyre with her worn-out body hitched to her cart and, sick as she was, dragging it, loaded with bread, to the market.

She couldn't stand the fact that Dodye's money was just trickling out, and his house seemed to be a regular "public place" (where everyone went in and out as they pleased). And when she saw the open table drawer, she got really angry.

Dodye, however, did not allow her to interfere. He was a stubborn bullhead in general and used to resist doggedly and stubbornly.

They just couldn't stand each other - and as for her, she had no other name for him than "Trup", which means "corpse". It probably had something to do with his appearance: he had a sparse light blond beard, which sprouted only on his chin. And both the beard and his face always looked the same yellowish pale. He had a lot of strong hair on his head, but it was never combed and always dusted with flour.

He loved to play cards with a good sip of brandy. Towards strangers he was like a good brother, but to his own relatives he tried (to stay with his nickname "corpse") to bring suffering from "under the earth".

[Page 31]

But he was very fond of me, because I made life a misery for both my Mom and Grandma. I was a good buddy for him and could enjoy all the good things he kept for sale to the goyim.

I loved the fresh bread when it came out of the oven. And I had special fun with the challah bread. This was a type of bread that was baked foursquare instead of round, as normal breads were. And this bread had a special advantage: on two sides there were soft parts that I could pluck out. When I was done, some of the loaves looked more like gnawed corn on the cob.

But Dodye did not care. He knew that he would get his reward - in the form of the grief that I would bring to Grandma Rive.

He really liked my Grandpa, Khayim Osher. Because, first of all, he, Khayim, didn't even try to tell him what he thought. And secondly, he felt sorry for Dodye that he had such a woman for a wife. Grandpa was entertained by him with tea and small appetizers, and every Shabbat after the cholent meal, Grandpa would visit him for a cup of tea.

Dodye made friends with all the fools of the shtetl. His closest comrade was a klezmer, a musician named Kalamnovitsh. And his constant guest was a strange cranky one from the area, called Shloyme Dubrover.

Well, Shloyme was not a madman, as the insane are. In essence, he was more of a scoffer and a vagrant.

But the "vayse khevrenikes", the schoolboys, regarded him as "meshugge" because he spoke in proverbs and made his rhymes about everything and everyone, immediately, on the spot! He performed little plays in which he imitated the demeanor of the powerful and rich with gestures and grimaces.[2] For his songs and bon mots he was provided with food. He was always hungry, and a few times he even ate more than was tolerable and got sick. Yes, in fact, he performed all these antics only to get food and change.

The youth came alive when he came to the shtetl; they used to look at him expectantly. He came once a year, always in the summertime. Whenever he did not come, the shtetl longed for him. When he came to the shtetl, and used to go through Sokolker Street dancing and singing, his arrival in Krynki spread like wildfire.

Mainly he sang "Shloyme Dubrover the Elkone, an upright citizen, earns 10 rubles a week!", accompanying himself by hitting two planks together.

[Page 32]

Hundreds of schoolchildren then literally ambushed him and made their rounds with him through all the streets of the shtetl. It was simply that the whole town was stirred up when he arrived.

A few times, however, the members of gangs beat him up, and he had to drag himself sick and wounded to Uncle Dodye's stable, where the flour was kept. There he stayed for several days in pain, until suddenly he was gone. Just as one did not know when he would arrive, one never knew when he would disappear again.

Dodye usually looked after him and prepared him a bed for the night in the stable. In general, he felt affection for Shloyme and wanted to hold him tightly.

Dodye's warm relationship with the crazy comedian of the area, helped the musician Kalmanovitsh, who was also a wild bird, to become sincere friends with Shloyme.

The real name of Shloyme Dubrover was Dovid Sidrer. Oh, what crazy ideas this man had! He used to turn facts upside down and make them absurd, and he had an answer for everything. When asked about his claim that he was older than his father, he said, "Well, time doesn't stand still either, but I'm faster and have overtaken him!"[3]

On Shabbat evenings in winter, Dodye's comrades used to gather in his house. They played cards, ate geese and goose giblets (we called them "gribenes") and drank "bronfn" (brandy).

The course of these evenings was completely different from the normal way in middle-class homes. The custom on winter Shabbat evenings was actually to dip boiled unpeeled potatoes in herring sauce, which we called "lyok," and which could be bought in spice stores for a penny.

Yisroel Moyshe, however, was influenced by the customs he saw at home with his father. He learned to play cards while taking a good swig. For Dodye, it was fun to give his boy bronfn, making him a full member of his social circle.

Since he was a stubborn pigheaded man, he not only knew that he was annoying his wife and mother-in-law with this way of acting, no, he even tried to incite them even more by getting his son, who was practically still a child, used to all non-kosher things.

Grandmother's combativeness, however, was never broken, she only waited for a favorable opportunity to confront him with even more passion.

[Page 33]

He knew that she had given him the name "Trup" and provoked her. She, in turn, looked at him with a mixture of disrespect and pity. But when she saw Dvoyre pulling her bread wagon, she went into a rage.

She could not just accept all these things and did not give up the fight with Dodye. And on top of that, she had other children to keep a watchful eye on.

Previous failures forced her to arrange a match between her son Yisroel and one of the "Tsherebukh" family. She did not like the "Tsherebukh's" at all, but she had no other choice, because either she paired her son with Yisroel Toivye's daughter, or with another girl, which she did not want at all, because with her descent from joiners, she was out of the question.

[Page 34]

Aunt Dvoyre

Translator's footnotes:

1. no literal translation
2. This reminds me strongly of the "Jewish Till Eulenspiegel", Hersch Ostropoler.
3. I cannot exclude that there is much more behind this "funny" answer of Shloyme than one suspects at first. Possibly an allusion to the conception of the phenomenon "time" of the "old Hebrews" is behind it, which is different from today's conception.

[Page 35]

The Lovers

When Grandma Rive wanted to speak gently and tenderly, she always did so in her elongated Polish Yiddish - even in her old age, when her language was already very much influenced by the Lithuanian dialect.

When she talked about her children, and even when they were already fathers and mothers themselves, she called them nothing but "my little birds".

For her, they were never adults and independent people. She considered them not only as her children, but in general, as (little) children. And this view she passed on to her sons and daughters. My own mother, even when I was already in my forties, still treated me as if I were still under her supervision.

Grandma actually took her children under her wings like little birds, protecting them in her own way. However, other times dawned and the "little birds" began to escape a little from her wing.

She liked to recite this Jewish proverb freely: "As you make your bed, so you sleep." With this, she wanted to teach her children that it would not fare well for them to "bed down" on their own, without her direction.[1]

However, her children did not lead a happy life with the "destined ones" chosen by her. She never considered people from Krynki as spouses, although later she insisted that her sons and daughters-in-law become residents of Krynki.

Who can explain the mystery of her actions? What were her motives for not including Krinkers in her wedding arrangements, yet insisting that non-local partners then move to Krynki? Modern psychology will certainly be able to clarify this.

It is conceivable that she wanted to spare her children the discomfort that strangers were wont to experience in a new environment. It was strange, however, that she never considered marriage with Polish Jews. She alone forged the marital connections and determined the partners.

She, who herself was unhappy that her husband was chosen over her head, did not allow her children to choose their own spouses.

[Page 36]

Before a marriage match was made, she herself determined when the children were ready for a wedding. She never consulted with Grandpa so he usually learned about a wedding party only when the relatives of the future spouse showed up. She, the Grandma, also used to do the dowry negotiations and give the approval.

All her selections were a dilemma: not a single one of her match-ups turned out to be successful. Her children, whom she had married off, atoned for this with a life of torment. Something never fit as it should.

The eldest son, Perets, did not love his wife, and even Grandma did not like her. Daughter Malke fell into the hands of a drunkard and scandalmonger, and the second daughter, Dvoyre, was always clamped under a relentless yoke and never had peace.

Never able to dress cleanly and neatly, she (Dvoyre) was sick and tired and suffered from swollen legs and short breath.

To get rid of the worms in her stomach, she had to constantly chew certain candies that she was told were a cure.

Her son-in-law Dodye, whom Grandma had nicknamed "Trup" (corpse), was a disheveled, messy person. And the burden of life thus only weighed heavier on Dvoyre, so that she could not live quietly and normally.

However, all her actions that affected her children's lives did not cause her (Grandma) to think about it. She did not allow anything to change in her organization and when her younger children grew up, she repeated her former activities.

She did not concern herself with accountability and acknowledging that times had changed. And they had indeed changed a lot! New ideas had reached the youth in the shtetl. By then, the "Haskole"[2] was already considered old-fashioned. Rather, there was now the "Bund", which spread enlightenment among Jewish youth in Poland, Lithuania and Russia.

People already began to quietly sneak away from home to the study circles of the "brothers and sisters", where they exchanged praying together for singing the "Shvue"[3] and the song: "Salted Sea of Human Tears"[4].

And with perseverance they sang the conclusion full of pathos:

"Long live the Jewish Labour Bund of Russia, of Lithuania, of Poland"[5].

The new times did not leave Grandma's children untouched. Quietly, and without his mother knowing it, her son, Yisroel, also sought out the "brothers and sisters circles."

[Page 37]

A few workers of the factory where he worked had dragged him into it. At that time he was already a "Shagrinshtshik"[6], that is, he practiced such activity in the context of leather tannery.

Grandma did not let him become a tanner lightly. However, she had to agree; firstly, because of her deep poverty and secondly, what else could be done with a young boy in the shtetl that promised success? Tanning was the main source of income for the townspeople. All middle-class children were tanners. This trade promised good earnings.

It seems that Yisroel was not a radical "Bundist." He was a man of many contradictions. From his father he had the compliance and from his mother the firm conviction of himself which, however, immediately turned when he was manipulated by someone. He was very afraid of his mother and was fully under her influence.

The fear of his mother and the influence of the Slonimer Hasids stopped him like a fence and did not allow him to become a "Bundist" with body and soul. He attended the study circle because he did not want to be ostracized from the other young people.

"The brothers and sisters" knew that Yisroel was no safe "candidate" and put Sore'ke, Yone (Yona) the Stolyar's (joiner's) daughter on him to deepen his knowledge and teach him more "class consciousness".

Yisroel was a very handsome young man. To all appearances, he completely fulfilled the blessing that the Rabbi had given to his mother at that time when she did not want to go under the wedding canopy with that "little creature" because she was afraid that the children might take after him.

Yisroel was of tall stature, the tallest of all the other children, and had (otherwise) the appearance of his father. Grandma's children were assigned as follows: The boys had inherited their mother's stature and their father's handsome imposing face. The girls had their father's stature and a little bit of their mother's face. That is, the daughters were comparatively not as short as their father - but they were not very tall either.

Yisroel and Sore'ke joined together, and it became love.

And it was not just a little flirtation. The study circle regarded a romance between "a brother and a sister" with a frown. For the principle applied that love would distract the couple from the (political) movement and therefore they could not bring enough "light and knowledge" to the "masses".

[Page 38]

When the two felt that they were in love, they were downright scared. They had to hide their love from the "brothers and sisters"! Because if they had found out, they would have expelled them from the study circle with shame. Yisroel would not have minded very much, but Sore'ke was very devoted and serious about the matter. However, she was very much in love with Yisroel, and this won out over her loyalty to the circle.

Yisroel also had to be careful of his mother. He knew only too well that she would never allow a marital union of this kind because, first of all, she had something against the lineage (of the girl). But the main reason was that her child had dared, and without her consent, to look for a spouse by himself.

When Grandma found out that Yisroel was "hanging out" with Sore'ke, a dark cloud began to gather in the house. Grandma mustered all means to prevent Yisroel from marrying Sore'ke.

She fainted. She cried and threatened that she would not survive.

When things got too hot for him, Yisroel promised not to meet with Sore'ke again. However, he did not keep this promise.

Sore'ke, who had already sacrificed her loyalty to the "study circle" for the sake of love, felt shaken by Yisroel's fickleness. This fellow was constantly wavering between his mother and Sore'ke, not knowing what to do or how to decide.

Grandma did not believe in Yisroel's promise not to see Sore'ke again. She dragged my mother, who had a child of her own by then, into a conspiracy against her son's mistress and sent her to spy on her brother.

My mother accurately and punctually delivered her report to Grandma about what she had found out about the love. And after each report, the house filled with Rive's anger and spite.

She now tried another way, by badmouthing Sore'ke.

The poor girl had small eyes, and so she only called her "the Blind One."

She used to give Yisroel a hard time, teasing him with the pointed question, "What is that Blind One doing?"

[Page 39]

When the young people saw that this story would never end, they decided to flee to London.

This decision was immutable as long as they were together. But when Yisroel came home, his decision became shakier. Never was he able to decide with certainty what to do - follow his mother or his sweetheart?

Rive felt that Yisroel would slip away from her if she did not take matters firmly into her hands now. As a result of my mother's report, she knew that Yisroel was meeting with Sore'ke and not keeping his promise made to her. So Grandma decided to act quickly and consistently.

She put up with suppressing her hatred for the "Tsherebukh's" a little in order to check the possibility of a marital union with them.

Her brother-in-law, Yisroel Toivye, who had taken possession of the inheritance for himself alone, was already in the "Oylem-Hoeemes"[7]. His wife survived him only a few years. What remained was a house full of orphans: four sons and six daughters.

The eldest of the daughters, Khaye Sore, had taken over the "korobke" ("Kosher Tax") from her parents. The other adult daughters were all very talented and knew how to run businesses. Daughter Khane was very successful in running the "dub"[8] trade. Daughter Mere ran the housekeeping and the other three were still small.

Grandma was now trying to forge a marital union between Yisroel and the orphan, Khaye Sore, his biological cousin.

Translator's footnotes:

1. I understand it to mean shaping and organizing one's life
2. השכלה= haskole, Haskalah, Jewish Enlightenment Movement of the 19th Century.
3. שבועה = shvue, holy oath, / the Shvue: Anthem of the Jewish Socialist Labor Movement, see https://www.youtube.com/watch?v=w4W0LUnohVw
4. the "salted sea of human tears", https://en.wikipedia.org/wiki/In_Zaltsikn_Yam
5. "Jewish Labour Bund of Russia, Lithuania and Poland". https://en.wikipedia.org/wiki/General_Jewish_Labour_Bund
6. *shagrinshtshik*= One who worked shagreen leather, a type of leather that was given an artificial embossing by grains pressed into the leather while it was still wet; no literal translation
7. עולם-האמת= oylem-hoemes, the world of truth, abode of the deceased
8. see page 15.

[Page 40]

Forced Marriage

Grandma was very serious about her activities to break the love between her son Yisroel and Sore'ke. For her, it was considered a done deal that she would marry her son to the orphan, Khaye Sore, by virtue of her authority. Nothing was to stand in her way. All possible complications had to be removed beforehand. First, she had to make a guest visit to Yisroel Toivye's eldest son, Khayim Gershon.

Khayim Gershon was not only the oldest, but also the most respected of the four brothers. He and two younger brothers were leather manufacturers.

Khayim Gershon was the poorest and most pious of them- an ardent Slonimer Hasid.

Khayim Gershon, a tall, confident man with a red beard, dressed not only himself in Hasidic garb, but also his only son, a pot-bellied fellow with a round face, who stood out from other boys by the way he dressed and his peyes, his temple curls.

The two younger brothers had turned out completely differently from Khayim Gershon. The youngest, Yoshke, was still a boy and was under the supervision of the sisters.

The second brother, Ayzik, nicknamed "Zhuk" (beetle), was a broad-shouldered and steadfast man. He did not interfere in the business of the others.

His wife, she was not from Krynki, was a personality. However, she was punished by God, because she had no children, and especially her husband was very depressed because of that.

His wife used to travel far away, as far as Volhynia, to visit all the "good Jews"[1] and came back to the shtetl full of confidence every time. She would then trustingly tell the women in the family about her visits to the "good Jews".

After some time had passed, however, she used to be depressed and full of doubts again. She began, however, to change a great deal and to resign herself to it. Her husband, Ayzik (or, as the name is pronounced in our area, "Eyshik") would not hear of a divorce and made peace with his fate without dying "Kadish"[2] an eldest son.

[Page 41]

The third, Moyshe Velvel, thought nothing of combining Hasidic piety with his idea of how to do business. His motto was "What belongs to God belongs to God, and what belongs to man belongs to man"[3].

He was not a Hasid with passion. Only on Shabbat did he come to pray in the Slonimer Shtibl and, although he was highly regarded and respected by the Rabbi, he was not one of those who divided the "shirayim"[4] among themselves. In general, he behaved a little misnagdic.

He wore a black, short-shaven beard and loved to make "lekhayim"[5]. He concentrated all his energy on the factory. He had set his mind on surpassing Nokhem Anshel, the largest leather manufacturer in Krynki and the surrounding area.

He was not a kind-hearted person and used to avoid charity. In the shtetl they hated him. And later, when he had already achieved his goal and had become richer than Nokhem Anshel, the townspeople cursed him. But this did not bother him very much. He, an influential person, thought nothing of being sorry for anything. He used to say:

"You don't get rich from regretting!"

After the First World War, he became the main leather manufacturer and very wealthy. He continued to live in great wealth and remained a hard and selfish person.

Grandma Rive's visit to Khayim Gershon caused great astonishment in his house. Although she liked him better than Yisroel Toivye's other children, he continued to be a " Tsherebukh" to her.

Grandma did not like to get right to the point. She used to warm up the mood a bit first with a conversation that had nothing to do with the real issue.

She loved preserves, and her greatest joy was when they served her cherry compote for tea.

When she finally came to the request and suggested that Yisroel be betrothed to Khaye Sore, Khayim Gershon immediately acquiesced and held on to it, as they say, with both hands. Together they worked out the details of the marriage contract.

They determined the day of the "tnay"[6]. The two younger brothers, Ayzik Zhuk and Moyshe Velvel, agreed with the marriage arrangement.

What Khaye Sore thought of it interested no one and remained a secret.

[Page 42]

Khaye Sore was not a significant personality. Among the six girls there were two beauties - Mere and the second youngest, Sheynke. But the others were not "krasavitses", not pretty women. Khane was ill and later died of tuberculosis ("skhote", as we said in the shtetl).

The younger daughter, Rashke, emigrated to America together with Shoshke (her aunt), who was the sister of her father and my grandfather.

Yisroel was handsome, and he earned well. Besides, he was one of the family. Such a match for Khaye Sore was extremely desirable! In essence, Khaye Sore certainly would not have minded, for Khayim Gershon took the position of father to her, and she was a devout Slonimer Hasidic woman, according to the tradition of her father and brothers.

Grandma Rive did not tell anyone about the matchmaking. In the morning on the day of the engagement, she only instructed my Grandpa Khayim Osher to go to Khayim Gershon at about two o'clock.

When Yisroel came for lunch, as factory workers usually did, to his amazement, Grandma instructed him to wash and put on his good "Shabbes" clothes. To his question, "what holiday is it?", Grandma did not answer, and he only performed in amazement as she ordered him. She did not even tell him that they were going to Khayim Gershon.

Just as one takes a small, awkward boy by the hand, she silently led him inside to Khayim Gershon. Yisroel saw the tidy house filled with "Tsherebukh's".

In addition - a set table with food and drinks and a boisterous mood.

Before Grandpa went to Khayim Gershon, things seemed strange to him. He knew that Grandma was up to something and went to his eldest son, Perets. He informed him about Rive's sudden friendship with the "Tsherebukh's" and that she had gone to Khayim Gershon as a guest on a simple weekday.

Until Grandpa and Perets arrived, Yisroel still did not know the reason for this festivity; only when Perets told him the secret did he know that they were about to betroth him to Khaye Sore.

He felt sick. He simply could not rise to the occasion, and it was difficult for him to comprehend what was happening around him.

How could he be engaged when he was so much in love with Sore'ke?

[Page 43]

All the plans to escape to London were already matured: she, Sore'ke had covered the expenses by subsidy from her relatives, and the plan was for Yisroel to secretly take a few shirts and sneak out of the house.

It was agreed that they would meet in Bialystok and "smuggle" themselves from there across the border to Germany.

Perets could not simply accept his mother's manipulations. The hatred and contempt his mother had instilled in her children proved stronger at that moment:

He pulled Yisroel to him, "Just come away from the 'Tsherebukh's," he said in front of everyone, and took the stunned and confused Yisroel outside. Granny went after them, grabbed Yisroel by the hand and clearly informed him that she had given her word and would not allow an orphan to be shamed.

Perets left the place, not wanting to be present at the engagement. Yisroel came back in, quiet and depressed, to be betrothed to a girl he hardly knew and did not love.

The news of the engagement spread in the shtetl and Sore'ke left for London immediately, full of shame.

In London she became involved in the socialist movement among the immigrants there. She began to study and further her education and married an English teacher who later became a famous professor.

A few years later they emigrated to America and settled in Los Angeles. Yisroel was already staying in the country there. He had never forgiven himself for not escaping with Sore'ke. When he learned that she, now a widow, was in Los Angeles, he asked a relative who lived in that city to seek out Sore'ke and greet her.

She, however, replied that she had never heard the name "Yisroel Khayim Osher's" and did not know it. This was her reckoning with Yisroel for the disgrace he had done to her. She had completely repressed her memory of him.

After the wedding, Yisroel surrendered to his fate. The brothers-in-law made him a leather manufacturer. He engaged in the trade, and just like his older brother Perets, he too replaced his unlived life and longing with Hasidic piety.

[Page 44]

He became one of those who were allowed to sit very close to the Rabbi at the top of the table, and when his older brother Perets died, he took his place and became his "noyse-keylim"[7].

He was given an influential position with Nokhem Anshel. He was the only one of Grandpa's children whom Nokhem favored and gave the opportunity to run his factory without obstacles.

Yisroel began to distance himself a little from the family: ignoring what little was left of "Bundism" in him, he became a partner in the factory owners' "khevruse"[8].

Now and then he used to come to my Grandpa on Friday evenings and sing psalms with him.

He brought up his children in a somewhat modern way, but this was contradictory in itself. He sent them to the modern Reformed elementary school, but their views were influenced by Zionism.

After World War I, my parents brought Yisroel to America and did everything possible to give him the opportunity for a pleasant, dignified life.

Yisroel returned from America to Poland and got stuck there. My parents sent out a search for him and rescued him, just as World War II was breaking out.

Translator's footnotes:

1. I think that here the (Hasidic) rebbe or Rabbi is meant, who was visited, often also in his role as "miracle Rabbi", and for whom it was acceptable to travel long distances. Such a Rabbi, who enjoyed a special reputation, could be a charismatic figure and take on many roles. First and foremost was the role of an intercessor who interceded before God on behalf of those who came to him with their troubles and illnesses. The Rabbi also played the role of a "good Yid", a "good Jew", to whom the Jews could describe their problems and who would give them the best advice, blessings and certain rituals of action that could contribute to healing.

2. קדיש= kadish, the Jewish prayer for the dead, usually said by the eldest son for his deceased father every Shabbat for a year. The eldest son is often called "kadish".

3. "What belongs to God belongs to God, and what belongs to man belongs to man," probably expressing that religion and morality are seen as two contrary realms. According to this, religion has to do with fear of God and morality has to do with fear of man. According to this conception, it is enough to offer sufficient praise and prayers to God.

4. see page 25.

5. makhn a lekhayim= to raise one's glass, drink a toast.

6. תּנאַי= tnay. condition, engagement agreement.

7. נושׂא-כּלים= noyse-keylim, "weapon bearer," helper, fellow fighter next to an important leader.

8. חבֿרותא= khevruse, partnership.

[Page 45]

Secret Love

Of Grandma Rive's children, my mother was the only one who chose her future husband herself, and, in addition to that, it happened through romance.

But this did not fall into her lap.

It was rather a whole novel with the complete color of small-town love stories. It fed the youth of the shtetl, be it with gossip or songs, to which suitable rhymes were added about the "heroes" of the romance and the schemers who disturbed it.

The words and the melody of the song of her daughter's love reached my Grandma's ears. She too knew that the town youth had woven into her song something about a kind of witch who was trying to interfere in an evil way with her daughter's love.

At that time, a new zeitgeist was forming in Krynki: "worldliness." "Akhdes"[1] groups began to form. The youth, young men and girls, started to meet in the forest or in the house of a young man or girl, even if they were not of noble descent.

An "enlightened" youth appeared in the little town, which was also quite natural in an area where almost all the inhabitants were engaged in the same manufacturing.

The shtetl had just been famous for its weaving mills. Later, however, this production moved to Bialystok, Horodok and Vashlikove (Wasilków).

The weaving mills there began, thanks to modern machines, to produce higher quality and cheaper. Krynki could not compete with Bialystok, on the one hand because the necessary capital for modern machines did not exist here, but also, because Krynki had no railroad connection. Both import and export still had to be done by carts.

Krynki had produced a cheap commodity, such as "Tiger", "Koshbi" and "Eskimo." However, Bialystok and Lodz began to surpass Krynki in all areas of production. Krinker factory owners fell behind; either they did not want to or they could not adapt to the new and modern conditions.

In addition, there were fierce disputes among the factory owners, and this contributed to the fact that manufacturing went downhill quickly.

[Page 46]

The decline continued until one day all the factories came to a standstill and the shtetl had to come to terms with the fact that weaving was over.

When the weaving mills were still in operation, the shtetl was noisy and bustling. People worked in different ways: There were hand looms, where one could spin by moving with the feet or hands. But there were also factories where production was done with steam. Water from the rivers was used for this purpose.

The larger and wealthier manufacturers already had factories where the work was done exclusively with the help of steam. At that time, everyone was engaged in weaving: wherever there was an attic, a cellar or a stable, they set up a weaving machine and worked on it.

Back then, weaver workers earned six or seven rubles a week, which was a high wage by the standards of this time. For a girl, marriage to a weaver was considered a happy match, and therefore, the Krinker girls used to sing at that time:

"Mama, let me marry and give me a weaver for a husband; the day after the wedding I will drive in a carriage with rubber wheels."

When the weaving mills ceased operations, the need became so great that alms were collected for the Krinkers in the surrounding towns. The shtetl was simply going from bad to worse. At that time, quite a few weaver-fabricators joined forces and started making leather. And after a short time, Krynki was already counted as a major center, manufacturing leather of all kinds.

In the face of such (significant) manufacturing, it was understandable that the youth developed self-confidence and the various movements that arose in Russia also reached the Krinker youth.

From time to time, wandering groups of actors and circuses would come by. In addition, books were brought to the shtetl and the young people used to gather to listen to someone read from them. Because of (Russian) (press) censorship, it was customary for the reader to explain the "real intentions" of the book's author.

At that time, books with novels were already making the rounds, and through them the youth became acquainted with the lives of other humans and nations. Popular was an agitation booklet by Dovid Pinski, "The Story of the Four Brothers." They lived quietly and fraternally in the forest.

[Page 47]

The moral of the story was to show how the encounter with civilization makes one brother rich, the other poor; the third it makes a fighter, and the fourth it makes a pious man who accepts with love whatever may come. However, the four brothers were eventually turned against each other. In the book, there was a song that the poor brother used to sing:

"I go over fields, I go over woods, I hear the wind rustle and sing. A fright, a dear brother, a terrible cold; it is hard, dear brother, to live in the world."

The youth usually sang the song with great enthusiasm. The melody was melancholy and stretched. Girls used to cry when they sang the words.

A wandering group of actors aroused the young people's desire to put on a play themselves. One of the actors was stopped in the shtetl and began to teach the young people how to play theater. The repertoire consisted of works by Goldfaden.[2] The songs were sung by young and old.

Many elders looked with suspicion at the new behaviors and ideas of the youth. However, there was no fanaticism in the little town. A large number of young lads helped to take on the duty of earning a living, and this caused the elders to look quite closely to catch the gist of the performances.

With regard to the plays, however, people did not yet dare to give women a role, so the "heroes and heroines" were all men. This also helped to avoid "interferences" by the adults.

The girls, however, did attend the circle where they read from the books and prepared for the theater plays.

My father was a passionate young fellow. He liked to attract attention and was fond of showing off. As a result of this passion, he always tried to make an impression. He had a good grasp of things, which is why he could absorb and implement everything very quickly and very precisely.

He liked to get involved in all the events that concerned the youth. Not long ago, he had come from Bialystok, where he had studied in its Yeshive (Yeshiva), the Talmud school.

My Grandpa, Yankel Bunim, brought him back to Krynki due to great sorrow in the family because the eldest son, Ahron Velvel, had joined the "Buntovshtshikes", the Bundists, and was already in Bialystok prison for leading a strike of the weavers. And the second son, Yudel, had been drafted as a soldier.

[Page 48]

So Grandma insisted on bringing the son Leyzer Hersh home. He should no longer stay in a foreign country and eat "teg"[3] there with the Bialystok relatives. When my father came back to Krynki, my Grandfather gave him in apprenticeship to learn the craft of tanning.

My father immediately joined the youth circles. He considered himself a metropolitan man and had already secretly snuck into a circus in Bialystok to watch a performance. Therefore, he considered himself a great expert of theatrical play.

My father had a fertile imagination and it was his nature to overdo and exaggerate things.

He was a passionate, romantic and sensual fellow.

At a meeting of the "Akhdes" circle in the forest, he met Mashe and soon burned with passion for her.

Both were beautiful people, my father took after his mother and had pitch black hair. In contrast, my mother had brown hair ("shatin" as we say)[4] and a round face, red cheeks, a finely curved ("getokt", turned, as we say) mouth and a beautiful nose.

I still remember my mother when she was about 20 years old, and how her beauty was praised. My mother took after her father completely. My Grandfather Khayim Osher was small in stature but had a very imposing face.

Now when Leyzer Hersh caught sight of Mashe, he did not leave her side and in fact also very quickly announced that he was in love with her. He was an impatient person and could not suppress a mood, a feeling or a thought for long.

She liked him, too. Only she was frightened by his boldness and directness. Besides, she thought that nothing would ever come of it anyway: it would be nullified as soon as her mother got wind of it.

Leyzer Hersh, however, did not mind when Mashe stopped coming into the circle; he simply waited outside her house and then went after her. He began to have success with her, and his persistence drew her to him.

They used to meet in secret. With Grandma, however, it was hard to sneak out of the house. One had to stay in her sight all the time. The two people actually suffered as in the novels in the books. Finally, their meetings could no longer remain hidden.

[Page 49]

My Grandma found out about it and simply locked her daughter in the house and held her captive.

Leyzer Hersh stayed in front of her windows, and she, secretly, gave him a glance or a smile.

The romance became known in the shtetl, and kith and kin turned to the subject, gossiping and whispering about the "affair" between Yankel Bunim's son and Mashe Khayim Osher's.

Cliques gave the two lovers a song, "... they can't meet because her mother is standing there like a gendarme, holding the poor little bird captive."

In the factory, the workers, especially the married ones, used to tease the young lad and make his life difficult. The youth sang in chorus the song about his love affair.

My grandmother saw that things were not going well. There was talk in the shtetl, and the lad would not step away from the window. So she began to hatch a plan to marry off her daughter to another fellow. My mother had many suitors. There were several young men who would have liked to take Khayim Osher's daughter as their wife. But when Leyzer Hersh learned that Rive was bent on betrothing Mashe to another, he announced a threat; and this was a threat whose memory was recalled not only by jokers, but even by my mother many times when she wanted to tease Father.

My father could not pronounce a "shin"[5] correctly and used to interchange it with a "sin".[6] In his threat, he announced that he would shoot himself if he was not allowed to marry his love. He pronounced it something like this, "If I don't get Masenke, I will soot myself!"

Translator's footnotes:

    1.   אחדות= akhdes, Unity or identity
    2.   Avram (Abraham) Goldfaden (1840-1908), Yiddish folk poet and composer, founder of modern Yiddish theater
    3.   Esn teg= ...refers to the once widespread custom in Eastern Europe of supporting teachers and education by inviting Talmud students to one's home for meals on certain days of the week, with stays probably changing from day to day.
    4.   chestnut brown
    5.   שין= Shin, name of the 20th letter in the Hebrew alphabet.
    6.   שׂין= Sin, name of the penultimate letter in the Hebrew alphabet; it corresponds to a typical peculiarity of the Lithuanian dialect of some regions that, among other things, the two letters shin and sin were "interchanged", which not infrequently caused ridicule.

[Page 50]

The Soldier

My father's warning that he would "soot himself" if he did not get "Maseke" (as a wife) spread in the shtetl. Why the townspeople found out about it, is not known.

But one must assume that Dad, who could not hold back any feelings or emotions, had confided in someone, and so it was spread not only among the women and factory workers, but also among the jokers.

My Grandpa, Yankel Bunim, an "enlightened" man who was considered a "maskl" (educated person) in the shtetl, was startled when he heard talk that his son was considering taking his own life because of Khayim Osher's daughter, Mashe.

Grandma Rive, however, attached no importance to the gossip. On the contrary, she only became stricter and did not let her daughter out of her sight.

The girl used to sit there and cry. Leyzer Hersh had not really carried out his threat yet, but who knows? It wasn't out of the question after all! Through Mashe's brother, Yisroel, the two lovers sent messages to each other. At one point, Mashe also snuck out of the house and left to meet her lover.

But where could one hide in the shtetl? There were always eyes watching everything. The encounter of the couple in love was immediately reported to her mother, who gave her daughter a severe punishment.

Mashe used to tell later that she had felt guilty and therefore did not contradict her mother with a word. She just sat there and kept silent. However, as it turned out, her taciturnity only irritated her mother even more. She used to get into a rage until she convulsed. This once went so far that she grabbed a knife that was lying in front of her eyes and threw it at her daughter.

It will forever remain a wonder what kind of energy gave Mashe a jolt and made her jump up. The whole scene of throwing the knife lasted only seconds after all. Rive's fright from her own rage and the daughter's hysteria obviously had an effect.

[Page 51]

She cringed at her own unrestrained ferocity that she had just displayed and began to soothe and calm her daughter.

Obviously, her outburst of anger had reached a peak, which made Rive realize that she was putting her child's life in danger. This incident caused her to give up resisting her daughter's love for Yankel Bunim's son.

When Yankel Bunim realized how his son was "perishing," he decided to go to Rive to confer with her about the love between their children. Rive was a patient listener.

She used not to get excited during the conversation but took every opportunity to speak up or express concerns. In turn, she used her silence to think of a response.

By the time Yankel Bunim arrived, Rive had already decided not to object to the wedding arrangement. His visit coincided exactly with the incident of the knife throwing, so she listened to him gladly and patiently. Moreover, the families of my Grandpa Khayim Osher and Yankel Bunim were connected by "kroyveshaft"[1], and they stood by each other like members of one family.

After the conversation with Grandpa Yankel Bunim, she agreed to the marriage. However, her condition was that the coupling of the young pair should not be based on the "love affair" alone, but through a (formal) union, which is why she insisted on hiring a "shadkhn", a matchmaker.

Yankel Bunim, who was also a stubborn man, albeit a smart one, knew when to compromise, so he gave in. Rive presented her terms to the matchmaker. She could not give a dowry, so both my Dad and his father should do without. She insisted on exempting the young man from the "Priziv", the conscription.

This was already something of a "customary right" for her: To exempt the sons and sons-in-law from military service.

The (future) in-laws started their guest visits and the couple used to meet in public. However, Rive did not let her daughter go to the groom's house. She thought that once a girl dared to have a love affair, she had to be guarded.

And so she insisted that the meetings take place in her house, where she could keep an eye on both of them.

The first thing she tackled was to exempt the groom from military service. My father, who was already like a family member to her, used to explain to her again and again that he was still young and had enough time to think about how he could be exempted.

[Page 52]

He was 18 years old at that time. There was still a period of more than three years until the "priziv."

Rive allowed herself to be convinced. Her motives for agreeing to the couple's marriage were very clear to her: First, she did not think much of a young couple "hanging around" for a long time. After all, who knows if it could be "saved" (from the consequences)?

Secondly, she was very sure that she would succeed in freeing my father from the "priziv." After all, hadn't she already freed her son Perets and son-in-law Dodye? And "with Mazl" they fixed the day of the wedding.

However, my Dad had not told her the truth. He had concealed from Rive the fact that his father had registered him in such a way that he had to be drafted not at the age of 21, but already at the age of 19. The fact that my father hid this secret from her, caused my grandmother's sympathy for him to wane later on. She labeled him a liar, and not only did he lose his good reputation with her, but she also discredited him with all those close to them.

There were reasons why he should go to military service at the age of 19. This had to do with a confusing mess in the family. Besides, my Grandpa Yankel Bunim said that if you really wanted to serve the tsar, you should be very young, so that if you were later released (from military service), you would still be young enough to create a livelihood for yourself.

Grandpa had not registered his children in Krynki. His family came from Semyatitsh[2], a town located around Bielsk and Brest-Litovsk. He used to brag about his relatives from Semyatitsh. Their name was "Kadishevitsh."

Actually, that was also my Grandpa's former family name, but when the family moved to Krynki, they changed the name from "Kadishevitsh" to "Krinker."

The "Kadishevitshes" from Semyatitsh were large landowners. They owned estates and ran business on a large scale. Grandpa's biological cousin from the Kadishevitsh family was a lawyer and used to travel even to St. Petersburg.[3]

The "Kadishevitshes" had their own "castle"[4] near the shtetl. Those who remained from this family, a mother with her son, rarely used to come to Semyatitsh. They kept away and alienated from Jewish life and Jewish society. The son did not speak Yiddish, only Russian. He was considered a little "meshugge."

He used to dress in robes that had strange and bright colors.

In addition, he wore red boots.

[Page 53]

He especially liked to hold a short stick, (a "palke" as they call it), and wag it. Grandpa once had an exchange of correspondence with them. Because of birth certificates or other legal documents he needed from Semyatitsh, he used to go there and visit the family on this occasion.

Even before a year had passed after the wedding, my father was called to the "priziv." He had to go to Bielsk because he was registered in Semyatitsh and Bielsk was the competent district town.

Grandpa Yankel Bunim did not believe that his son would really be drafted. He thought that Leyzer enjoyed a privilege, therefore he did not have to serve in the military.

But, it was quite different; obviously, it was Leyzer Hersh's desire to be a soldier. He loved the military parades and the attention a uniform brought.

Rive had not expected her son-in-law to be called up for military service so young. She couldn't accept that the young man had kept the truth from her; to her, it was a hoax.

So she had prepared herself to work right from the beginning of the summer to exempt him from military service. And when, right after "Sukes", the "Festival of Booths", everyone was to get ready for "Priziv", she had already prepared everything. But, what a "misfortune!" She was not ready for what happened next!

She planned to go to Bielsk with her son-in-law, and an opportunity would surely present itself there. It was the rule that recruits had a few more days off after registration and she wanted to use those few days to find ways to free her son-in-law (from military service).

But things turned out differently. After he was admitted and registered, he stayed there. There was some reason why they didn't release the draftees that year for a few more days, as was usually the rule.

Grandma ran to the "Kadishevitshes." She introduced herself to them and asked for their help. But either they didn't want to or couldn't help; anyway my Grandma came back to Krynki disappointed and depressed. She took her daughter to her place; she did not want to leave her alone.

She also wanted her daughter to give birth in her house.

[Page 54]

My Dad, when he was in America for the first time

[Page 55]

My mother at the age of 25[5]

Translator's footnotes:

1. קרובֿהשאַפֿט= kroyveshaft, relationship, friendship
2. Semiatycze, https://de.wikipedia.org/wiki/Siemiatycze
3. This sentence can also mean that his influence reached all way to St. Petersburg.
4. „Shlos" actually means "castle"; however, it can be assumed that it was a magnificent, palatial manor house.
5. Mashe Pruzhanski Krinker (later Cohen)

[Page 56]

Songs of Sorrow and Longing

A few months after Leyzer Hersh left for military service, his child was born. Someone now had to support the young woman with the child, but one could not rely too much on her father's income.

In the shtetl they knew only too well that Khayim Osher could be fobbed off with a trivial amount of money. He never demanded something nor did he ask for something to be given to him. If one slipped him something, it was of course good, but if not, he was not angry either. He believed that as a Shames he had to do his duty as it suited his own requirements and that no one was obliged to give him a reward.

Rive took this very much to heart but, after all, she couldn't follow him!

When he came home, whether from a wedding, a bris[1] or, God forbid, a funeral, Rive immediately instructed him to hand over the money; at least, the money that he used to bring her. He never found it easy to perform a task. She used to pour out all her anger and bitterness on him.

He swallowed everything and rarely gave her an answer.

Why Rive did not go into business herself or engage in an activity that would have helped supplement the income was probably connected to a number of deep psychological reasons. Perhaps the main reason was that she wanted to be like the (other) wives in the family. They conducted themselves with pride and pomp and did not bother with such things as helping to earn an income. Her bitter envy of the rich relatives did not allow her to deal with earning her own bread. This was not suitable for a relative of Nokhem Anshel K(i)nishinski.

She used to take every dime Khayim Osher brought. He kept the money in a large cloth that was in a back pocket of his caftan. When he came home, he would quietly take the tied cloth out of the pocket and place it on the table.

Rive then used to recount the money and deduce whether he had been treated fairly or unfairly.

[Page 57]

Grandpa liked to give his grandchildren gifts. He, continually, used to give me a whole kopek. Before he came home, he hid several coins in the tobacco box and left them there until a grandson came and demanded "his coin". As for me, there were already fixed days when I got my kopek.

Besides my Mom, there were three unmarried children in the house: Yisroel, Meyshke and Yente.

My mother moving into the house, which consisted of only two rooms in which a family of six people had to "live" with a small added child, meant a great burden for everyone.

My mother not only had to support herself and her child, but also had to send money to her husband in Oryol, deep in Russia, where he was doing military service.

As a way out, she had to learn a trade, so she started an apprenticeship in sock knitting.

When she finished her apprenticeship, she bought her own machine and attached it to a board near the window.

I still remember how the work of knitting socks was done. The machine was long and had many needles. At one corner of the machine was a spool of cotton attached to an iron rod. The cotton was connected to the needles.

On an iron rod was a handle that could be moved back and forth, and the machine then shifted in the same way as a typewriter, only a little faster.

With one hand you moved the handle and with the other you held the sock form at the bottom, which helped finish the sock.

Mom used to sing sad songs to the beat while knitting: songs that lamented failed love romances. Her brother Meyshke had already begun to participate in the "Skhodkes"[2], bringing songs to the house that lamented the fate of poor people and called them to fight.

Their most popular song was "In Storm and Struggle" by Edelshtat[3].

Sadly and with a tearful voice, she used to drag out the melody: "In storm and battle my youth has gone, of love and happiness I never knew.

Just bitter tears and aching wounds, have pressed my soul."[4]

[Page 58]

There was another melody she loved: "Footsteps of tyrants could be heard at 12 o'clock in the night, at that time a star dropped down at our place, such a one that sparkles in the night".

Whether she had understood what the songs intended and what they were aiming at, I don't know. But as small as I was, the songs had an effect on me. Curious and excited, I used to sit and listen to the sadly drawn-out melodies that my mother sang, in keeping with her disposition and mood.

She herself wrote a "poem" lamenting her miserable "fate". She gave it a melody and she used to sing the song more often than the others.

> "You knew you were going to be a soldier,
> why did you come to me?
> You knew you were going to be a soldier,
> so why did you flirt with me?
> Here you have the sack, now pack your bag
>
> and go to the station.
> While you go to the station,
> I don't have a dime to earn,
> I go around and shout for help,
> give me a dime to earn.
> If I only earn a dime,
> then I don't want to complain.
> I already live a life quite fine,
> I remember the husband mine,
> oh, he is not here, the boy shall be no burden to him,
> though he longs for his father,
> oh, his father is not here!"

As an encore, she had this song:

"What do we want to eat, brothers? Soldier's pap; brothers, soldier's pap is not good, the Russian is tapping our blood."

Mama was friends with very few people. She no longer liked being with her girlfriends who had remained unmarried. Young women her age who could have suited her, either didn't exist or she didn't want to get acquainted with them.

Besides, she was much too busy with her work. Only on Shabbat, together with her brother Yisroel, she used to go for a walk, as the Krinker youth usually did.

A very great friendship had developed between them, which lasted until her death. When my mother and Yisroel went for a walk outside, people would watch them. Both of them were important personalities.

They used to talk to each other while walking and usually got to Shishlevitser (Swisloczer) Street where the youth used to meet. Sometimes, they also went to visit.

In later years, my mother was very close to Nokhem Anshel's daughter Alte. Alte lived on the "Vigon" (a common pasture) in a "castle"[5] surrounded by a large garden.

[Page 59]

I used to play with her children and pick fruit with them in the garden. In addition to apples, pears and cherries, gooseberries also grew there, and I was particularly fond of this "fruit" (gooseberries).

(My mother) was also close to Nokhem Anshel's sister-in-law, Sheynke, who was the sister of his wife Roshke. Her husband, Yisroel Hertske, ran a large factory. He himself was a modest man. Sheynke had a higher social status than he had. They had four children, a daughter, Mezhi, and three sons. One of the sons was segregated from the others. He was an "idiot" and was locked up in the house.

They dressed him in children's clothes even when he was a big lad. From time to time they used to let him out into the garden next to the house.

The garden was fenced with iron bars, and even if he had wanted to go out from there, it would have been impossible for him.

His vocabulary was very limited. The few words he could speak, he only mumbled. Most of the time he was friendly, but when he burst into a rage, you had to tie him down.

I was usually a little afraid of him, he was already growing a beard! His mother Sheynke, however, insisted that I play with him when we came to visit; a thing I had little desire to do. And that is why the visits to Sheynke were a punishment for me. The "madman" literally, smelled that I didn't want to play with him, so I was a "mortal enemy" to him.

One son had just succeeded in taking a leading position in his father's factory. But Sheynke was not fond of the other (third) son either[6]. She sent him to the Bialystok "Private Gymnasium". He used to come home in a uniform with shiny buttons. The garment looked good on him and fit him like a glove.

However, he was not a respectable person, and his mother sent him to live with her brother in Chicago.

Her daughter Mezhi[7] had a contorted face all the time. She was not ugly, but had a crooked odd expression that distorted her appearance.

Mother also used to visit Roshke's second sister, Hode. She was the poorest of the sisters. Her husband, Nisl, was a weaver and came from Bialystok. She had two girls who were "one heart and soul", as they say. Both girls were at odds with the noble Roshke, and they used to say many unpleasant things about her.

[Page 60]

It also happened that Nokhem Anshel himself invited my mother and Yisroel to a meal.

But this happened very rarely and only by chance. On the way to Hode or Sheynke, one had to pass by his house. If he was standing on his porch on Shabbat, after tsholent[8], and caught sight of my mother with Yisroel, he would invite them to join him.

He enjoyed a privilege towards me: he had been my sandek[9], and when he met me on my way to school, he liked to pinch my cheek so that tears would come.

He never gave me change, but once, satisfied by the answers I gave him (to his questions) about where and how I would learn, he gave me a ruble bill.

I will never forget my joy and the strong impression!

[Page 61]

Grandpa Khayim Osher

Translator's footnotes:

1.   Bris= "Covenant with God", circumcision ceremony
2.   Skhodkes= Illegal meetings of the Jewish labor movement
3.   Dovid Edelshtat (1866-1892), famous Jewish anarchist
4.   The title of this song is "Mayn letste Hofnung", "My last hope". Contentwise there were versions with small textual deviation. I translated "soul" instead of "breast" for sound reasons.
5.   shlos= castle, but I think this was more likely a palatial mansion
6.   The author writes "also", referring to the fact that the first son was mentally handicapped.
7.   Mezhi= derived from "Miriam"
8.   tsholent= a stew with potatoes, vegetables and meat. The typical Jewish stew for Shabbat was already pre-cooked on Friday and cooked at low heat until Shabbat noon, and in the past usually in communal ovens at the baker's, where it was then collected after attending synagogue.
9.   sandek= the man holding the child on his lap during circumcision

[Page 62]

A Shabbat with Grandpa

Grandfather and Grandmother were both neat people. Despite the great poverty, they kept themselves impeccable. And so was the house.

Their poor clothes were always clean and dapper. Grandpa often used to go "tvilen"[1]. Grandma loved to wash herself with a bar of fragrant soap. She always calculated to have a few pennies left over for such a bar of soap.

Grandpa's beautiful thick beard was never disheveled; he kept it neat and combed. Only on his lower lip was a brown trace of snuff.

My strict Grandma, despite her desire to rule and dominate, was never vicious and resentful. Her dominance and supervision of her children stemmed from the fact that she had never had a person to rely on: After all, she was a stranger, a wretch, without parents, without sisters, brothers and close people. Her husband was someone who cared little about real and practical things.

She had completely taken over the education of her children and insisted that they be permanently guided by her influence, even when they were already adults.

The part of the work that she handed over to my Grandpa was to teach respect for Judaism and to take over the spiritual education of the children. Apparently, she herself did not have much respect for the Hasids. She never went to the Slonimer Shtibl and would not even come out to see the Rabbi when he came down to Krynki.

She liked the Bes-Hamedresh and her bench on the east wall, for which she had fought so doggedly so that the brother-in-law, Yisroel Toivye, would not usurp it.

Her sons, however, were indeed Slonimer Hasids. They followed their father completely in terms of their Judaism.

Only in her own domain, the granny wanted to be all-powerful. She ruled out matchmaking with Hasids.

[Page 63]

The only marriage arrangement with a Hasidic woman was with Yisroel Toivye's daughter Khaye Sore. But that had been a "marriage of necessity," a way out to save her son Yisroel from his love for Sore'ke by a quick marriage to the niece[2].

She didn't think much of superstitions. But when her younger son, Meyshke, got "a rose" (shingles) on his foot (which I imagined in my childish fantasy was like a flower), she would bring a Tartar "quack" to "cure" him from the neighboring village of Krushenon (Kruszyniany).

In the end, however, she had to go with him to Grodno, to the famous Doctor Zamkov, who actually healed him.

She was very insistent that the children should show respect to their father, which she herself observed through warmth and understanding. She also felt great reverence for her father-in-law and mother-in-law.

After the death of Yosl Tsherebukh his wife Sheyne continued to live together with her daughter Shoshke. Apparently, there was sufficient livelihood. However, they were also supported by Yisroel Toivye, who then held all of his father's business in his hands.

All the children showed their great-grandmother[3] the greatest respect and never contradicted her. She conducted herself as before, in a noble manner. However, she was very thrifty and avoided spending any left over money she had unnecessarily. She thought a lot of "takhles"[4] and had a special relationship with her son, who ran the business.

She[3] also loved my Grandpa. Only she was bothered by the fact that he completely turned away from the earthly world. It is said that my grandmother (Rive) never contradicted the great-grandmother[3], who was her mother-in-law. She used to listen silently to everything she said to her.

It was a tradition for the grandchildren to visit her every Friday, and she used to give them a small "Challah", a wheat flour bread, which she had baked for them herself. But being stingy, she also saved on the dough, and therefore the little "Challahlekh" were hardly seen.

My great-grandmother liked my grandmother and therefore promised to bequeath her fur (coat), which my grandmother liked very much. From this incident comes the story about the fur that Yisroel Toivye had given to my Grandpa as compensation for the "benches" in the Kavkaz Bes-Medresh.

[Page 64]

Rive was very envious of her mother-in-law's beautiful fur coat. She dreamed about it and probably tried it on thousands of times in her mind.

However, it happened that after the death of great-grandmother Sheyne, as a result of a mishap, the fur remained with Yisroel Toivye. To the great annoyance of Rive, he kept it. She used to bring this up and demand the fur coat. Apparently, however, Yisroel Toivye could not accept that "a have-not" should adorn herself with his mother's fur coat. He kept it in the attic, and when it was already worn out, he used it as a means to wrest the benches from Grandpa.

The regimen in the house was divided in two by Rive; the physical-practical part she took over, and the spiritual part she left to Grandpa.

Shabbat belonged to the Kingdom of Grandpa. Still during the Friday she handed over the scepter to Grandpa. She stopped bothering him with everyday things. She was no longer obstinate and demanding, nor did she trouble him with income matters. In general, she kept herself in the background.

With her, the Shabbat evening did not begin on Friday, but on Wednesday. On that day she already went to buy the flour for Challah and cleaned the candlesticks. On Thursdays she bought meat, fish and food for the tsholent stew. At night, she prepared the Challah dough. She used to put the dough in a large brass bowl or in a wooden trough, cover it with a clean linen cloth and drape it with an object like a bedspread or other heavy blanket.

Until late at night, the women performed various tasks. Still in their clothes, they lay down. After about an hour or two of sleep, Grandma used to wake up all the daughters to "take Challah"[5].

The wood at the stove had been provided earlier. Grandma used to put the wood in the oven and light it, and each daughter would pinch off a little dough, shape the dough with both hands under a blessing, and then throw it into the fire. When the dough was baked, my Grandma would go to the market to buy what was missing. Towards the end of the first half day, it was already Shabbat-festive in the house.

[Page 65]

The "tsholent" was already in the pots, it was only necessary to take it to the baker. The floorboards were mopped, and a clean tablecloth was spread on the table, decorated with the candlestick and the covered Challah breads.

In our area, it was traditional to eat brown bread every Friday (we called it "rozeve bread"), and porridge with it. Often greaves and some lard were put in the grits.

After the meal, my grandmother went to the mikve. When she returned, well combed and half her face wrapped in a shawl, she used to put on her Shabbat clothes. When she had dressed and adorned herself, nothing from everyday life was to be discussed. Not a single thing was to be remembered that had any relation to money, to work, or to commerce.

She did not even want to listen to the trouble that her married children experienced at home. As soon as Grandpa came out of the bathhouse and put on his festive clothes, every trace of ordinariness was completely expelled from the parlor.

Grandma had only a few festive dresses in her entire life, which she wore solely on Shabbat, on a holiday, or to a wedding. They suited her very well and were tastefully embroidered. Rive was confident and tall. One of her dresses, it was made of velvet, had a waist that made her appear younger. From the waist down, the dress widened and was pleated. People used to look at her askance when she wore this fitted dress, because they whispered that it looked like a crinoline.

At that time, there was a famous Maggid[6] in Krynki, Avroham Yakev Levitan, who was a follower of the manner of the Dubner Maggid[7]; and just like him, he also waged the same battle against crinoline dresses.

R'Avroham Yakev Levitan, the old Maggid, was a very interesting figure. He had a fine pronunciation, and in addition to being a preacher, he was also a judge in the shtetl during the time when R' Avromtshik Kharif[8] was the Rabbi there.

After Avromtshik's death, R' Borekh Lavski became the Rabbi. And as soon as the latter took over the rabbinate, he began to make life difficult for Avrohem Yakev Levitan. He deposed him as a judge and made him leave Krynki. R'Borekh felt that he did not need a supporter, because he alone could provide the shetl with sufficient spirituality.

Avrohem Yakev Levitan took over the rabbinate in the neighboring shtetl. At the same time, he drove around towns and cities, preaching.

[Page 66]

He liked to be known as "the Krinker Maggid." However, he could not settle in a place where he had not lived before. He had a strong longing for Krynki. In his old age he came back to the shtetl. He took a job as a teacher, and taught and recited to the community in the Kavkazer Bes-Medresh.

Grandma loved her velvet dress very much and used to watch her reflection in the mirror. She did not relate the Maggid's anger at those kinds of dresses to herself, with the excuse that a crinoline dress had fish-legs or a hoop skirt at the waist, and her dress did not. However, she wore the dress and dressed up in it on Shabbat and holidays.

She did not go for a walk with Grandpa even once. And even to pray she did not go with him. After all, as a Shames, he had to be in the Bes-Medresh before they began to pray.

As soon as the stores closed their doors, she used to walk out to the Bes-Medresh: confident, dolled up in her dress, with a white silk scarf and a prayer book under her arm. She liked her shoes to be polished, and she used to put a shine on them with the help of "shoe wax" (that's what we called it).

She always planned it so that women were already present when she arrived at the "Ezres-Noshim" (Women compartment in the synagogue). She used to walk with confident and sure steps to her bench on the east wall.

Translator's footnotes:

1. Although this spelling is unknown to me, I think it refers to going to the ritual bath, the "mikve" and immersing oneself there to ritually cleanse the body.
2. It seems that in this case he means "cousin".
3. Sheyne
4. תכלית= practical goal, purpose, serious business, result. In German, it is also applied with the meaning "talking sense".
5. to take challah= a religious ceremony in which some dough is removed and burned with a blessing to commemorate the later giving of some dough to the high priest.
6. מגיד= maged, Maggid= preacher, religious orator.
7. https://www.jewishencyclopedia.com/articles/8465-jacob-ben-wolf-kranz-of-dubno-dubner-maggid
8. חריף=kharif: perceptive

[Page 67]

Grandpa's Songs on Shabbat Eve

On Friday evening, my Grandpa did not come home from the Bes-Medresh right away. He used to rush over to the Slonimer Shtibl and stay until the end of the prayer, which took longer there than in the misnagdic houses of prayer. With great pleasure, he celebrated the reception of Shabbat there according to the Hasidic way, "Nusekh-Sford"[1].

My Grandma Rive used to wait with calm and patience until he came home. She would run out to receive him and greet him at the door with "Gut Shabes!".

Khayim Osher liked music. His own versions of songs, which he interpreted with great feeling, were a mixture of heartbreak, joy and pathos.

He composed melodies himself, and matched them with passages of text from the Tanakh (Hebrew Bible). His "Sholem Aleykhem, malakhey hashareyt, malakhey elyon"[2] was unique in the shtetl.

With sweet melting in his voice, my Grandpa sang from the Shir Hashirim[3]:

"We have a little sister who has no breasts; what shall we do for our sister? "

His singing from "Kabole-Shabes"[4] was simply touching:

"To greet Shabbat let's go, let's be gone, for She is the wellspring of blessing".[5]

His "Adon Oylem"[6] was filled with spirituality, and he let it swell to a great pathos.

His "Ribon Kol HaOlamim"[7] was a very extraordinary song. He used to let it begin very sadly but then increase to ecstasy:

"Oh, help me, sweet Father!"

It went like this:

‏"כאשר צויתני לזכרו , ולהתענג ביתר נשמתי"

- Oh woe, sweet Father!"[8]

The old Slonimer Rabbi, the father of the famous "Shmulekl"[9], adopted many of my Grandpa's melodies and spread them among his Hasidic followers.

Every Friday night, all the sons (of my Grandpa) and even the sons-in-law who were Misnagdim, used to come to sing Shabbat songs with my Grandpa.

My Grandma usually didn't sing along. She would just tap her finger on the table to the beat. The other women used to sit a little away from the table and hum along with the melodies. But they never sang along loudly.

[Page 68]

The hospitality in honor of their guests at my grandmother's house consisted of cake cut into pieces, tea, preserves and nut kernels. They sat together until late at night. The conversations were about family matters.

However, Grandma did not allow any defamation or gossip to take place.

On Shabbat morning, her daughters and daughters-in-law would come to her (my Grandma's) house to pray together. Surrounded by those closest to her, she used to sit full width on her bench with her daughters and daughters-in-law right next to her.

For Torah reading[10], women would gather around her, and she used to read from the "Taytsh-Khumesh"[11]. She also liked to look through the "mekhitse" (partition wall) at her sons-in-law, who had their pews on the east side. Her sons prayed in the Slonimer Shtibl.

After cholent, it was her custom to go to her daughter Dvoyre, the baker's wife, for tea. (Otherwise), she rarely went to visit, or to an invitation to eat and drink. Her children and relatives knew that one had to come to *her* for a hospitable meal.

My grandfather was rarely at home when guests came. After a nap, which he took, he went to the Bes-Medresh, because he only studied a little at home. My Grandma went without him to visit. Often he would join her later.

Most favorite of all the children, Grandma Rive went to visit her oldest son Perets. She considered him to be a very smart person. However, she could not stand her daughter-in-law Khaye.

The poor daughter-in-law tried to buy her mother-in-law's kindness. She wanted her mother-in-law to be kind to her.

But the latter already considered Khaye a hopeless case. Even if her mother-in-law had not behaved that way, her fate would not have been better. Because, apart from my Grandma, her husband did not love her (Khaye) either.

Aunt Khaye was kind-hearted, but she was a depressed, already elderly woman. She rarely went to the neighboring town of Sokolka, where she came from. Sometimes, however, a relative would stay with her, but Khaye would be depressed and embarrassed, and in the end she was glad when her closest ones did not come. Because she usually wanted to get (everything) off her chest, Grandma insinuated that she was not in her right mind, and did not put up with her.

[Page 69]

However, my grandmother did not stay too long with her son. Before the day was over, she was on her way home. She still wanted to accompany the Shabbat out of her house. Because, she used to say, "I helped bring Shabbat in, so now I want to escort it out!"

Before night fell, her daughters, who (still) lived with her, had to be home.

They used to sit at the table and talk quietly. My Grandma would sit near the window and wait for the sun to set.

As long as it was still light, she would read from the "Taytsh-Khumesh". When it became darker, she remained silent for a while, moving only the upper part of her body now and then. As it grew more gloomy, her shadow used to expand and move, bent, from the wall to the ceiling of the room.

When the night came, Grandma disappeared together with the shadow. The darkness had covered and swallowed her.

What was my grandmother thinking in those hours at the end of Shabbat? Probably her thoughts wandered to her youth, to her home and all who lived there? To her shtetl, to her brothers and sisters and to all those from whom the disdainful life had separated and alienated her?

In her mind, Grandma certainly went back to her days as a young girl, talking and discussing in her Polish-Yiddish dialect with all those who were dear to her. And she merged with her own past years.

She was never the first to light the fire again. I remember my mother asking her to light the lamp because the neighbor's house was already lit.

But Grandma waved her hand away:

"Apikorsem are living there!"[12]

These events filled me with gloom and sorrow. Small as I was, I already felt the great change that was taking place in the house with the approach of the (new) week.

I used to sit on a chest and observe everything that was happening at home.

My grandmother's silence, her movements and the image of her shadow used to weigh on me and wrap me with longing and sadness.

I felt great sorrow that the Sambatyen[13], (the legendary river), would soon begin to "play" again and the Reshoim[14] would once again begin to torment themselves in the "Gehenem"[15].

My Grandma had told me all these stories and I usually visualized with mental pain that the Reshoim were tortured. I had no idea what the stories actually meant.

[Page 70]

According to Grandma's explanation, human rishes[16], were atoned for. That is, forgetting prayers, but above all, not sanctifying the Shabbat, as a Jew must do. My grandmother did not tell me about other religious duties or sins[17].

Who knows if those evenings at the end of the week, my grandmother's behavior and mood, and the pain of the transience of Shabbat, did not greatly shape my life and my mind?

When my grandmother decided it was time to let the week (beginning) into the house ("you mustn't retain Shabbat too long," she used to say), she would quietly get up from the chair and instruct the daughters to rise.

Together they touched a window pane with their fingertips, and in the room, there spread silently and restrained:

"God of Abraham, of Yitskhok and Yakev, dear Shabbat is now leaving after all. Lord of the world, may you bless us with happiness and well-being, success and rest during the week. As the holy Shabbat fades away, so shall sorrow and suffering depart from our families and from all Israel.

Protect us and your people Israel from evil and from enemies, Amen".

She did not let anyone else light the (kerosene) lamp. Slowly she used to go to the table, take the glass insert from the lamp, screw the wick higher, strike the match, light the wick with it, and only wished "Good week" when the glass was already fixed in the lamp again.

The luminosity at the beginning of the week was a melancholy and darkened one. It seemed to be the same lamp, the same wick. But Friday night the light was more cheerful and brighter.

As soon as the light was on, a pot of potatoes in their skins was put on to boil.

But this was done only in winter on Shabbat evenings. One of the children would then go with a small jug or bottle to buy "lyok," (herring sauce) for a penny, into which they would dip the boiled potatoes.

Saturday night, just like Friday night, my Grandpa was at the Slonimer Shtibl and spent time there with the Hasids.

Before sunset, they usually sat together and told each other stories.

Then before they lined up for the Minkhe prayer[18], the Hasids used to stand in a circle, put their hands on (each other's) shoulders, dance around the bime[19] and sing:

"All that the Holy One, blessed be He, has created in His world"[20]

Ecstatically, they then cried out:

"And (I) say, G'd shall reign forever and ever".[21]

Each tried to outdo the other's enthusiasm, but it was always Shmuel Khonen's voice that rose above all others. He used to shout out the "voed" (and ever) with great impetuosity and pathos.

[Page 71]

I remember that my grandfather did not reach the shoulders of his fellow dancers when he danced, so he leaned on their elbows. He used to close his eyes, throw his head down with his beard in front, and adjust to the dance with extraordinary nimbleness. The Hasids had the habit of suddenly slowing down the dance and pawing their feet as they took steps.

In the semi-darkness, one did not recognize any faces, only black shadowy figures moving in the round dance.

As soon as the Hasids approached the Orn-Koydesh[22] where the dance ended, my Grandpa left the shtibl to go to the Bes-Medresh alone and perform the Havdole[23] ceremony.

When Grandpa came home, the lyok was already on the table, and right after Havdole, the boiled potatoes (still with skin) were brought. The skins of the potatoes were wet, and steam rose from the plate. My Grandpa performed the blessing-.

"Boyre-Pri-Adome"[24].

And again, the heavy, dreary week began.

Translator's footnotes:

1. סערד= nusekh-sford., "Verses from Spain," canon of prayers commonly practiced among Hasids.
2. Text of the song "Peace upon you", sung on Shabbat. https://www.chabad.org/library/article_cdo/aid/528331/jewish/Shalom-Aleichem-Text.htm, https://www.youtube.com/watch?v=913jZFL1bdE
3. שיר השירים= Shir Hashirim, the biblical "Song of Songs," the first words and name of the first megillah, which includes the love songs of King Solomon
4. קבלת-שבת= KabolesShabes or Kabalat Shabbat= series of prayers which are spoken or sung in the synagogue on Friday night to welcome Shabbat.
5. לקראת שבת לכו ונלכה כי היא מקור הברכה= Verse from the welcome song for Shabbat "Lekha Dodi"
6. אדון עולם= Lord of the Universe, opening words of a hymn in the Jewish liturgy, https://de.wikipedia.org/wiki/Adon_Olam
7. רבון כל העולמים= Beginning of the song "Lord of all worlds", https://www.youtube.com/watch?v=u_21caKG-DA
8. כאשר צויתני לזכרו , ולהתענג כאשר צויתני לזכרו , ולהתענג ביתר נשמתי= roughly: "...as I was commanded in His memory, and to rejoice in my additional soul (= "neshome netera", the additional Shabbat soul)", excerpt from the "Ribon Kol HaOlamim". The full phrase in the song would be " כַּאֲשֶׁר צִוִּיתַנִי לְזָכְרוֹ וּלְהִתְעַנֵּג בְּיֶתֶר נִשְׁמָתִי אֲשֶׁר נָתַתָּ בִּי". The essence of these songs does not come from the literal statement alone; rather, it is revealed through a careful analysis of his ambiguous words, their word roots, individual letters, and relationships to one another. Meditative immersion and/or fervent singing were, or are, a means to enter a state of trance, or ecstasy, and to experience the longed-for "closeness to God". I can well imagine that Khayim Osher got into a state of "God rapture" and uttered the following Yiddish words, where by "Father" he surely means G-d./ One of the existing versions of the prayer can be found here, with English translation http://www.zemirotdatabase.org/view_song.php?id=106&recordings=1
9. "Shmulekl" =Rabbi Shmuel Weinberg of Slonim (1850-1916). https://en.wikipedia.org/wiki/Slonim_(Hasidic_dynasty)
10. קריאת-התורה= kries-hatoyre, reading from the Torah in the synagogue
11. טייטש-חומש= Taytsh-Khumesh or "Tsene-rene"= Ashkenazy translation of the Pentateuch in ancient "ivre-taytsh" script
12. Apikorsem= skeptics, heretics, non-believing Jews
13. Sambatyen/Sambation= legendary river, which divides the known world from the land of the displaced and lost 10 tribes of Israel (also known as "Red Jews"). According to the legend, the Sambatyen is a raging torrent that throws stones for a whole week and is impassable. It rests only on Shabbat, but because of the religious regulations the exiled Jews are not allowed to cross the river then.
14. רשעים= bad, malicious persons, Jew-haters

15.   גיהנם= "Gehenem" is usually translated as "hell". In fact, however, there was a real place, "Gei-(Ben)-Hinom," the Valley of (Son of) Hinnom, a narrow, deep ravine on the southern border of ancient Jerusalem. This used to be the city's garbage dump, where corpses were also deposited. In the past, a fire burned there constantly to burn remains and to cleanse the place of impurities. In the religious sense, "Gehenem" is the state or place of spiritual purification and repentance, which – depending on the faith – is accompanied by external or one's own torments and chastisements.

16.   רשעות= rishes: wickedness, badness, hostility to Jews

17.   עבירות= aveyres: sins, transgression of commandments, wastefulness

18.   מנחה= Minkhe, a prayer which is prayed after noon or before the sun sets

19.   בימה= Bime, Bimah= Podium from which to read the Torah

20.   כל מה-שברא הקדוש, ברוך הוא, בעולמו= Mishna, Traktat Avot

21.   ואומר, יי ימלוך לעולם ועד = this praise to G'd, sometimes only slightly modified, appears in several Jewish prayers and religious songs.

22.   ארון-קוש= orn-koydesh: Holy Ark, cabinet for the Torah scrolls

23.   הבדלה= havdole: Distinction between sacred and common, ceremony at the end of Shabbat or a holiday

24.   בורא-פרי-אדמה= Boyre-pri-adome: Creator of the World.

[Page 72]

Two Soldiers in a Picture

The only picture in our house showed two soldiers. On a small table next to them lay an open book. The soldiers' pants, wide and puffed up like sacks, covered half of their boot shafts. Their hats, they were without visors, had slipped sideways and were close to their ears.

One soldier kept his one hand outstretched on the table, and with the other clutched a small sword scabbard. From his shoulders hung a bit of cloth, a sign that he served in the "musical section."

Years later, my father, rest in peace, used to tell exciting stories about how he became a military musician.

In civilian life he had never played on an instrument and had no ear for music at all. But, because he quickly acquired military doctrine with his good skills, he found recognition from the "Rotne Komandir", the company commander. He promoted him and brought him together with the "Rotne Shrayber", the company's secretary.

This secretary, the second (soldier) in the picture, a converted Jew, was a heavy drinker and a bon vivant. The company commander, an elderly, sick person, had befriended him (the secretary) and usually left him in command of the soldiers.

A deep friendship developed between my father and the secretary. He used to tell my father that he longed for Jews and Judaism.

When he was drunk, my father told me, he used to cry and reproach himself for having been baptized.

He had done this in defiance of his grandfather, who was a cruel man and had tormented him, an orphan, to such an extent that he had to run away from him.

He began to wander all over Russia until he found himself in Samara. There "utshitel", teachers, fostered him and supported him until he was 20 years old.

One of the teachers tried to introduce him to Christianity. However, he did not allow this.

[Page 73]

When he felt that it became a burden for him to continue being with the Christian family, he went back to his Polish shtetl.

As soon as his grandfather, who had become even more angry and dogged in his old age, saw him in non-Jewish clothes and without any beard growth, he prophesied to him that he (his grandson) would still convert, and chased him out of the house. The latter, just to hurt him, went to the Orthodox priest and was baptized.

When he became a soldier, he was already a goy with a gentile name. He quickly became popular in the company. The little knowledge his teacher had taught him in Samara now came in handy, so when the "Rotne Shrayber", (the company's secretary) had completed his military service, he took his place.

The "Rotne Komandir" (company commander) began to treat him as his own child and relied on him completely for everything. When the meshumed[1] finished his military service, he decided to become a professional soldier. He did not know where he could have gone, and he had already completely finished with his past.

In the 1905 revolution, his company was transferred to Krynki. He came to visit my father, but Dad was already in America. He brought my mother a gift, a purse made of "patsherkes" (beads). It was a rare antique piece.

Whenever he had time, he came to visit us. There was a constant smell of spirits coming from him. My mother could not stand it and was not very happy when he came.

His wife, a tall and skinny goy, smoked and coughed incessantly. He (the meshumed) had a boy my age and a younger girl. He often took me with him to play with the boy.

The girl's name was Tseroshke. He proudly explained to my mother that she was named after his mother's name, Tsirl.

Even though he did not lead the company himself, he walked alongside the commanding officer when the soldiers were led out into the field to practice.

Often I went along with him. With pride and haughtiness, I used to stand next to him and have fun watching the other children look at me with awe and envy.

[Page 74]

The soldiers knew me and played with me. I loved to ride on the shoulders of a soldier and pull him by the ears as if they were reins.

When Dad did his military service with the meshumed, the latter lobbied for my father to be "relieved of his rifle" and transferred to the music company. There he became "Starshi Polkovoy Barabanthisk" (the main timpanist and timpanist elder of the regiment).

Timpani playing became such a part of my father's life that even years later he enjoyed showing off his timpani skills. He could then continuously and for hours drum various notes with two sticks.

I liked the two soldiers in the picture. Mother and Grandma instructed me to call one of them "Papa", although I did not know what this name meant. The second one they called "Berl." When they wanted to call me to order, Mom and Grandma used to threaten me that the soldiers from the picture would come to me and punish me if I didn't keep quiet.

However, they never proved that anything followed their threat. I was much too boisterous. I liked to scuffle with boys my age and no punishment, even from soldiers, deterred me.

In those days, we lived with the carpenter Itshe Shakhnes.

He was a hot-tempered Jew. His wife, a bent, worn-out person, all skin and bones, used to cough constantly with a dry croak. She was a kind-hearted woman. They both loved me as much as their own grandchildren, with whom I used to play. They used to say about me and their son's girl, as a joke, that we were a real wedding couple. Itshe Shakhnes and his wife I called Grandpa and Grandma.

Every Friday morning she would bake a little challah bread for me, and Itshe would give me a penny. Even years later, when we were no longer living with them, I would come to them every Friday for a challah bread and a penny.

When Itshe Shakhnes and his wife emigrated to America to join their children, they said goodbye to me with great heartbreak, as if they were abandoning their own child.

I was always dressed neatly and nicely. But the outer finery lasted only at home. Often I came back from outside twisted and with torn clothes. Angrily, my grandmother used to pinch me very hard. But it didn't help a bit, and as soon as I got back outside,

[Page 75]

I forgot my resolution to behave appropriately.

Grandma's grief over my behavior was great. She no longer knew how to cope with it and used to complain to her eldest son, Perets. I then heard her say, "May only Leyzer Hersh come at last." (My father). But, who Leyzer Hersh was, who would deliver Grandma from me, I did not know then.

Often she would say in anger, "It took three days for him to be born. Surely this is not a child, but a shed"[2].

Later I inquired in more detail how it had been with mother and my difficult birth. To ease her pain, they had "measured the grave"[3] and "torn graves at the ancestors".[4]

Lights were lit in all the Bote-Medroshim, and with the Torah shrines torn open, people lamented and prayed that the mother might survive the difficult birth safely.

Even the Torah shrine in the "cold" synagogue was opened, which was customary only in times of great misfortune, may the merciful keep us.

I was born, but I did not cry or scream. It took a while before the accoucheurs revived me.

When my grandmother told this story, she used to shake her head with a strange regret.

Translator's footnotes:

1. משומד‎ = a Jew who has adopted a foreign faith, renegade, outcast
2. שד‎ = shed: Demon, term for a wild child or an evil person

3.   mestn feld, mestn kvorim: a custom to measure a grave with a small rope, which will serve as a wick-such a light is considered an amulet for a long life, or for a terminally ill person

4.   raysn kvorim: to raise a cry, to weep violently at the grave of parents, ancestors, or wise scholars, and pray in the hope of bringing about help (this should be distinguished from "necromancy," which is forbidden in Judaism).

[Page 76]

The First Teacher[1]

My mother couldn't be bothered with me. She was too busy with her work, knitting socks. Grandma Rive had the supervision over me. She used to dress me, wash me, and even take me to the market for shopping.

Besides her, everyone in the family wanted to replace my father a bit – especially Grandma's oldest son Perets.

Who was who, and what they had to do with me, I didn't know. Only my grandfather and grandmother I called "father" and "mother".

My Grandpa Khayim Osher began to deal with me when it was time to learn. When they took me to the first kheyder (the Jewish elementary school), I already knew the "Alef-Beys".[2]

Jewish boys were not allowed to remain children for long, and very early they were accustomed to the duties of Judaism and the Torah.

When I was three years old, my mother did not want me to be put into a kheyder so early. Grandpa negotiated a compromise with her – for the time being, until I was older, I should learn only two hours a day.

My first teacher, (Rabbi) Shmuel Tentser, had a kheyder where about a hundred boys were learning at the same time. There was not a boy who was not in his school. To relieve the workload, the teacher had several helpers.

The school itself was a huge room with a sticky floor and three large, wooden tables set up in the shape of a "khes".[3] Long benches had been placed around both sides of the tables so that the children sat facing each other.

The Rabbi sat at the horizontal table. He called out the subject matter loudly and audibly. The helpers stood around the tables or walked among the children, making sure that everyone was quiet and listening to the Rabbi.

From the kheyder, several flights of stairs led to another room, the Rabbi's apartment. There it was dark and dirty. The walls were completely soaked.

[Page 77]

They virtually steamed from the moisture and fumes from cooking.

The room did not have a single window, and since kerosene was spared, it was constantly shrouded in darkness.

Peye, the Rabbi's wife, had pus constantly running from her blind eye. How she could work at all in this darkness remains truly a great wonder.

The parlor was full of children, all with snotty noses, unkempt and unwashed. Their pants and dresses were soiled, (the boys' fly was open), and their "little tails" peeked out.[4]

Peye's mouth was never closed. She screamed or scolded incessantly. Usually only her voice reached the kheyder. She could only be seen when she rumbled into the kheyder, looking ragged, with her blouse unbuttoned and cursing.

Then she hurriedly ran to her husband and took out on him everything that had accumulated in her bitter mind. Then again she used to tear herself away from the place with impetuosity to run up the four stairs to the apartment. For a while she stopped (at the top), looked around, let out another curse and disappeared.

These scenes, which repeated themselves a few times a day, did not affect Shmuel Tentser. He did not even turn his head toward his wife, but continued the lesson material as if there had been no noise of a human voice, but only the buzzing of a fly.

Peye's shouting and cursing mingled with the children's voices, "Komets Alef o, Komets Beys, bo."[5]

Grandma, Grandpa and my mother took me to the kheyder. Shmuel Tentser was already coming to greet us. His first welcome was a pinch to my cheek. The pain and the smell of snuff made me cry profusely.

For the children, this was a real holiday. They stopped studying and laughed. I broke away to run, but I was taken to the Rabbi's bench, on which there was a cushion (so that the Rabbi would sit higher and keep a better eye on the children).

[Page 78]

Shmuel Tentser sat me near him. Grandma, Grandpa and my mother stood behind me. Shmuel Tentser ran a long, wooden pointing stick over a piece of paper tacked to a blackboard.

Satisfied that I had done a good job of repeating "Alef, Beys, Giml," he gave me another pinch, and a coin fell on the blackboard:

"An angel threw it down to you, if you study well, you will get a whole kopek!"

For punishments, in the kheyder there was a "kine", a corner where a child who had "sinned" had to stand. This "kine" was closed by a door that reached up to the child's head.

The "sinner" had his little hat with the cap twisted backwards. In one hand he was given a broom, in the second a stove hook. The other children used to surround the "kine", moving their right and left index fingers together, contorting their faces and shouting: "Be, be byushim".[6] This continued for a few minutes. Then they went back to continue learning.

How long the punishment lasted depended on the magnitude of the "crime." Once a child had to stand for an hour – and then another.

As for me, the "kine" punishment took over. I made life so difficult for Shmuel Tentser that I was a frequent "stayer" there....

Shmuel Tentser was fed up with me, so he went to my Grandpa, Khayim Osher, to complain. Khayim Osher then spoke to me in his level-headed way. I liked to listen to and followed him. I was very fond of him. Today, when I reflect on my feeling toward him, it seems to me that it was characterized by pity.

I liked his quiet manner. His silence had a strong effect on me. When my Grandma began to criticize him and make her demands, his eyes would be filled with sadness. He rarely gave her an answer. Often he would get up in the middle of a meal, grumble a "well" and walk out.

After such scenes, I felt overwhelmed by grief and never stopped crying. Often I would run after him.

[Page 79]

He used to go to the Bes-Medresh, to sit right there and immerse himself in a prayer book.

When he was busy with some work, I loved to help him. I liked to give him a hand, sweep the floor, and bring the wood for heating in the winter. I also replenished the water in the ritual washing bowl and helped polish the candlesticks and the menorah.

On Friday nights, I usually went with him to the Bes-Hamedresh. I would stand on the bime, very close to him, and get the first sip of the kidesh (Kiddush) wine. At Havdole he would then let me smell the spices.

Early on Shabbat, my uncle Perets used to take me to the Slonimer Shtibl. My grandfather insisted that I follow the Hasidic path. When the Slonimer Rabbi came to Krynki, I was seated next to him at the "praven tishn" (see page 25) and he saw that I was assigned Shirayim.

In the middle of the week, especially in winter, I used to visit my Grandpa at the Bes-Hamedresh. Rarely was anyone there; sometimes a batlen[7] would be sitting next to the stove, or from a corner one could hear the nign[8] of a student. Once "little" Ayzikl, an interesting Jew, came in. He used to brag that he had undergone torture like a "Nikolayevsker soldier" and had remained faithful not only to the Jewish religion but also to the Yiddish language.

He lived a few houses away from the Kavkaz Bes-Medresh. In his old age he could walk only poorly, nevertheless he dragged himself up to the Bes-Medresh. There he would sit until one of his children or grandchildren came to accompany him home.

He always sat by the stove, nasally singing one nign with the same words all the time:

"Home, home, you have to go".

My Grandpa loved to warm up and stare motionlessly into the void. He could be silent for hours without interruption. It was hard to engage him in conversation, and he didn't like to answer. He liked to indulge his own thoughts and listen to the people around him.

I was a wild and restless boy. The excessive attention that Grandma's children gave me had "spoiled" me. I could not stay seated in one place.

Inside me was a mixture of anger and gentleness, of mischief and patience, of inflicting pain and subsequent suffering over having caused pain, of breaking and destroying and of regret.

[Page 80]

I resisted moral sermons, but could sit for hours listening to fables with moral lessons.

I had a great desire to be grown up and imitate adults, but at the same time I was engaged in foolish, childish games. I could be beaten half to death without giving the thug the pleasure of hearing me cry.

But those whom I loved could win me over with a single word, a movement, an expression, by an interjection that did not even make use of any words, but was simply a regret. Certain expression in the corner of their eyes.

My grandfather Khayim Osher did not use words to punish me; I just sat next to him and listened for hours to his silence.

Translator's footnotes:

1.   (original)מלמד= melamed, teacher in Jewish elementary school (kheyder)
2.   אַלף-בית = Alef-Beys, Alphabet
3.   ח = חית = Khes. Name of the 8th letter of the Alef Beys, the number 8
4.   a song describing this situation...here the word "veydl" is not pronounced out of shame, https://archive.org/details/nybc214738/page/73/mode/2up
5.   קמץ = Komets: the vowel sign, which in Yiddish means an "o", so that the first letter, Alef, is then pronounced "o", and the second letter, a Beys, is then pronounced "bo".
6.   „Byushim": I don't know if the word comes from Russian (from "beat") or if it has something to do with the Yiddish word "bushe"=shame.
7.   בטלן = batlen: devout Jew who sits in synagogue continuously
8.   ניגון= Nign, a (Jewish) melody that can, i.g., have a plaintive and joyful character, it can be a mystical-religious melody, an accompaniment to a festive affair (dance) or a melody at festive meals in the presence of the Rabbi.

[Page 81]

Grandpa's Speech

My Grandpa, Khayim Osher, used to say, "A Jew must not weep, for this distracts from trust in God. – What befalls a person is God's will alone, which must not be questioned or profaned by lamentation!"

Grandpa diminished his own grief by singing sad songs. His youngest son, Meyshke, used to say to this, "Father 'puket' himself." By this he meant- he stifles sorrow within himself. There was much sorrow around Grandpa. Life at home oppressed him. He felt guilty toward his wife, for he knew she was right and her heavy lot spoke from her.

He was no good at earning a living, and even his poor position as Shames had to be secured for him with vigor. Only the merit because of his father, who had built the Bes-Medresh at that time, helped my Grandma undermine the attempts of the Gaboyem[1] to push him, Grandpa, from his position.

Two main Gaboyem were targeting him and making his life miserable. One of them was "Borekh Khokhem" (clever person), the surname being ironic and meaning the opposite. Not only was he a giant, but he was also getting broader. His big belly and the golden chain he wore gave him authority.

Actually, he was a simple Jew who had worked his way up. As an upstart, he loved to kiss up to others. From those who depended on him, however, he demanded subservience. My Grandpa did not like bootlicking, and did not use to "dance around" the rich gentlemen. Precisely this omission and the fact that he was also an "unlucky person" exacerbated the rejection from the Gaboyem.

The main Gabe, Berl Fishke's, a biological nephew of my (other) grandfather, Yankel Bunim, was a tall, thin Jew with a blond beard. He was an industrious Jewish student, but a very vicious person. Wherever he was the "balebos"[2] and held influence, he insisted on being obeyed.

Berl Fishke's was a great wood merchant and apparently expected my Grandpa Khayim Osher to serve him as he was accustomed to, as a "menial".

[Page 82]

He was targeting my Grandpa and making his life difficult. But the Rabbi stood behind Khayim Osher and maintained his position as Shames. Due to my grandfather's credulity and naiveté, there was once a story that actually reduced his income again considerably.

Krinkers had the reputation of being very hospitable. Paupers often arrived in the shtetl, not only from the surrounding area, but also from as far away as Ukraine.

In order to control who moved about the houses, the council of the community divided the shtetl into districts. Each district was assigned a certain color, which also contained the begging box that the beggars received. Twice a week the colors were changed. Together with beggars there also arrived a tall and strong Jew who pretended to be a discharged "Nikolayevsk soldier". He spoke Yiddish with a strong foreign accent.

This Jew liked Krynki, and he entered the "Kavkazer" Bes-Medresh, which became his hostel. He began to make himself useful to Grandpa: He brought water, helped sweep out and clean, brought wood, supplied the stove, and did other work as well.

My Grandpa supported him and let him watch. He used to go around and ask the balebostes[3] to give this Jew some extra income.

When the Jew saw the Gaboyem opposing my Grandpa, he began to try to outdo him. With soldierly obedience he began to do errands for the rich gentlemen. In bad weather he brought their children hot food to the kheyder, and many children he carried home on his shoulders.

Rive did not like this Jew right from the start, and she used to tell my grandfather to beware of him. The latter, however, resisted her talk, for it did not occur to him at all that this broad, coarse Jew wanted to do him any harm.

It did not last long, the Jew was declared the Sub-Shames. And the latter was now wildly determined to outstrip my grandfather. He learned the respective blessings, became the prayer leader at weddings, brisn and other festivities. He actually became the Shames!

My Grandpa's income was now almost completely reduced as a result. In the bes-medresh he had become superfluous, he was not even allowed to call anyone to read Torah.[4]

[Page 83]

My grandfather was completely confused. He did not understand what was going on around him. Grandma made a huge fuss, and fortunately the Rabbi disapproved of the circumstances in favor of my Grandpa. He decided that Grandpa had a privilege to the Shames position and no one could take that away from him.

The Jew disappeared – and just as one did not know where he came from, one did not know where he had gone. The events, however, shook Grandpa very much. Apparently, he had had no idea beforehand of such human wickedness that would attack and assault him. It hurt him deeply that a Jew whom he had supported would turn against him in such a way.

His pain was written all over his face. He became even more silent. He did not like to answer and did not like (anyway) to take part in conversations. He went to the Slonimer Shtibl even more often. When he was in the Bes-Hamedresh, he used to retire to the stove or to a corner, and hum a nign.

I had a longing for him. From playing or from the kheyder, I would sneak to him in the Bes-Medresh. It was not Grandpa's way to caress or stroke you, but his eyes expressed everything: pain, sadness, love and glee.

Exactly during the time when the (described) story took place, a great misfortune happened in the family: the eldest son, Perets died! His death disturbed everyone. Before the funeral, the women were in an uproar. My grandfather sat huddled in a corner.

But when he was asked to pray the first Kadish in the cemetery, his voice failed him. He was overwhelmed by his pain and his own words, which he spoke to the deceased even before the Kadish. Perets had died quite suddenly.

He had suffered continually from headaches and had discomfort in one eye, which had been "made sick" so that he would not have to serve. He could hardly see anything in this eye. Because of the permanent headache he often used to lie in bed for whole days.

On Friday evening, right after the blessing, Perets had not felt well at all. As if they had foreseen the tragic end, his sons ran to tell the family about his illness.

[Page 84]

As a result, everyone arrived at Peret's family home – even the "Tsherebukhes".

The visitors sat in the large front room, drank tea and talked. Only my mother, peace be upon her, stayed with the sick. Suddenly Perets rose fell forward, into her lap. When the visitors came running in response to her screams, he was already dead.

My mother could not get rid of the idea that she had breathed the last breath of the dying man. She was then taken to reputable doctors in Grodno and Warsaw. My grandmother again took over the supervision of (her) four children.

When Perets passed away, my Grandpa left the room where the corpse lay so as not to disturb Shabbat.

After the Shabbat meal, he went to the Slonimer Shtibl. Before the Minkhe prayer, my Grandpa danced with the Khasids in a circle, faster and more boisterously than usual, and sang in a loud voice.

After the havdole, when the corpse was lying already on the floor, my Grandpa arrived. He recited several psalms. When the first Kadish[5] had to be said at the grave, the Jews asked, "Reb Khayim Osher, say the first Kadish!"

Grandpa stepped to the edge of the grave and began broken, filled with deep pain:

"My son, it is not you who will now say the Kadish after my death, but I must do it after your death, woe is me!"

Soon he straightened up and after saying:

"G'd has given, and G'd has taken away," he began the first Kadish for his eldest son.

Translator's footnotes:

1. גבאים= gaboyem, Plural of "Gabe, Gabbai": Synagogue functionary who performs responsible duties for the congregation, charity supervisor
2. בעל-הבית=balebos: householder, owner, boss, citizen, leader (etc.)
3. בעל-הביתטע= baleboste: female form of balebos
4. קריאת-התורה= kries-hatoyre: reading aloud from the Torah at prayer in front of the congregation
5. קדיש= Ka(d)dish: name of the Jewish prayer at the grave of a deceased person, name of the firstborn to say the Kadish for his deceased father. https://www.myjewishlearning.com/article/text-of-the-mourners-kaddish/

[Page 85]

Grandpa's Confidence

The grief of Perets' death and my mother's illness caused my Grandpa Khayim Osher to shrink and made him even smaller. He could not bear the pity of his relatives and Grandma's sudden kindness.

He only came home for a small hot meal and to sleep. During the day he was either at Bes-Medresh or with his daughter, the baker's wife. He used to crawl on the oven of the bakery, crouch down, lie down and think. He could not hide his pain and sorrow.

Great strokes of fate had struck the family, and my grandmother Rive used to say: "Job's sufferings have poured down on us!". Everything happened at the same time: Perets had died, his younger son Meyshke was in Grodner prison for a revolutionary activity, and my mother's illness had worsened. Her obsessive idea that she had breathed Perets' last breath simply could not be exorcised.

Exactly two years and one day after Perets' passing, his eldest son passed away. Khatskel, a well-bred young man, had been a very strong person who could actually bend iron.

He, Khatskel, fed his family well and was, as they say, a fellow who was devoted to God and man. That year he already had to face the "Priziv", the conscription. Grandma had already made all the preparations to exempt her first grandson from military service, as she had done earlier for her sons and sons-in-law.

Khatskel was a quiet and pious young man. He was not interested in the movements that had won over the city youth. He was devoted not only to his parents but to the whole family.

He was popular and always ready to do someone a favor.

Since Khatskel relied heavily on his strength, he paid little attention to the cold he had contracted.

[Page 86]

He neglected it until it forced him down. In the shtetl there were two doctors and ten royfim (healers): Feyve the Royfe, Avrohem Mair Pyaves, Motl the Royfe, Yankel Motl, Shimen Ber the Royfe, Peyshke the Sherer and Simkhe. The latter was already called by the modern name, Feldsher.

However, the other royfim, besides Peyshke or Simkhe, were rarely visited. The last two enjoyed the sympathy of the townspeople. The most successful was Peyshke. Apart from the craft of a feldsher, he additionally engaged in hair cutting, shaving, cupping and treatment with leeches.

He usually charged 15 kopecks for a visit to the sick. People were happy to let him come and he became the royfe of choice.

The second, Simkhe, was actually considered the better feldsher. Nevertheless, he was not called so often, because the townspeople did not trust him, which was connected with a strange relationship that Jews had with Jewish doctors.

In the shtetl, a Jewish doctor did not have much luck and did not use to stay there long. In fact, the Jewish community used to accommodate a Jewish doctor, but the Jews made little use of him. They had confidence only in a gentile doctor, a Pole.

Doctor Dzhitkovski, a giant-sized goy with thick hair on his head and a big, thick mustache, lived down Shishlivitser Street, among the goyim.

He came to the center of town either when he had to visit a sick person or just because, for medical rounds.

Jews used to treat him with respect and friendship.

Those who met him, used to take off their hats and greet him, whereupon he always had the same answer; his "gut Morgn" (good morning!) he used to pronounce extended as "g u t M o r g n".

Dressed in a pelerine (shoulder cape) and with a thick stick in his hand, his figure caused great awe among the Jews. The children liked to run up to him, pull their caps and shout, "g u t Sh a b e s, g u t Sh a b e s!"

He could speak Yiddish very well, but was actually an anti-Semite. One suspected a little that he was not fond of Jews, but that did not diminish one's confidence in him.

Only after World War I, when Krynki was in Polish territory, he became an open leader of anti-semitism and incited the goyim against the Jews.

[Page 87]

He even boasted that he had, with full intent, delivered many Jewish sick people to the afterlife.

Doctor Dzhitkovski had favored 'Peyshke the Sherer'. This consolidated the latter's (professional) situation in the shtetl. Simkhe, on the other hand, who felt close to the Jewish doctor, unfortunately, had to share his fate as well.

At first, Peyshke was brought to the sick Khatskel. But when he saw that he could not give any advice, he sent for the Polish doctor. The Jewish doctor was then the last choice – and he gave the order to send for the famous Doctor Zamkov in Grodno.

Grandma had collected a few hundred rubles among the rich relatives and went alone to bring Zamkov. By the time he arrived, however, Khatsel had already died in great pain.

In addition to all this, at that time there was a quarrel with Grandma's son-in-law, Dodye the baker. Often it was suspected that Dodye was only thinking about how he could harm and cause pain to Grandma.

Grandma had the idea of adding a small attic apartment (for herself) to Dodye's house. He, Dodye, agreed to it for the price of 400 rubles. The sum was to be paid in installments.

But when Grandma obviously could not pay the last 100 rubles, Dodye would not let her into the attic apartment.

To hurt her even more, Dodye rented the apartment to a soldier who had just completed his military service, a dull, coarse young man.

The "soldiering" had gone into his bones and determined his whole demeanor. He moved hastily like a soldier marching, throwing his arms with impetuosity. His hat he wore after the manner of soldiers: on the side.

The lad was a troublemaker.

His father, Dovid Shloyme, a village tailor, had a lot of grief with him. His son used to make him scandals and torment him with malice and cruelty. He mocked his father for taking a young wife.

The wife of David Shloyme the Tailor had suddenly, on a Shabbat evening, died in the Kavkaz Bes-Medresh. Several years after her death, he took a wife from the neighboring shtetl Sokolka.

[Page 88]

But his son was deeply annoyed by the fact that his stepmother was younger and more beautiful than his own wife, and so he began to make life difficult her.

He used to get drunk and break the windows of his father's house. Full of rage, he would then go after the young woman until she finally packed her bags and fled from Krynki.

Once he cut his hands on the broken windows. Thereupon he ran to my uncle Dodye, scandalized there, stirred the flour with his bloody hands and then smeared them on the stove.

As a result, Doydye threw him out.

Granny, however, did not keep quiet. She had litigated against him and finally got justice. However, she did not enjoy living with her son-in-law because he made her life difficult.

Grandpa did not interfere in these conflicts. His son-in-law's behavior caused him great suffering, which, together with the great blows of fate, crushed him.

His pain filled me with deep sadness. I was ready to do many things for him to make it easier for him.

The day before Yom Kippur, I came to him in the Bes-Medresh very early in the morning and helped to take the candles and place them in the boxes filled with sand.

On Sukes (Feast of Tabernacles) I carried "the etrog and the lulav (palm branch)" into the houses. At the end of that (festival) week, I brought him the kopeks that the women had paid for the blessings. He used to rely on me because he had made it clear that if I bit the tip off the etrog, I would pay dearly for it.[1]

I was the only one of all his grandchildren who felt a deep love for him. Therefore, he often spoke to me as if I were an adult. Once, in the middle of the day, when no one was at the Bes-Medresh, I found my Grandpa sitting there huddled by the stove.

His face was marked with sorrow. Seeing him like that made me cry intensely.

"Grandpa, why are you so sad?"

"God is punishing me!"

"What is God punishing you for?"

He averted his eyes from me.

Suddenly he stood up with a jerk. I was startled by the sound and the passion with which he had torn himself away from the stove.

I had never seen such impulsiveness in him before.

[Page 89]

He walked forward a few steps, then suddenly stopped and shuffled exhaustedly to the bench by the stove.

Obviously he felt that I had gotten a fright.

He took my hand:

"Well, understand, if it were not a punishment, my pain would not only be more severe, but also senseless! Confidence, my child, makes it easier to endure agony".\

Translator's footnote:

1.   The fruits that Yosl delivered to the households had to be completely undamaged in order to be allowed to use them for the feast. The present sentence is a bit ironic and also

ambiguous. In fact, biting into the etrog tip is said to have a positive effect on fertility, and biting off the etrog tip was a well-known child's prank and a saying.

[Page 90]

"Dad" Has Arrived

When her younger children began to earn money, Grandma Rive moved to a larger and more comfortable apartment. In addition to Yisroel, the younger son, Meyshke, was also going to the factory. Grandma gave her youngest daughter, Yente, to relatives in the store of a manufactory. Meyshke already began to be involved in the group of "brothers and sisters".

A Russian elementary school ("Narodnaya Utshilitshe") opened in the shtetl. The teacher Krupnik was employed by the "center" to agitate there and educate the youth in the spirit of the "class struggle." Most of the students came from middle-class families. By the time it became clear what was being taught in the school, it was already too late. Most of the young boys had already been infected by socialist propaganda.

After the police had came to arrest teacher Krupnik, he was never seen again.

Without Krupnik, however, the young people felt left alone. They decided to stick together and educate themselves autodidactically, so to speak.

For their meetings, the group chose Grandma's apartment.

This was the most suitable place for the youth. At that time, Grandpa was a gemore[1] teacher, and from the outside, Grandpa's teaching post provided a kind of protection, so that no suspicions arose in the first place.

Meyshke managed to convince Grandma to let the group meet at her house and educate each other. Thus it succeeded, and so in one room young boys sat together learning Russian and listening to propaganda speeches.

In the other room, Grandpa taught the young boys the subject matter of Jewish religious books.

When Grandma realized that the group members were talking against the rich and the government, she did no longer let them in.

Often I came into the room where the "brothers" had gathered.

[Page 91]

There it was completely different from Grandpa's room, where the teaching content was "sung" with a nign.

Where Meyshke was, people sat and were silent; only a young man, standing up, made incomprehensible speeches.

There I heard for the first time speeches about "poor and rich". Rich people, for me, were only Nokhem Anshel and the "Tsherebukhes", about whom my grandmother spoke many unpleasant things.[2]

I liked very much to listen to the songs, which the lads sang softly. I remembered the "nigunim", the melodies, and also the words. The song of Edelshtat, which they sang with much feeling, had a deep effect on me.

Silent and sad, they sang:

> "We are hated and driven,
> we are hunted and persecuted,
> and all because we love
> the poor, languishing people."[3]

I could only attach meaning to individual words: "poor"-that was my Grandpa and Grandma. "working people"-those were my uncles Yisroel and Meyshke.

Once, there was unrest in the house – a message arrived that father was released from military service and was on his way (home).

Mother immediately began to look for a (suitable) apartment. She ordered furniture from Itshe Shakhne's son, a famous carver. His carvings adorned holy Torah shrines and the estradas of many Bote-Medroshim.

The furniture, two beds and a wardrobe, were real works of art. Who knew the value of these carvings even then? I still remember what the figures on the cabinet looked like.

The upper part of the cabinet was on the shoulders of very strong men, their facial muscles were tense, but they gave the impression of carrying the load with agony, but also with heroism.

On the cabinet doors were carved some groups of people. Next to one of the groups were vessels on small tables filled with food: confectionery and various fruits. The bodies of the people were thick, and satisfaction and energy radiated from their faces.

Beside them, thin and hunched people stood submissively and with sad faces.

These figures, with their depiction of social "classes," exerted a great influence on me that resulted in my later association with the labor movement in America, and which I internalized like a pointer to injustice in the world.

[Page 92]

When the furniture was brought on a gentile cart to the apartment at Alter Milbn, downwards Kavkaz, Itshe Shakhne's son placed it with great care. He looked at the figures on the cabinet for a long time and lovingly stroked them like living creatures.

When father arrived, I was at the market with Grandma. On the way home, Feygele, the daughter of Yente Avremtshik, came running toward us with outstretched arms to tell us the news.

Feygele, a relative of ours, was a good but unhappy child. Her sick eyes were constantly watering and her eyelashes were always stuck together.

Her father and mother did not live together in family harmony. Her father was from Ponevezh, the area around Kovne (Kaunas), and talked with a sharp "Rish" and a "Sin".[4] He was a "kamashn-shteper"[5], but apparently he did not earn enough income in Krynki and therefore went back to his hometown. He promised to catch up with his wife and child, but rumors spread in the shtetl that he had a mistress in Ponevezh and aspired to divorce his wife.

His wife Yente was not a big personality. The grief and her crying had made her ugly, and she used to talk and cry constantly only about her gloomy lot.

Feygele must have been 10 years old when her mother, Yente, asked my mother to take her in and teach her how to knit socks. She, Feygele, also helped to take care of me and Mama fed her in return and once bought her a dress.

After a few years, Feygele's father's behavior brought even more grief to the already bitterly depressing life of wife and child. He drove to wife's house with his mistress, whom he passed off as his sister. The carters soon scattered the news that Avremtshik's son-in-law had arrived with an "impudent woman." Thereupon, the entire shtetl took up position under Yente's window to catch a glimpse of the man and his mistress.

The strange girl, or miss, was so frightened by the crowd that she fled the house.

[Page 93]

Feygele's father chased after her and asked her to come back. The next morning, the two of them had disappeared from the shtetl. Yente became even more confused by this story until she finally lost her mind completely. Feygele, however, had already come to stay with us.

When we (me, Feygele and Grandma) came back to our house, it was already besieged by people standing at the windows to see my father. (What was the use of newspapers, radio or telephone? The coachmen already made sure that the townspeople got all the news from them faster than through the newspapers).

Inside, the house was full of people. A person in a soldier's uniform hurriedly got up from the table, reached for me and lifted me to him.

I recognized him right away, it was the same as the one in the picture – "Papa" had come!

[Page 94]

My cousin Yisroel-Moyshe

Translator's footnotes:

1.   גמרא= gemore, Gemara, part of the Talmud that explains the mishna
2.   כּל-דבר-אָסור= kol-dover-oser: everything you are not allowed to say, everything that is not nice to say
3.   a version of the song can be heard here
https://www.youtube.com/watch?v=P8H1SiaH9cA
4.   He spoke the typcal Northeastern Lithuanian dialect.
5.   Gamashn-shteper (Gamaschen-Stepper) = tradesman who sews a shoe/boot upper to the sole.

[Page 95]

The Grandchildren

Grandma Rive desperately wanted to keep her grandchildren under her influence, only she couldn't, because by now they were too far out of sight. So Grandma had to content herself with giving her sons and daughters advice on how to deal with their children. Her sons and daughters-in-law, however, often did not want to follow it.

Now, as for her son-in-law Dodye the baker, Grandma had no success at all. She used to give him instructions on how to raise his only son, Yisroel Moyshe. However, Dodye only laughed at this and did just the opposite; only to make her suffer.

Her daughter, Dodye, was too tired and exhausted to engage in conflict with her husband. Of course, she also could not talk back at all, much less argue.

However, Dodye certainly did not want his only son to spend his time drinking liquor and playing cards at such an early age either. Yisroel Moyshe, however, had begun to hang around with bullies much older than he was and who were after his money, of which he had plenty.

Apart from the fact that the drawer in the bakery was always open, and Yisroel Moyshe could take heaps of coins from it, he had also found out that his father hid money in his mattress. And since Dodye never kept records, it was easy for Yisroel Moyshe to take as much money as he wanted.

Yisroel Moyshe became more and more estranged from me, and this annoyed me and made me angry. I couldn't stand that he was making friends with those louts and hanging out with them in inns.

Yisroel Moyshe was taller and fatter than me, and yet he was afraid of me. I was more aggressive than him, and in my anger I faced even boys who were older and stronger than me. Once I grabbed and hurt him. From that time on, he completely avoided contact with me*[Page 96]*

When Dodye realized that he was in danger of going completely astray, he decided to send him away from Krynki, to his sister in the surrounding shtetl Bodke. He spruced him up and adorned him with a silver pocket watch with a chain. Then he put him on a cart and told him to stay in Bodke until Passover.

However, Yisroel Moyshe did not stay there longer than two weeks. On a Thursday evening he arrived back home. When Dodye saw him, he wrung his hands (in despair). Yisroel Moyshe remained sitting quietly at home for only one day. On Shabbat, immediately after praying, he sought out his gang again. The boys got drunk and went to sled on the (frozen) "Sazelke" (pond).

Yisroel Moyshe fell, and the louts jumped over him and mocked him.

A boy came to Dodye to tell him what had just happened to his only son. Everyone who was at Dodye's for tea at that time ran to the "Sazelke".

Yisroel Moyshe, accompanied by rascals, was carried home. He had lain there motionless, blue-frozen, stiff and with torn clothes. There was no trace of the pocket watch with the chain.

For a whole week he wrestled with death. When he got up, pale and haggard, he talked to no one and sat melancholy and withdrawn in a corner.

Exactly when he was in this mood, I goaded him then and provoked a scuffle. He never forgave me for this. Until I left for America, he was angry with me. He did not answer my letters to him from America.

When Yisroel Moyshe was an adult, he became a communist activist and became deeply involved in municipal affairs. He perished, along with millions of martyrs, in the crematorium at Auschwitz.

The children of the eldest son[1] were more inconspicuous. Perets' son Khatskel, was obedient, as were the other two older children, Moyshe Yosl and Yente. Yente took after her grandmother completely; a tall, confident, but very quiet woman.

Perets' son Shimen, who was younger than his sister Yente, was a little twisted. From childhood, he loved to trouble people with strange questions. When he learned a little Kabbalah, it got to his head.

He used to dream about strange and incomprehensible things.

[Page 97]

He talked a lot and usually annoyed people with questions they couldn't answer. The death of his father and eldest brother then finally drove him out of his mind.

Shimen's mother Khaye, who was herself psychologically distressed, took him to Warsaw to a "good Jew." Her sick son, however, secretly slipped away and wandered through the city. When the police found him after a few days, he was frozen stiff. His hands and feet had to be amputated.[2]

The body of the seriously mentally ill man lay in bed for years until God had mercy on him.

Perets' boy Feyvl had a funny habit of snorting with his nose, so I called him "Shnants".[3] This nickname remained with him all his life. He was the same age as me and was the only naughty one of Perets' children.

After the First World War he became a great leather manufacturer in Krynki, however, he too lost his life along with the martyrs in the crematorium.

Perets' remaining two children, the girl Khane and a younger boy, are hardly remembered by me. I was informed that Khane was a good but very poor woman who always struggled to make a living. Perets' youngest son is now residing in Uruguay.

Granny's oldest daughter, Malke, had an only daughter, Sheyne Blume. Malke lived in Glusk, in the Minsk gubernye, and Sheyne Blume and I wrote to each other regularly. When I was in Russia, I did not visit the family. Sheyne Blume and her husband had gone to Moscow at that time to visit me, but I was out of town at that very time. When I got back to Moscow, I just couldn't bring myself to go see them.

That's something I still can't forgive myself for today.

The children of (Grandma's) son Yisroel kept their distance and rarely came to visit Grandpa and Grandma. Yisroel himself had completely switched to the side of the "Tsherebukhes".

I was Grandma's most popular grandchild. I was constantly under her influence, and she considered me not as her grandson, but as her own child.

However, I offered her no reason to take pleasure in me. I used to hurt her and insult her.

She showered me with privileges, but my insolence and pranks filled her with anger and rage.

[Page 98]

I resisted her and took pleasure in causing her grief.

After a too wild prank, I fell out of favor with my Grandma Rive. She treated me only very coldly and even turned her head away when I spoke to her. I often did something that hurt the whole family and made them despair.

I used to envy the adults and wanted to behave like them. Above all, I wanted to act like the revolutionary lads. And as soon as Mom's brother Meyshke and Dad's brother Mair (Meyer) got involved in the movement, I ran after them and was often with them at their "skhodkes".

The lads began to use me for themselves. I often went out and did various courier runs, delivered proclamations, stood guard and let them know when the police arrived.

One sign that I was growing up was a suit (for me) with a breast pocket. Another sign- smoking cigarettes!

From Dodye's drawer I stole money for cigarettes. But in addition, Dodye also sold cigarettes without a band, which were in his open drawer.

Many times I filled my pockets with cigarettes and then used to take some of them to trade with Dodye. He never realized that they were really his own.

But I especially liked those cigarettes that were in a box with a picture of a young woman on the lid. She was sitting in the bathtub, covering her upper body with her hands. When I got my new suit, I used the breast pocket I had longed for, to put a pack of "Babushka" cigarettes in it.

That Friday night, when I first dressed up in my new suit, Grandma had asked me to spend the night with her. I was to pick her up at her son Perets', to whom she was paying a visit to the sick.

On the way to Perets' house, I calmly walked past the Rabbi's house with a lit cigarette. Students from the Talmud school who had been sitting on the porch saw me, came running out, grabbed me and gave me a good thrashing.

I therefore arrived at Perets' house with a reddened face. I explained to my grandmother that I had become so red from running so fast.

[Page 99]

The Rabbi immediately sent someone to my Grandpa Yankel Bunim with the news of what his grandson had done.

When I had already taken off my clothes, my father came storming into Grandma's house, agitated and angry. From sheer excitement he had lost his speech. He muttered only two words incessantly, "woe, woe, what grief!"

My father was so upset that he actually could not tell Grandma what had happened. My Grandpa Khayim Osher sat to the side, confused, looking at my distraught father.

Impulsively, Dad grabbed my clothes and took out the packet of "Babushka" from the breast pocket. Grandma's eyes grew huge. She looked at me sharply for a while, then got up from her bench and slapped me with all her might.

Then she ordered me to leave her house.

Grandma never forgave me for desecrating Shabbat and shaming the family.

In our house, father took my clothes. For a few days I was tied up in bed and was not allowed to go outside for weeks.

Translator's footnotes:

1. The sentence concerns the family of Khayim Osher.
2. hent und fis= hands and feet, but also possibly meaning arms and legs
3. possibly the term means something like "snout".

[Page 100]

Rive and her Son Meyshke

For none of Rive's children did life turn out to be really easy and successful. Even my mother, who chose her future husband herself, had a hard lot, because on her lay the burden of raising her children and supporting them.

A few months after the wedding, my father left for military service. She was pregnant at the time and had to move in with her mother. Later, when she already had three children, the Russo-Japanese War drove my father away to America. Mother had to move back in with her parents and once again provide for the living alone.

My mother's bitter and difficult life increased Grandma's sorrow and worries. None of Rive's children, however, brought such excitement to her life as her youngest son Meyshke. She was constantly on the road because of him. For several years Grodno was her second home. What happened to him made her drop everything and spend her time only with him.

Figuratively speaking, she moved in with him in Grodno prison. She was driven by an overpowering urge to free Meyshke from the detention.

Who knows, it may very well be that the excitement around Meyshke even rejuvenated Rive. Her life would certainly have been hard for her to bear if everything had gone quietly and smoothly.

Rive had already become accustomed to the worries of her married children. She was not able to change their lives. With all of them, a certain order had already set in. But as far as Meyshke was concerned, she could let her impulsiveness run its full course, loosen stiffness, and liven up again.

Her involvement with Meyshke had the effect of keeping her busy. However, her enormous activities on his behalf were linked to the message to him that he had to fulfill obligations to her; for without her, he would be rejected and lost, and his life would end behind prison walls. He therefore did not belong to the "movement," but only to her.

[Page 101]

Meyshke's role in the 1905 revolution went far beyond the borders of Krynki. The anarchist group to which he belonged had designated him and Nyomke, the son of Yonah the Stolyer/Carpenter (a brother of Sore'ke, with whom Yisroel had a love affair) to carry out an assassination attempt on the mayor of Odessa.

Nyomke had remained in Bialystok, but Meyshke went to Krynki to say goodbye to his family.

He arrived in merchant's clothes, with a Karakulene fur hat[1], a fur coat with a collar of Karakulene fur, a gold pocket watch with chain, and pockets full of money.

When Grandma Rive saw him dressed up like this, she knew immediately that something was not quite right. Rive soon began to make hysterical scenes. The whole family gathered, Perets talked at Meyshke, Grandma fainted, and my Grandpa helplessly tucked himself away in a corner, muttering sad nigunim.

Meyshke himself was drifting around lost and desperate. At that time, Avrohem Yitskhok the Vilner, leader of the anarchists of Krynki, lived in Grandma's neighborhood. All conspiratorial plans were prepared in his house.

Rive stormed into Avrohem Yitskhok's house crying and pleading. For several days in a row she did not give him any peace. The end was that Meyshke remained in Krynki.

Meyshke was a serious young man. He liked to get to the bottom of facts. He read a lot and was, as they say, a person with an "open mind".

On Meyshke, the propaganda of Krupnik, who taught at the Russian elementary school, had had a great effect – as on a large part of the youth in general. Right at the beginning, the young people belonged to the "general socialist movement". Later, the "Bund" received great support in the shtetl, and most of the Jewish youth became "Bundists." There were also social democratic groups and the "PPS" organization, the "Polish Socialist Party."

The first to establish an anarchist group in Krynki was Yankel "professor" (the well-known author Yakev Krepliak, peace be upon him).[2]

[Page 102]

Meyshke liked the speeches about targeted actions. He became an anarchist. He and Yankel "Professor" became devoted and close comrades.

There were quite a few anarchist groups that had absolutely no connections with each other and carried out actions on their own responsibility.

Meyshke was not a hot-tempered young man. He was thoughtful and did not do rash things. Apparently, Meyshke was not a fanatical revolutionary either. He was somewhat sentimental and strongly attached to his family, especially to his mother. He felt deep sympathy for his father, and at that time when the Gaboim came upon him, Meyshke came to protect him with great devotion.

Immediately after the outbreak of the 1905 revolution, he spent several months in the Grodner prison. When he returned, he was (even) more serious and thoughtful – but had now become completely an anarchist.

His collaboration with the revolutionaries aggravated the "war" between us and the rich relatives; Nokhem Anshel, especially, was very angry. He used to severely criticize my Grandpa Khayim Osher for his son's activities. Several times he quoted Grandma to him, but she did not want to cross his threshold.

Rive tried in her own way to talk Meyshke out of allying with the "Buntovshtshikes", the rebels. She used to argue: "Why are you interfering? People will manage without you. Settle down, get married, and conduct yourself as a Jewish child should. If something comes out of their activities, it's very good, but if not, well, what do you want to sacrifice yourself for (your ideal)?"

But Meyshke answered her, "If everyone listens to their mothers, then nothing will ever change!"

Grandma moved heaven and earth to dissuade him from the "Buntovshtshikes", but it was of no use. Meyshke began to be at home less often, and when he did come, he met secretly with Avrohem the Vilner.

Meyshke's silence and disappearance filled Rive with shock and worry. It annoyed her that he did not listen to her. All at once she realized that he had broken free of her influence and was estranged from her.

Translator's footnotes:

1. Karakul sheep pelt
2. Yakov Krepliak or Yankel Kreplak, this link leads to an obituary, in „Forverts" 16 Oktober 1946,
https://www.nli.org.il/en/newspapers/frw/1946/10/16/01/article/22/?srpos=5&e=-------en-20-1--img-txIN%7ctxTI-%d7%a7%d7%a8%d7%a2%d7%a4%d6%bc%d7%9c%d7%99%d7%90%d6%b7%d7%a7

[Page 103]

Daughter Yente's Shidekhim[1]

Unfortunately, Grandma Rive had not known what misfortune had dawned. Meyshke's dealings with the revolutionaries did not upset anyone in the family as much as her.

All at once she relinquished supervision of her other children and no longer attached any value to other matters. Meyshke was now the center of her life. He was constantly in danger and stayed more in prison than in freedom.

At that very moment, there was also grief with the younger daughter. Yente was a decidedly quiet girl and conducted herself like a bourgeois child. However, the revolutionary mood that had fascinated the Krynki youth at that time also influenced her.

At that time, those who kept aloof were considered unsophisticated and backward people, and in such a mood it was simply not pleasant for a young person not to belong to any of these groups or parties. The entire city youth was involved in the revolutionary movement.

It is a historical fact that the first workers' council was formed in Krynki. Three days before the outbreak of the revolution in Russia[2], the boys of the "Brothers and Sisters" had occupied the few government buildings and Jewish communal institutions, arrested quite a few people of the police, declared a "workers' republic" and administered the shtetl until soldiers and Cossacks marched up.

The townspeople liked to spend time in the woods during the summer, and therefore this was the appropriate place for secret meetings.

At such gatherings, people listened to speakers who had come from a big city.

[Page 104]

Together, they discussed, read and sang fight songs by Edelshtat (Edelstadt), Bovshover, Reysen, Vintshevski and Rozenfeld. Once such a secret "skhodke" was stormed by the police. Yente had to serve two months in the Grodner prison. When she was released, she had completely changed.

She followed her mother again, as a middle-class girl should.

Grandma, however, had become afraid and was now striving to marry Yente off as quickly as possible. She no longer allowed her daughter to have any contact with young people from Krynki.

On the occasion of Yente's matchmaking, they began talking to a fellow from Narew(ka), a shtetl south of Bialystok. The fellow, a good and intelligent person, was older than Yente. Like all young people of the merchant class, he felt attached to Zionism.

In the beginning, my grandmother did not like him at all. She made fun of his appearance, his nose and his small eyes. After a short time, she gave up looking for a spouse for Yente for the time being.

Finally, however, she invited the young man again. This time, though, she again regretted her decision, because it crossed her mind that he was not allowed to be chosen as a spouse, since he had the same name as Grandpa Khayim Osher – namely Osher.

But Grandpa voted against this rule. That one time Rive listened to him and finally agreed with this shidekh.

After the wedding, Grandma Rive even accepted that Yente moved away from her to settle in her husband's shtetl.

Now she was completely occupied with Meyshke. He was the only "little bird" that she still took under her wing.

She was now in "competition" with Meyshke's comrades. She wanted to defeat them in the struggle for influence over Meyshke. For all at once she felt that a strong enemy had risen against her, who wished to diminish her influence over her child. Meyshke began to perform actions at her place that she normally would never have tolerated. Thus, she agreed to allow the boys and girls to meet in her house.

Among the anarchists at that time Reyzl Tevl Liptshiks took a leading position.

[Page 105]

She was a well-bred, educated girl, with a good knowledge of Russian, Yiddish and Hebrew, and she was also quite well-read. For the movement, she occupied herself with enlightening, teaching and educating the youth.

Reyzl was nimble and lively, but also headstrong. She remained true and devoted to her ideal until her last breath. In London, she was killed by a bomb she had thrown herself.

Meyshke persuaded my grandmother to let Reyzl teach classes in her home. At the very beginning she (Reyzl) came to our house twice a week. But it didn't take long at all, and the little young woman with the blond curly hair moved completely into our house (we were living with Grandma at the time, father was already in America).

Reyzl's move effectively turned Grandma's house into an anarchist center. I still remember how she (Reyzl) gave her propaganda speeches to the group. Grandma used to sit quietly in a corner and nod her head. Reyzl agitated constantly, even from bed, making clear to Grandma and me the importance and indispensability of the struggle for a happy future.

Grandma Rive did not use to argue with her. My mother, on the other hand, I remember, was already arguing with her.

She (Reyzl) taught me to read and write Yiddish and gave me my first Russian lessons.

It happened that she and Meyshke could not be found for a few days or weeks.

Then Grandma could not sit still. She used to walk around the house sad and tense and could not bear with me and my two brothers.

When Meyshke and Reyzl were not there, none of the boys and girls came to our house. Grandma used to go out to see one of the group to find out where Meyshke had gone.

But every time she came back sad. Once, when Meyshke and Reyzl were not there, soldiers and guards stormed into our house. They searched and rummaged in every corner. They actually turned the whole house upside down. But they left empty-handed.

[Page 106]

Reyzl used to put her books and literature in the "kotakh" (a kind of cellar room near the oven). The place was covered with potatoes and wood, which was usually kept in this place. After the "revision" (the house search) Reyzl did not show her face in our house. She had left Krynki. When Meyshke came back, the house was not like before.

Translator's footnotes:

1. שידוך, shidekh, Plural shidekhim: (Matches) connecting people through a wedding, marriage, matchmaking
2. The Russian Revolution broke out on January 22, 1905, and encompassed a series of revolutionary events and activities until July 16, 1905. It was triggered mainly by the bloody suppression of a peaceful workers' demonstration in St.Petersburg

[Page 107]

A Bomb Injures Meyshke

Soldiers and Cossacks kept the shtetl in fear and terror. A large number of the youth were taken to prisons and many left Krynki, but those who remained did not back away from danger and responded with attacks on the rulers and the "bourgeoisie" (which the youth pronounced with hatred). Attacks were carried out on individual powerful lords[1] and on cruel policemen.

At this very time, a large number of expropriations, confiscations, started as well. In the neighboring town of Sidre, quite a few Krinker "bokherim" (boys) raided the post office. Some officials went to the attic and shot down from there. One young man, Dovid, the son of a bricklayer, was killed.

(Individual) young boys from Krynki emigrated to other towns, and news of their exploits spread in the Shetl. At that time in Krynki the factory owner Shmuel "Amerikaner" was shot. He, a Jew, was a great braggart and blowhard. He used to brag that he had once been to America and therefore had been given the nickname "Amerikaner".

Shmuel "Amerikaner" took special pleasure in coming to the market where the youth met, showing them his revolver and emphasizing that he was not afraid of anyone. When warned that he had better stop these antics, he only laughed at them and even intensified his provocations towards the young fellows.

On the last day of Passover, when Shmuel came from praying and was walking together with a group of Balebatim[2] who also lived on Gabarska Street, he was shot. The attackers had hidden under a bridge that Shmuel had to cross.

[Page 108]

Out of the darkness, a voice had warned the companions to run away. When Shmuel turned around, a hail of bullets pierced him like a sieve.

At that time there had also been planned the assassination of the mayor of Odessa, which Meyshke and Nyomke, the son of Yonah the Stolyer (the carpenter), were to carry out.

After Meyshke's dramatic farewell to his mother and the scenes of wailing and lamenting at Grandma's house, Avrohem the Vilner, the leader of the Krinker anarchists, had taken action and relieved Meyshke of his mission.

However, this was done only in pretense. In fact, Meyshke did not go to Odessa, but he had to do another job. Things were bubbling up among the Krinker lads! So how old were they at that time? They were 14- to 15-year-olds, and if one of them was 18, he was already considered an old bokher.

They were Jewish children who fought with devotion and willingness for the ideal of "Akhres-Hayomim"[3], to dedicate it to their fathers and grandfathers. They set out to liberate and fraternize the world, sacrificing their lives along the way for their ideal and their faith.

Not two weeks had passed after Meyshke's return home when he disappeared again. Grandma went to Avrohem Yitskhok the Vilner to find out where Meyshke was. Avrohem Yitskhok, however, did not come out with the truth.

After a few days, the news came that Meyshke had been injured by a bomb in the shtetl Horodok. Meyshke had been ordered to bring a bomb from Horodok to Krynki, which was to be thrown into a gathering of factory owners in the "great" Bes-Medresh.

Meyshke was very skilled in building "wick bombs" (bombs with fuses). He had received instructions on how to do this from Yankel "Professor" (Yakev Krepliak, peace be upon him).

A new bomb was tried out in a field near Horodok. Meyshke had lit the fuse but apparently missed running away in time.

[Page 109]

The bomb exploded next to him and injured his face and his right hand, from which the middle finger was torn off. His comrades were afraid to bring him in to Horodok. When his wounds were bandaged, they took him on a farmer's cart to the neighboring town of Shishlevitsh (Svisloch in Russian), to Doctor Bitner. The doctor promised not to betray Meyshke. But as soon as the group of comrades left, he reported to the police, and they took Meyshke to Grodno prison.

As soon as this news reached Krynki, Rive set off for Grodno and, in effect, lodged with the Gendlers, who were very hospitable people.

Avrohem Elye Gendler, and especially his wife Khaye (the author Karlin's mother-in-law), whom Grandma could not praise enough for her beauty and kindness, made Rive's stay pleasant and helped with whatever she could.

Russia was in a state of war at that time. Trials against Revolutionaries from the "tkhum-hamoyshev"[4], were held in two specific regions. In Warsaw there was a "field court" where the death sentence would always be pronounced. In the second region, in Vilnius, there was already a court with a jury (the "Okruzhnoi sud", District Court). Those who were sentenced there could consider themselves lucky.

Now when Grandma heard that Meyshke was to be sentenced in Warsaw, she fell into fear and panic. She knew that Meyshke would be lost if she did not intervene.

Where did this old-fashioned Jewish woman, expelled from her Polish-Jewish homeland to a hilly Lithuanian shtetl, get all her strength?

She did not know a word of Russian. Her knowledge of foreign languages was limited to a few Polish words she remembered from her childhood. However, she mustered all her strength and not only managed to contact the governor of Grodno, but even succeeded in getting respected advocates to defend Meyshke free of charge.

The governor had the power to annul the decision to try Meyshke in Warsaw. But who could make contact with him for Rive? No one.

She had to do it on her own.

[Page 110]

Rive began to lay siege to the governor's apartment from the outside for an extended period of time. Every day she sought out his office. It didn't help that they chased her away. She came back!

Fortunately, the secretary of the office felt sympathy for her. He liked the tall, self-confident Jewess with her dignified bearing. She did not make a noise or shout, but only asked to be let in to see the governor.

And so he interceded for the governor to hear her out.

Proud, confident and flawless, Rive walked in to the governor. She bowed, approached him and kissed his hand.

"What do you want, Mamuchka?"

Using the few Polish words she knew, she described her son's situation. She pretended that he had nothing at all to do with the "Buntovshtshikes." He had only visited relatives in Horodok. And on a walk he had accidentally come to the field where the bomb had exploded. Therefore, she asked that her son not be sentenced in Warsaw.

"Don't worry, Mamuchka, everything will be all right!" the governor told her.

"Angels stood by me then," Grandma used to say.

When Meyshke's trial was transferred to Vilnius, she went to Petersburg to get advocates.

Why she could be there at that time without "Pravozhitelstvo" (the right for Jews to reside in cities outside the tkhum-hamoyshev), I cannot explain.

In Petersburg she made her way up to (the lawyer) Grusenberg and to a Russian advocate who was famous at that time as a defender of revolutionaries. Both advocates agreed to provide legal representation free of charge.

But before Meyshke was sent to Vilnius, Rive learned from him that he did not want to defend himself at all, but on the contrary, wanted to admit everything.

Grandma could communicate with Meyshke through a young woman who knew the prisoners' finger language. Right next to the Grodner prison stood a building from which one could look into the prison yard. Relatives of detainees could watch their close ones walking in the prison yard every day.

[Page 111]

Since the prisoners were well aware of this, they usually looked up, to the roof. And so, with the help of the young woman, my grandmother learned that Meyshke did not want to defend himself.

At that time, arrested revolutionaries liked to use the court as a platform to publicly proclaim their ideas and views. Therefore, instead of defending himself, Meyshke planned to declare that the bomb was made to "kill the servants of the autocracy."

After Rive realized that she could not talk Meyshke out of this, she came up with an extraordinary plan. When they transferred Meyshke to Vilnius, she called her son Yisroel to her by telegraph.

Every morning, when the detainees were led from the prison to the court, surrounded by policemen with bare swords, my grandmother and Yisroel would follow them all the way along the sidewalk.

And during the walk, Grandma discussed with Yisroel so loudly that Meyshke should hear it. However, she addressed him not as Yisroel, but as Meyshke!

"Meyshke, remember, you are not to say anything, but to deny everything. If you do not do this, I will commit suicide. Remember that, because you will never be able to forgive yourself if something happens to me!"

At the trial, Meyshke denied everything, and the jury acquitted him. However, Meyshke did not remain at liberty for long. After six weeks, the prosecutor reopened the trial. A gendarme arrived from Grodno to interrogate Meyshke. And the new sentence was now 4 years in prison.

My grandmother Rive was simply not destined to find peace. She settled back in Grodno, knocking on doors again, looking for ways to get Meyshke free.

End of the first part

[Page 112]

My Uncle Meyshke

Translator's footnotes:

1.   גבירים= Plural of Gvir: a powerful, rich, distinguished man (also seen politically)
2.   בעלי-הבתים= Balebatim: plural of balebos= the owner, landlord, boss, citizen, proprietor
3.   אחרית-הימים= akhres-hayomim: end of days, messianic times, when mankind is redeemed from all wickedness
4.   תחום-המושב= tkhum-hamoyshev, territory within which Jews were allowed to live in tsarist Russia

[Page 113]

<u>Second Part</u>

Father's Family

[Page 114]

My Grandfather Yankel Bunim, my Grandmother Sime-Feygl and my Aunt Sore

[Page 115]

Grandpa Yankel Bunim

Grandpa Yankel Bunim's children were passionate and impetuous. Their world of thoughts lacked structure and balance. Their kindness and warmth of heart simply bordered on stupidity many times. They were I and believed everyone. They did work for the community with zeal and dedication. They were ready to sacrifice themselves for an ideal, and when they did something for a person, they always thought it was still not enough.

Yankel Bunim himself was not exactly a placid person either, but he did not have the effervescent temperament of his children. It may be that in his youth he had also been as hot-blooded as his sons, but he probably had to adapt his behavior to the customs and mood of the times.

Yankel Bunim was able to come to terms with a situation. Impoverished as he was, he processed the changes from his former personal, economic and social circumstances in a philosophical way. He tried to settle into his situation and calmly accept his fate.

Yankel Bunim was not a doubter. He scared away emerging sadness and melancholy. He loved life because he loved his wife from the bottom of his heart and, as sick and broken as he was, he did not accept moods of skepticism and small-mindedness.

Yankel Bunim did not try to impose his definite and clear philosophy of life on his children. He taught and explained to them his views about the world, God and people. However, he did not insist that they behave as he did.

His views were different from those of Grandpa Khayim Osher. They were also different from that small minority in the shtetl who had an objective worldview. After all, there were not many people in the shtetl who had such a broad general education. He was a Jewish scholar, well educated in Talmudic knowledge, who was also interested in world literature.

[Page 116]

Yankel Bunim himself tried to write. His written reflections were clearly and directly formulated and of great scope. He usually wrote novellas and kept his literary works, which he guarded with great care, wrapped in a blue ribbon. If he had lived in a big city, he might have made something of himself.

But his illness and love for his wife bound him firmly to Krynki and did not let him go out into the wide world to fight for a place within the burgeoning Yiddish literature. As far as I can remember, he wrote in the style of Mendele Moykher Sforim[1].

Yankel Bunim was influenced by the Haskalah[2] and counted himself among the representatives of this philosophy. In Krynki, however, he was unable to significantly advance the impact of the Haskalah movement, and so he was content to fight the Hasids.

Moreover, he considered Hasidism to be idolatry and felt that it seduced, deadened, and did not let the Jews out of their dull corner into which the exile had forced them.

Yankel Bunim spoke excellent Russian. Despite his poverty, he subscribed to the Russian newspaper "Retsh" ("Rech") and the Hebrew "Ha-Tsfira".

He was one of the few in the shtetl who could add and multiply well.

He liked to discuss and did so passionately and impatiently.

Yankel Bunim considered himself a spiritual aristocrat. Usually he turned off and away from a man whose views he did not accept. Essentially however, he was tolerant and even conducted his fight against the Hasids with forbearance. He was in the habit of severely chiding adults for letting their schoolchildren attack the Slonimer Rabbi.

He considered this a great sin.

Because of Yankel Bunim's love for the Enlightenment movement, he did not oppose his sons when they began to join the rebellion against the government.

He understood that times had changed and that one could not turn off the new thoughts that were spreading among the youth.

After all, he himself was different and he knew how difficult it was to fight against deeply rooted views and concepts of life.

Yankel Bunim did not want to prevent the sons from joining forces with the "brothers and sisters". However, he demanded that they not do anything that would shame him.

[Page 117]

Grandpa used to encourage his children to leave Russia, knowing only too well that he could not make them stay at his side. And in addition, he was aware that their participation in the revolutionary movement put them in danger not only of losing their freedom, but also their lives.

Yankel Bunim's sons joined the revolutionary movement body and soul. Loud and hotheaded fellows they were, and when they committed themselves to something, they did so with fire and passion.

In the shtetl there were only two families, that of Yankel Bunim and of Yonah the Stolyer, whose sons and daughters were almost all active in the first ranks of the revolutionary movement, not only in Krynki but also in Grodno and Bialystok.

Most cruel blows of fate befell Yankel Bunim. He was a sick person. His shortness of breath used to torment him. In order to facilitate his breathing, he used a kind of tube, which he formed from a book cover. Inside the tube was absorbent cotton soaked in carbolic[3]. This mixture gave off oxygen as it evaporated rapidly[4].

He held the tube to his mouth again and again. Without it, he could not breathe.

He was never able to sleep peacefully through the night. He got up dozens of times, because his shortness of breath always woke him up.

His illness, shortness of breath, was the result of a cold. A Grodner doctor instructed him to use the tube and showed him how to use it.

A while later, Grandma Sime Feygl fell ill, and her illness made her a completely different person. A gland stopped working, and this caused her to become obese, which interfered with her mobility and led to digestive problems.

They took her to the best doctors in all the towns around Krynki. She took remedies to lose weight. This did not make her lose a bit of weight, but at least it prevented additional fat accumulation. Grandpa's and Grandma's life was hard and poor.

Continuously they lived in hardship and misery. They could never afford to live in a comfortable apartment, it was always cramped, and often they lived in apartments that did not even have a wooden floor.

[Page 118]

Their largest apartment had two rooms. And I still remember some apartments that had only one small, narrow room. Grandpa earned his living by selling lottery tickets that promised a "big win." However, the lottery tickets not only did not bring a "big win," but no win at all. His lots brought no luck. The lots were bought only out of respect for him and because the youth appreciated that his sons were revolutionaries.

His sons, Yankel Bunim had six of them, can, with the exception of my father and an older brother, be called heroes of the revolutionary movement, both in the 1905 revolution and far earlier.

His youngest son, Mair, was torn apart by a bomb in Bialystok. This happened when he came with two other boys (one of them also from Krynki) from Zabludow, a shtetl next to Bialystok, to throw a bomb at a meeting of the highest officials with Brash, the Grodner governor. This (meeting) took place in the shtetl Vashlikove (Vasilków). On the way, the bomb exploded and the three boys and the coachman were blown to pieces.

When people did not want to buy raffle tickets because they had never won, he (Yankel) would equip himself with an object and raffle it off; a gold watch, a ring, a brooch for a woman or some other piece of jewelry. He kept the item in a beautiful box that was wrapped in either blue or red plush.

The jewelry was carefully wrapped in thin paper, and the box itself was also wrapped in a colored cloth.

His customers were mostly factory workers whom he visited in the tanneries. He then carefully took out the item and let the people admire it. In front of their eyes there was a lottery ticket on the article that had a chance of winning. The drawing of lots, however, took place either at Bes-Hamedresh or at the home of a respected citizen. A child usually drew a number. And everyone learned who the lucky guy was.

Translator's footnotes:

1. Mendele Moykcher Sforim, very famous Yiddish author, see https://en.wikipedia.org/wiki/Mendele_Mocher_Sforim
2. השׂכּלה=Haskalah, Jewish enlightenment movement that emerged in the 18th century. Some of the distinctive features was its interest in natural sciences, philosophy, grammar, literature and a renewal of pedagogy and Torah study. An emancipated society with separation of state and religion was sought.
3. Karbol= formerly used as disinfectant, formula C6H6O
4. This sentence seems incomprehensible to me, which is why I have translated it completely freely.

[Page 119]

I Distinguish Grandpa Yankel Bunim

My memory of my Grandfather, Yankel Bunim, does not go back to the time when my father was doing military service.

This is strange because I still remember his daughters, the elder Henye and the younger Sore, clearly.

I also remember the story told about Grandpa's oldest son, Ahron Velvel, who had been deported to Siberia, and the other two sons, Moyshe Berl and Khayim Shloyme, who had fled to America because of revolutionary events.

But my memory of Grandpa Yankel Bunim and Grandma Sime Feygl begins only from my "Pidyen-Haben"[1].

The Pidyen-Haben was organized when I was already exactly four years old. I was Yankel Bunim's first grandson (my father was his third son, but the first to marry), and he prevailed upon Grandma Rive that the ceremony would not take place until my father returned from military service.

The first memories of Yankel Bunim's figure actually come to me in connection with the Pidyen-Haben. And it was because he was continually kissing me. I liked that a bearded Jew was caressing me and leaning towards me. My Grandpa Khayim Osher, whom I called "Papa," never showed me such closeness, nor did he caress me.

In general, there was a big difference between the two Grandpas. Yankel Bunim, the sober Misnaged, was quick-tempered. In contrast, Khayim Osher was a serene and calm person, a passionate Slonimer Hasid, someone who lived in his particular Hasidic tradition and created fiery melodies for the Rabbi and the Hasids.

My Grandfathers often used to argue and have disputes. Yankel Bunim used to get excited and try with fierce determination to prove the " non-Jewishness of Hasidism" by referring to the Goan of Vilna[2] and his struggle against the Hasids.

Khayim Osher listened to him calmly, he used not to interrupt Yankel Bunim, only to answer quietly and calmly. And if he had no answer, he smiled naively and lost.

[Page 120]

Often the two of them had arguments because of me. Yankel Bunim would not allow Khayim Osher to take me to the Slonimer Shtibl and insisted on leaving me alone with it. And finally he prevailed.

I cannot say that I loved my Grandpa Yankel Bunim very much. I think this resulted from the fact that he had taken over the supervision of me after my father went away to America. He wanted to be too strict with me; however, I was also a wild and spoiled brat.

Not only was I naughty, but I was simply aggressive. I broke windows, fought with boys, stole money from my mother, and caused him (Yankel Bunim) great suffering.

A cabinet, attached to the wall, hung in the porch. It was used as a kind of "cool box". In the summer, various fruits were stored in it, and in the winter, Grandma stored beef lard and cherries there that she had stewed during the summer months.

I used to tear out the hinges of the cabinet, carry away the fruit and eat up the berries. With my fingers I used to pick the greaves out of the beef fat and get full of the cherry juice. Thanks to me, it was not possible to keep a little fruit or snack in the cupboard.

My Grandma was good-natured; she never got angry with me. There was never a curse coming out of her mouth. Her worst "threat" was, "Just make sure this doesn't end badly!"[3]

Grandpa, however, could not simply watch how rampantly I behaved and what damage I caused. Several times he slapped me and often he beat me with his stick.

In general, Yankel Bunim's surges of emotion were sorrowful and had a strange effect on me. Instead of compassion, it aroused a great satisfaction in me to see his rage boiling up.

Even when he was calm and relaxed, he could not do without his "trubke." When he was upset, he could no longer breathe, he threatened to suffocate, and instead of words, he only uttered a gasp and struggled for air. He would then turn blue, his face would swell, his eyes would pop out of their sockets, and sweat would break out.

When this happened, I would retreat to a corner and watch him struggle. Grandma, who could only walk with difficulty, used to run off scared to death, to bring him some water.

[Page 121]

He sat down heavily on a bench with his eyes closed. Grandma poured him the water and wiped his sweat. She brought him his trubke (the breathing tube) and held it to his mouth. When he regained consciousness, he would take a piece of sugar and stare blankly into space.

When such a sorrowful scene ended, I would flee and give him a wide berth for a while. Yankel Bunim used not to look at me after (such an episode). But my pronounced licentiousness usually brought him back to our house.

Often Mom would go to him and ask for help because she just couldn't handle me anymore.

Given my behavior, and because my father was rarely home, every male in our family was concerned with my upbringing and looked out for me.

The only ones who thought it was their job alone were Grandpa Yankel Bunim, Grandma Rive and Mama's oldest brother, Perets.

But Yankel Bunim wanted to play the main role. He insisted on interrogating me (literally) and often came to the schools where I was studying to inquire about my behavior and whether I was learning well. Since it was to be expected that the teachers would not praise me, I usually escaped just as I saw him coming to school.

I often made him suffer by annoying his youngest daughter, Sore.

All his children had moved out and scattered, and Sore was the only child he had left. She was about three years older than me, and I gave her a hard time. I beat her and put her out of commission. She was, as they say, Grandpa's and Grandma's "apple of their eye."

They spoiled her and their devotion to her was deep and boundless. None of my outbursts upset Grandpa as much as when I molested Sore. He literally fell into a panic.

Actually, Sore did like me very much. But like every child, she used to seek protection from her father, and spoiled as she was, she did this very distinctly and thus turned him against me. And at that time Grandpa didn't just accept anything, but immediately ran to seek me out. Since I was already expecting him, I usually fled to my uncle Dodye, the baker.

He was happy about my pranks and his home was always a kind of refuge for me.

[Page 122]

My lack of affection for Yankel Bunim must have resulted from the fact that he was a stranger to me; an outsider. Grandpa Khayim Osher was closer to me, I lived in his home and grew up in it.

I used to share in his fate and his helplessness and tragedy aroused closeness and compassion in me.

Moreover, he never hit me and did not try to dominate me or impose anything on me.

On the contrary, he spoke to me not as to a child, but as to an adult, and forgave my wildness.

Therefore, I avoided causing him grief. Even when I was caught smoking a cigarette on Friday night, he said nothing to me. He only groaned, then fell silent in screaming silence.

Yankel Bunim set heaven and earth in motion then. He talked my father into not letting me out of the house for a few weeks and was satisfied that my mother would tie me up for a few days. At times when I showed what we call "virtue," that is, behaved well, Grandpa Yankel Bunim was kind to me.

He liked to teach me and felt great joy when I listened attentively and made good progress.

Yankel Bunim did not think much of teachers (in the kheyder). He himself, when he was young, was taught by private teachers in all subjects, including Hebrew and Russian. But he taught his children the subject matter himself. Only later did he send them to teachers who taught adult young men.

If I kept quiet, Yankel Bunim usually wanted me overnight with him. Then he would study with me and tell me wonderful stories, which he would write down afterwards.

Yankel Bunim wrote at night. He loved to sit close to the window while writing, often looking out and contemplating the surroundings. He wrote small, fine letters on long sheets of paper.

While doing so, he used to sit bent forward and guide his quill. His hand moved slowly, but his legs fidgeted restlessly and quickly from the knees down. When he had written a sentence, or maybe a whole paragraph, he would read it to himself.

[Page 123]

He still wrote with goose quills and taught me to carve them.

I loved to help my Grandpa draw lots for items; sorting the slips of paper with the numbers or else the names of those who had bought the lots from him. He had written the names and (associated) numbers in a large book and used to transfer them afterwards onto pieces of cut out paper.

I used to cut the paper together with his daughter Sore. He insisted that they all be the same size and shape, because he didn't want anyone to suspect him of something; God forbid, not kosher.

The arrangements on the day before the numbers were drawn for the raffle filled him with activity and anxiety. He used to prepare himself as if some kind of holiday was coming up.

At the drawing, Yankel Bunim was sitting at the upper end with his yarmulke[4] slipped somewhat onto his neck. It seemed as if his shortness of breath decreased at these times and he used his trubke less.

When the winner's name was revealed, he beamed. He stroked his thinning blond beard, rose and stretched to his full height. He was of tall and straight stature. His large eyes and high forehead used to light up. Serenely and carefully he took the object out of his box, unwrapped it from the thin paper, and with joy handed it to the winner.

A few days after the raffle, however, Yankel Bunim walked around pensive and gloomy, and used to recite from religious books with a kind of sad nign. He yearned for that (festive) bustle and for the touch of the object that had become dear and familiar to him in the few weeks before the drawing.

One clock in particular took on the form of a living being for him. He used to yearn for the quiet restlessness of the ticking, the movement of the clockwork, and the jerking of the pointers, which he not only regarded as hands, but also called them so; just like human hands.

Translator's footnotes:

1.   פדיון-הבן= pidyen-haben/ Pidyon ha-Ben: "redemption of the son", ceremony in which symbolically the firstborn son is ransomed from the high priest as soon as he has reached the age of 30 days,   https://en.wikipedia.org/wiki/Pidyon_haben
2.   The Vilna Gaon (genius), see https://en.wikipedia.org/wiki/Vilna_Gaon
3.   literally, "You shall not be harmed!"
4.   yarmulke= Yiddish term for Kippah, probably from the Aramaic ירא מלכא, "yire-malkhe", "fear of the king"

[Page 124]

Yankel Bunim's Ancestry

My Grandfather Yankel Bunim was not a Krinker. He and his family came to the shtetl because of a tragic event. He, his wife and children were running for their lives at that time. Only by a miracle were they able to save themselves from the goyim in the village where they had lived. They had to leave behind even the few possessions that had not been stolen from them and settled in Krynki.

Grandpa was born on the estate "Meskenik", which was situated between Grodno and Kuznitse (Kuznica). His first three sons had also been born there.

My Grandpa's parents had inherited the estate, or "Hof" (farmyard) as they called their estate, from Yankel Bunim's Grandpa Yudel.

My Great Great Grandfather Yudl had been the richest landowner in the whole Grodno County at that time. He owned forests, estates and houses in and around Bielsk, near Bialystok, near Grodno and in and around Krynki.

In his will Yudl had divided his estate between three sons. The eldest got the estates around Bielsk and Semiatycze. The descendants of Yudel's eldest son were the

"Kadishevitshes". To the second son, Yosl the "Yishevnik"[1], as he was known in Krynki, he granted the estates in and around Krynki.

A famous city forest, later known as "Yente's Forest", was the property of Yosl the Yishevnik, whereby Yente bought the forest from him.

Krynki was once a famous weekend-home town, and the forest was home to the summer houses and cottages of its owners. Later, however, the shtetl "Druzgenik" (Druskininkai) cut it off, along with Grodno, and so Yosl Yishevnik sold his forest.

Yosl began to engage in granting interest-bearing loans to rich aristocrats. In doing so, he lent not hundreds, but thousands. In addition, he owned a tavern frequented by the richest people, and he also owned the hotel in the shtetl. The highest authorities used to drive up there.

[Page 125]

Later, the hotel became the property of his son Itshe "Lye"[2].

Besides the business with his hotel, Itshe "Lye" also traded in grain. His nickname "Lye" resulted from the fact that in Goyish the word for "yes" is "alye"[3]. But he usually mumbled the "alye" so that it became "lye".

Yosl the Yishevnik also had a daughter, Meri. She married a young man from Orla, Khaykel Orland. The latter was also a rich Jew who owned an inn frequented by the rich and the aristocrats. The townspeople nicknamed Khaykel "Khazer" (pig). He was a hard and nasty man who did not like to give alms. And so, not only was there no one to give him any merit, but they used to downright hate him.

Khaykel had about 12 children; his sons and daughters were all tall and broad and as hard-hearted as their father. They were not particularly bright either.

His third son, my great-Grandfather Mair (Meyer) Yonah, was given the estate near Grodno by his father Yudel.

There was a distillery on the estate, and Mair Yonah supplied the whole area with liquor.

Mair Yonah was a Jew with a sharp mind and was also very well suited for his business. He was already somewhat modern and thought highly of giving his children secular education. He made sure his children knew Russian, plus how to read and write.

He hired private teachers for them and later sent his son, Yankel Bunim, and daughter, Khaye Sore, to Grodno to a private Russian school.

Mair Yonah's daughter, Khaye Sore, was considered one of the most educated Jewish women in the area at that time. He married her off to the famous, distinguished bourgeois family of Avrohem Prilamer from Grodno. The son-in-law, Zundel Prilamer owned a spice store, however he himself sat days and nights (over his books) studying.

Khaye Sore did not love her husband. She was a great personality and also considered herself more educated than her husband was. There were constant quarrels and bad words between them. She wanted to divorce him, but he would not give her a divorce document.

[Page 126]

She did not depend on him financially, because her father, Mair Yonah, provided for her. She used to live completely separate from her husband.

The two had a son, Borekh Hersh. The quarrels between Zundel and Khaye Sore intensified with regard to the influence on their son. She did everything to alienate her son Borekh Hersh from his father and his family, and she had a tremendous influence on him.

Therefore, he was quite manipulated. The motive of her behavior was not love for her son, but his control.

When the time came for Borekh Hersh to do military service, she sent him away to hide in Krynki. In the shtetl he lived in the house of Itshe Lye.

He did nothing there, but loitered.

Borekh Hersh was a tall, handsome young man; and at that time, Sheynke Tabatshnik, the sister of Nokhem Anshel's Roshe, fell madly in love with him. Sheynke later married the factory owner Yisroel Hertske and had the "handicapped" son I mentioned in the first part of the stories.

Borekh Hersh apparently had no serious relationship with the young woman. As a loafer, he did not like to be harnessed into the yoke of caring for a woman and earning a living, but just wanted to have some good times with her. When he saw that the young woman really meant it, he began to stay away from her. But she was already very much in love with him and in her desperation decided to get him (as a husband) – if not by good, then by force!

During an argument, she threatened to reveal that he was avoiding military service.

When the young man saw that the story was becoming dangerous, he fled to America. His mother soon followed him. She spent her last years in New York. The relationship with her husband was completely cut off, they did not divorce, but they also never met again until the end of their days.

Yankel Bunim was married by his father to a girl of the famous Bialystok family "Barishes". My Grandmother, Sime Feygl, was of distinguished lineage. She was the granddaughter of the famous Bialystoker Rabbi R' Moyshe Zev Margolies, who was also known as R' Velvele, the "Mar'ot haTzov-ot"[4]

[Page 127]

Grandma Sime Feygl was a quiet and very fine woman. She spoke not only softly, but also tactfully. She was completely different from Grandpa Yankel Bunim. He was a hot-tempered and hot-headed man.

Her figure was also different. He was tall and straight, she was short.

When I was a child, my uncle, the jokester Dodye the Baker, used to tease me. As a joke, he would point out that my Grandparents must have been mixed up because one Grandpa was short and Grandma was tall, and opposite that, the other Grandpa was tall and Grandma was short.

Grandpa Yankel Bunim and Grandma Sime Feygl behaved completely differently from my mother's parents. Until the end of their days, Yankel Bunim was in love like a young lad with his wife and called her tenderly "Simenke".

Sime Feygl spoke little and usually behaved quietly. Never did a curse pass her lips. However, she was not free from superstitions, such as how to "avert the evil eye with a spell." She performed such things herself.

If a child yawned, it meant that someone had given him or her the "evil eye". She used to hold the child by the head, look into his eyes and quietly recite a spell. When she finished the spell, she used to move the head back and forth, spit out a few times and say, "To empty fields and wild forests!"

This was to drive away the "evil eye."

She also used to "tsingleven." This was a very strange act. If someone had a swollen cheek, either from the draft or from a toothache, she would fill a tea glass quite full of ashes. She wrapped it in a cloth and moved it over the cheek. This procedure, accompanied by a "spell", lasted about ten minutes. Then followed the control: if the ash had collapsed, it was considered a sign that the swelling would pass, if not, it was necessary to try again later.

Sime Feygl also eliminated toothache by a "spell". She put her little finger on the sick tooth and whispered words, which "killed the pain".

Yankel Bunim did not like this superstition. When his wife performed all these " uttering of incantations", he would·turn his head away. However, he refrained from offending her because of it.

[Page 128]

It may be that, at the very beginning of their years together, he enlightened her about the foolishness and futility of all her "incantations".

However, when she stuck to it, he made peace and let her do what she wanted. Yankel Bunim loved her not only for her virtue, but also for her beauty and quietness.

Grandma made friends with very few women in the shtetl. She avoided too close friendships. She was careful not to be drawn into intimate conversations, for she feared they might end in gossip.

Thus she behaved like her mother Reyne Gitl, R' Velvel's daughter, may she rest in peace, who did not want to have contact with women because she feared that from her mouth might come a word of defamation.

Grandma Sime Feygl loved to hear stories. She herself told very few. But Grandpa used to read to her the stories he had written down or tell her about a subject he was grappling with.

Sime Feygl never complained and never demanded anything. She used to accept everything as a sign of God's will and also never doubted His ways.

She relied on her husband for everything. She never opposed him or questioned his actions. The love between the two people was filled with tenderness and deep devotion. Her sons behaved in exactly the same way. Almost all of them were devoted, faithful and benevolent family men.

Translator's footnotes:

1.   יישובֿניק = yishevnik/ yishuvnik: Inhabitants of a "yishev", a village or settlement
2.   ליא = This word is pronounced Lye, but later in the book the nickname is spelled with a vowel sign and pronounced "Lya"
3.   אליע = alye: This is a Belarusian word that actually means "but" and is popularly used for "yes".
4.   מראות הצבאות = Mar'ot haTzov-ot: to the first word can be added the meaning "mirror" or "visions", the second word derives from "going to wars", "warrior", but also refers to holy actions for God's will, a kind of "militia sacra". Often this term is translated as "mirror of the armies". I choose to translate the Rabbi's epithet as "mirror of sacred efforts".

[Page 129]

Peasants Kill Mair (Meyer) Yonah

When my Great-Grandfather Mair Yonah received his inheritance share, the land and the distillery on the Meskenik estate, he dealt with widening and enlarging his property.

He provided his daughter Khaye Sore, who had turned away from her husband, with a pension. He involved his son Yankel Bunim, who was already married by then, in the management of his business.

Mair Yonah was very successful, so his inherited estates expanded. He bought forests in an area closer to Bialystok and Krynki. A few miles[1] from Krynki, he leased an entire village.

They (the family members) behaved like great aristocrats. My father, peace be upon him, used to tell that his eldest brother Aharon Velvel was wrapped in silk after his birth.

Father also told me that my grandfather taught them (the children) himself. But when they grew older, he sent them to Grodno to learn Russian and receive Jewish lessons. Every day they were taken to Grodno for this and the coachman waited there until he had to take them home again.

All the children of my Great-Great-Grandfather Yudel were well taken care of; both those in the Bielsk area, and the "Kadishevitshes" near Siemiatycze, and also the son Yosl Yishevnik, who settled in Krynki.

Yudel's family name was indeed Kadishevitsh, however, his son Yosl Yishevnik "because of the Cantonists"[2] changed this name to "Mastavlyanski".

However, while Mair Yonah's fortune was growing, hard and evil times began to dawn for Jews. The tsarist government endeavored in an even more evil and cruel manner to expel Jews from the villages and from their leased estates.

The edict declared as late as 1823 by Nikolai the First, yemakh shmoy[3], to drive Jews out of villages and prohibit the operation of leasehold estates, taverns, inns and post offices for them, applied only to the two administrative districts of Mohilever (Mogilev) and Vitebsk.

[Page 130]

At that time, the areas of the Polish Kingdom enclosed by the Russian Empire were in a privileged position. The "new Russian province" was endowed with a certain degree of autonomy, with a Polish government and "Seym"[4] – constitution. And this government held authority over the Jewish collective agricultural communities.

The situation of the Polish Jews in comparison to the Russian was comparatively exceptionally good. In fact, the Russian government even protected the Jews from Polish persecution.

It was not until 1842 that the Jews of the Polish province were put on an equal footing with the Russian Jews. They began to be conscripted as recruits, instead of being levied a recruit tax as before. Previously, they did not fall under the Cantonist Decree; there were no limitations on their living spaces (tkhum hamoyshev) or other cruel edicts from which the Russian Jews suffered.

When the Cantonist Decree was declared by Nikolai the First in 1825, it did not affect Polish Jews. Poles at that time had no general military service, serving in the military was the privilege of the "shlyakhte" (upper class).

Jews were counted among the merchant class and were free from military service. However, they had to pay 500 rubles for each enlistment. These payments caused the families to change their names so that their numbers were not recognizable.

When in the late years of the last century the tsarist decrees were further extended to the Polish provinces, it naturally affected Great-Grandfather Mair Yonah.

However, he did not follow the order to give up his estate and the inherited goods effortlessly or particularly quickly. He began to rush to Grodno and Petersburg. He had friends in the government circles of the district administrations who helped him to extend the deadline of the edict and to delay its execution.

Mair Yonah left the "Balebatishkeyt"[5] to my Grandpa Yankel Bunim and spent his time entirely knocking on the doors of various government offices.

At that time Yankel Bunim contracted a cold. He did not fully recover from the illness, but remained short of breath.

Meanwhile, the business was completely neglected.

Just at that time, a distant relative came to Grandpa's estate from the Grodno area. He was a well-educated young man with the ability to keep an account.

[Page 131]

This man was Nokhem Anshel, later, the powerful lord and the biggest leather manufacturer of Krynki. Nokhem-Anshel took the complete management of the business into his hands.

When Mair Yonah returned from his travels, he already met with disaster. Nokhem Anshel had robbed his store and fled to Krynki.

Not only the store, but his whole middle-class existence was destroyed and in disarray. Mair Yonah, however, did not want to let it get him down. He tried to build up a "balebatish" existence again, but this did not work out as it should, Moreover, the favors cost a large sum of money and, in view of the theft of Nokhem Anshel, it had become impossible to continue the management of the estate and the distillery.

For a small sum of money, he sold his property and the whole estate to a neighboring Polish nobleman and moved to a village near Krynki.

In the village of Kineshevitsh, Mair Yonah took over the tavern. His plan was to get back on his own feet and continue the struggle against the tsarist edict.

As usual, the village tavern was the center and the gathering place of the peasants. They came not only to drink and spend their time there, but also to hold their "skhodkes" (meetings).

Twice a year the farmers gathered: before the sowing and after the harvest.

The "skhodkes" served to determine the amount of taxes for both the central government and the needs of the village.

In the village there was still the Jewish family of the blacksmith, who had lived there for ages. Immediately a war broke out between the two Jewish families. And this was a heated war fought with all vehemence. The reason for this was competition, because the blacksmith also sold liquor to the farmers and thus drew customers away from the tavern.

But since the tavern and the house were Mair Yonah's former property, he naturally had the privilege of running the tavern and selling schnapps.

Mair Yonah dragged the blacksmith to the Krinker Rabbi, and he rendered his verdict in his (Mair Yonah's) favor. The blacksmith accepted this for a while, but this did not last long.

[Page 132]

Apparently he had little reverence for the Rabbi's judgment and secretly incited the peasants against Mair Yonah and his family.

The purchases for the tavern were made in Krynki. Grandpa Yankel Bunim used to buy the liquor in the Krinker distillery. He also obtained food from Krynki, especially meat and poultry. His older children studied there, and so there was a permanent connection with Krynki.

Once, when Grandpa Yankel Bunim had gone to Krynki and only old Mair Yonah and Grandma Sime Feygel were at home with their younger children, peasants raided the property, destroyed and looted the tavern and the house.

The blacksmith who had incited the peasants against the family was behind that. He had invited the "Sotski"[6] to a drink and persuaded him that the owner of the tavern was exploiting them all; he was getting richer and they were getting poorer. He assured the "Sotski" that he could sell the liquor much cheaper, but Mair Yonah and the Krinker Rabbi would not allow it.

The "Sotski" then summoned the peasants to a meeting at the blacksmith's to decide what to do with the innkeeper. The blacksmith, however, got them all drunk, and incited as they were, they fell upon the proprietor.

Fortunately, when they stormed into the tavern, Grandma Sime Feygl was in the apartment with her small children, and when she heard the noise, she grabbed the children and fled with them into the fields.

Mair Yonah, however, was killed by the peasants with their fists.

They demolished the house and the tavern piece by piece. They tore the bedding and broke the furniture. They carried and dragged out everything, leaving absolutely nothing of value.

An older son ran on foot to Krynki to tell his father about the disaster. He caught him just as he was already preparing to leave for the village.

(My) Grandpa immediately ran to the "pristav" (the chief official of the shtetl), and the latter sent two "Strazhnikes"[7]. They searched and found Sime Feygl and her children, who were scared to death, and with the corpse on the wagon the family left the village and "drove to Krynki".

They "drove" to Krynki? It's just a way of saying it. No, they were not driving, they were running for their lives.

Poor they were and broken, with not even a string. When Yankel Bunim wanted to sell his tavern, there was nothing left of it.

[Page 133]

They came to Krynki without bedding, without candlesticks, naked and barefoot, even worse than after a fire.

In Krynki, there were many members of the family residing and living in "rakhves"[8], among them grain merchants, forest traders, owners of taverns and hotels. Every single one of them was positioned big and broad.

And each of them was powerful and influential. Both those who descended from Yosl Yishevnik and those who descended from Mair Yonah's wife Henye. The latter's brother, Fishke the Kaliker[9], was a great forest trader. All of his children were wealthy, well integrated, and well cared for, and were among the most respected balebatim of the shtetl.

The body was brought to eternal rest with a grand funeral. But what was to be done with the living?

The family gathered and agreed that Yankel Bunim could not be taken care of. Should they give him a forest? Or a grain store? Or even a tavern? After all, one needed money to run a business. And none of them was willing to help him out with it.

Should they perhaps include him in their business? But what kind of business should he be offered?

After all, he was an asthmatic man who had no air, constantly held a trubke in front of his mouth and could not breathe without it. The most suitable plan was: trading lottery tickets. They would buy lots, they would also contribute[10] a big prize, and with that they would already help the unfortunate, impoverished relative (enough).

Translator's footnotes:

1. Original: vyorst= verst (ca. 0,66 miles)
2. kantonist: drafted soldier in Czar's army
3. ימח-שמו= may his name be blotted out
4. Seym= Polish parliament
5. Balebatishkeyt= household, order, economy, property, a kind of bourgeois respectability
6. „sotski"= a kind of bailiff
7. strazhnik= country policeman, security guard
8. רְחבוּת= rakhves: comfort, well-being, wide space, vastness
9. Kaliker= I do not know the meaning of this word. "Kalike" means cripple, which in this case should be excluded. " Kalika" is used in Polish in connection with, for example, the youngest son.

10.   The author uses a Hebraism (בעלנים) that is ambiguous. The word "balonim" in this connection in Yiddish means "persons who have desire/interest in something." On the other hand, the root of this word also indicates "owners," among other things. It is not quite clear whether the family members wanted to provide the prize thanks to their wealth, or were keen to win themselves. However, I assume the former, since Yankel Bunim could probably hardly both cover his living expenses and buy expensive items from the income from the lot sale.

[Page 134]

Great-Grandmother Reyne Gitl

Yankel Bunim did not consider himself an impoverished person. He never complained and avoided talking about his wealth at that time. He also did not like it when people expressed pity for him and his situation. When reminded, his response was, "it could have been worse, thank God we were able to save our lives!"

First of all, he had to take care of his wife and children. Yankel Bunim knew that Krynki would be his last home, he would not go anywhere else. "Thinking about what once was will not ease my situation," he used to say, and so he began to pitch and consolidate his tents on the Krinker earth.

Since it seemed to him a symbol of his resignation and destiny that had brought him to Krynki, Yankel Bunim changed his name, Kadishevitsh, to "Krinker." This was likewise an assurance and determination that he would not move from there again. So now he was a Krinker – not only as a resident, but also with his name.

The first concern now was to find a pillow, a blanket and a bit of home. I still remember the dark, gloomy apartments where he lived. I think back to an apartment with one room, a sticky floor, two beds, a closet, a table and two benches. There was a sliver of window between the drab walls, which brought a drop of sun and a bit of daylight into the unhappy apartment.

The plans of his rich relatives to deal in lots were indeed good. Only they did not bring him any income: Yankel Bunim's lots used "to be obstinate and did not want to win".

But the family was large, how could they all be fed? How could the children be educated?

And the grief of Yankel Bunim became very great when at some point his children were far apart and scattered, since he had to send them out into the world to earn their own living.

[Page 135]

The eldest son, Aharon Velvel, who was wrapped in silk after his birth, was already a big lad. He had to be taken care of immediately (with work).

There was no room for all of them in Krynki, for such a large family there were simply too few places to sleep and too few things to eat. And so Yankel Bunim sent Aharon Velvel to Bialystok. The rich relatives there were supposed to find him a job. In addition, (Grandpa) sent my father to study at the Bialystok Yeshive and to "esn teg"[1] with the rich family.

In Bialystok there was a weaving factory owner, Fishke the Kalik'ns, the son-in-law of Grandpa's uncle, and he sent Aharon Velvel to him to learn weaving.

Later, when Aharon Velvel was drawn into the revolutionary movement, the Bialystok relative threw him out, and he went to a relative in Horodok, Yudel Kronheym, to work for him.

But he did not last long with him either and came back to Bialystok to look for a job. Grandpa sent his younger children away to become tanners. The very youngest, Khayim Shloyme, was just 10 years old when he went to work in a tannery.

Wages at that time were between two and three guilders a week, a sum averaging 30 to 45 kopeks. However, this at least helped to reduce my Grandpa's financial pressure. It seems, however, that fate played a trick on Grandpa, because apart from adding three children born in Krynki, Grandma's mother also moved away from Bialystok and in with him.

My Great-Grandmother, Reyne-Gitl, was an exceptionally strange woman and a rare character. It is as if I still see her alive before my eyes now; in general she is unforgettable to me.

She was Reb Velvele's youngest daughter. When he died, she was around 5 or 6 years old. But she never tired of telling stories about him, with as much detail as if she just remembered clearly.

Usually Reyne Gitl talked very little. She never used to take part in conversations.

[Page 136]

She thought that if one was not careful about speaking, one would be tempted to gossip.

She used to read the "Taystsh-Khumesh"[2] constantly and without pause, and her common speech consisted only of necessary words of daily use. She did not speak more than that.

Only when she spoke of her father, she lit up and had a large vocabulary. She ate little and was only skin and bones.

About her father, Reyne Gitl told wondrous stories that were simply fantastic. She reproduced all the legends about him that made the rounds in Bialystok and interpreted them as facts.

I found many of these legends about her father, Reb Velvele, in the "Pinkas Bialystok"[3].

My Great-Grandmother used to recall with particular pride that her father had been titled "Mar'ot haTzov-ot", after his religious book of the same name.

She loved my father because he (Leyzer) was named after Reb Velvele's father Reb Eliezer, a Rabbi in Halusk (Hlusk). A very great impression was made on her by Grandpa's eldest son Aharon Velvel, who bore one of her father's names.

Reyne Gitl especially liked to tell a story that was very common in Bialystok. According to it, Reb Velvele, zts"l[4], was such a saint that the horses of the peasants jumped up with their carts to make way when he, on his way to teach or pray in the old Bes-Medresh, passed over the yard there.

No one was allowed to touch her father's many religious books, which she kept bound in cloth. She especially did not let the children get close to them. I remember that she had wrapped one of the books, "Agudas Ezov", with colored book covers held together by a colorful string. She kept the books, her wedding dress, a small bag of soil from the "Land of Israel" and her "Takhrikhim"[5] in a straw basket under the bed.

As I could see later from the records in the "Pinkas Bialystok", Reb Velvele zts"l is counted even today among the greatest scholarly Rabbis. He used to correspond with Rabbi Ekiva Eyger[6] and Khayim Volozhiner[7].

He exchanged ideas concerning "Shayles-u-Tshuves"[8] with the greatest Rabbis of his time and was a friend of the Warsaw Rabbi R' Shloyme Zalmen Poyzner.

[Page 137]

For a time he was the Rabbi in Tiktin, a town near Bialystok. R' Velvele was particularly concerned with the issue of the agunes[9]. He felt happy when he succeeded in giving an agune a (religious) permit[10].

Although he came from a very rich family, the "Barishes"[11], Reb Velvele disliked the rich and powerful and used to put them down.

He kept himself very modest and used to sign himself "haKotn Ba'Ezov Moyshe Zev".

As "Pinkas Bialystok" reports, Rabbi Akiva Eyger titled him with "haRov haGodel haGoen hoEmesi Nosi Yisroel"[12], and the Pinkas comments, "In this regard one must know that at that time people were very accurate in their judgments and stingy in giving titles. An average Rabbi and Talmudist was not usually titled "Goen" (Gaon, genius). "HaRov haMur haGodl"[13] was really a great honorific title.

Great-Grandmother Reyne Gitl married a great learned Jew who was a Rabbi in Volpe. When he died, she went back to Bialystok with her only child, my Grandma Sime Feygl.

Later Reyne Gitl married a merchant who did business with foreign countries. During a trip to Germany he died in Leipzig. Reyne Gitl remained a widow until the end of her days.

From her husband, Reyne Gitl was left a small fortune. Because her husband had died abroad, and so suddenly at that, she knew neither the extent of the fortune nor possible debtors or creditors. Nevertheless, she had capital that was enough for (her needs) for more than twenty years. All this time she lived in Bialystok and occasionally visited her daughter and grandchildren while they still lived on their estate in the village.

But all of a sudden she became weaker and ran out of money. So she came to her daughter in Krynki, exactly at that time when Yankel Bunim was already impoverished.

I remember two moments clearly: one day, when everything was smooth outside, she fell and hurt herself. She broke her leg at that time. My parents lived not far from Grandpa, and Father took me with him to pay her a sick visit.

[Page 138]

It really seems to me as if it happened only now, as she lay there like that by the window. Her leg was already plastered and the pungent and caustic smell of iodoform was spreading throughout the house. The bandages over the cast were discolored yellow from the iodoform.

At that time, Grandpa lived in two rooms. The first room was large and was used for eating, sleeping and staying. On the side was the kitchen, a dark room with no air and no windows. That was where the cooking was done. The floor was sticky, and the moisture and dampness literally ran down the walls.

I (at that time) liked to eat herring very much, so Grandma entertained me in the kitchen with a piece of herring. The smell of the iodoform, however, was so strong that when I took my first bite, it was not the herring that was in my mouth, but only the smell. I felt sick and since then, to this day, I can no longer smell herring.

The second story led me with harshness to a first encounter with the death of a human being. For a long time it was a custom in our house that I came to Grandma's on Friday morning to eat porridge with lard.

Both Grandma Sime Feygl and her mother were invalids at that time. It was after the great fire, in which almost the entire shtetl had been destroyed, and both women were housed in the Jewish "Bolnitse"[14].

They had been given a small room, and besides the two sick people, my grandfather and two younger children lived there- Mair and Sore.

It was "real life!"

On Friday, when I came to eat porridge as usual, Great-Grandmother was very sick. She simply could not sit up. Grandpa straightened her up, pushed her pillow under her and "fed" her grits.

Her face was a little covered with soot. This stayed in my mind from that time on as an omen of death. (Great) Grandma Reyne Gitl considered my Grandpa to be a Jewish freethinker ("apikoyres") who, in her opinion, was not pious enough. When she was satiated, she blessed him and said:

"You are truly an apikoyres, but with a golden heart! May you have a long life!"

[Page 139]

That very night, right after the blessing (on Friday evening), Mair and Sore came to our house to bring us the news that (Great) Grandma Reyne Gitl had died. Father took me with him (to her), but she was already lying there covered up. At that time I did not understand the meaning of "died". I lifted her blanket and father gave me a slap on the hand. When we were already on our way home, I asked my father:

"What is this, death?"

Then, my father did not take me to the funeral on Shabbat evening.

Translator's footnotes:

1.   Esn teg: …refers to the community custom, once widespread in Eastern Europe, of supporting teachers and education by hosting yeshive students for meals in private homes on certain days of the week, with stays probably changing from day to day.

2.   Taytsh-Khumesh= "Yiddish" translation of the Torah with interpretations and commentaries, edification book (end of 16th century), also called "Tsene Urene" and "Women's Bible", written in Yudeo-German.

3.   פּינקס= Pinkes/Pinkas: municipal chronicle, protocol, account book. The term is often used in the context of memory books (Yizkor Books). Pinkas Bialystok, see https://digitalcollections.nypl.org/items/c5ccd680-8fd5-0134-27ea-00505686a51c/book?page_start=left#page/1/mode/2up

4.   זצ"ל= sekher tsadik liwracha, the memory of the righteous be a blessing

5.   תּכריכים= takhrikhim, white linen clothes in which a corpse is wrapped

6.   Rabbi Ekiva (Akiva) Eiger, preeminent Talmudic authority (1761-1837), see https://en.wikipedia.org/wiki/Akiva_Eiger

7.   Chajim ben Isaak Woloszyner or Chaim of Volozhin, Rabbi and Talmudist, (1749-1821),   https://en.wikipedia.org/wiki/Chaim_of_Volozhin https://de.wikipedia.org/wiki/Chajim_b._Isaak

8.   שאלות-ותשובות= shayles-u-tshuves= "Questions and Answers," also: Title of Jewish books containing a Rabbi's analysis of certain halakhah issues.

9.   עגונות= agunes, women abandoned without a divorce contract or whose husband has perished and who are no longer allowed to marry according to Jewish law.

10.   surely the permission of a second marriage is meant here

11.   Barishe(s)= I think that this family name refers to the town "Paritz", also called Parichi, Paritchi. Paritz was a town near Szcedrin, in Minsk County. From another source we learn that Reb Velvele had a brother, Reb Zalmen of Paritz or Paritzer, https://jewishlibraries.org/wp-content/uploads/2021/03/LevyHandoutSeven2020.pdf, http://www.sichos-in-english.org/books/sefer-hatoldos-admur-maharash/17.htm

12.   the great personality, the genius, the true prince of the land of Israel.

13.   the genius, the Rabbi, the light, the great personality

14.   bolnitse/balnitse: a hospital complex in Krynki

[Page 140]

Grandpa's Relatives

Grandpa Yankel Bunim did not like to argue with the rich relatives. He didn't envy them, but he begrudged all of them what they possessed. Among his relatives there were some he liked, but also some he kept away from. He did not judge them by their wealth, but by their interpersonal behavior.

From the family of his father, Mair Yonah, he liked the son of "Yosl the Yishevnik's", Itshe "Lya"[1]. Apparently Itshe was a smart man, because this quality was one of those virtues that my Grandpa was attracted to.

According to my memory, Itshe "Lya" was an invalid. As a result of his haste, impetuosity and constant tension, he became paralyzed and was confined to bed for many years. As an invalid, however, he conducted his business with the same bustle as before, when he could still walk and hurry to and fro.

He had two daughters and a son. His son, Yosl, was lazy and did not like to deal with his father's business. He made friends with the bourgeois loiterers, preened himself and behaved stiffly and arrogantly.

Since he was the only son, Itshe "Lya" ignored his behavior. He (Yosl) was not a corrupt person, but still a lazy and haughty one.

Itshe "Lya's" daughters took after their father and were completely different from their brother. In particular, Yospe, the older one, was a very active person. Grandpa thought very highly of her. She managed both the business and the bookkeeping.

Breyne, the younger one, also had good skills and energy, but was still very different from her sister. Not only was her demeanor different, but more importantly, so was her appearance. Yospe was taller and more beautiful. She had tact and was calmer and more businesslike than Breyne. Yospe used to walk more slowly, speak more quietly, and be more patient.

[Page 141]

She could hold a quiet conversation as well as be a quiet listener.

When Itshe "Lya" fell ill, his two daughters took over the management of the business. He issued instructions from his bedside, which they then carried out. Yospe, the older one, dealt with the management of the hotel. And since the aristocrats and highest government officials came to the hotel, she conducted herself like a "grand dame."

Breyne ran the grain business. Her role was to negotiate with the farmers and traders, to weigh and measure (the goods) and to make the receipts and expenditures.

Grandpa Yankel Bunim used to rest at their house. Since his shortness of breath meant that he got little sleep at night, he used to lie down during the day to take a nap. Nowhere else, however, could he slumber as well as at Itshe "Lya's" house.

Itshe's house, it can be said, was spacious and comfortably cut with large, airy and light-filled rooms. The reception room, where Itshe used to lie during the day, was large and bright.

Yankel Bunim did not want to go to another room. In the reception room, his chair was already waiting in that little corner where he loved to sit.

Ithse's whole family behaved very respectfully to Yankel Bunim. The family members loved to talk to him and also consult about business.

They already took it for granted that Grandpa came to the house of Itshe "Lya" to take his nap.

To sleep during the day, Yankel Bunim did not lie down. He had a rather strange way of resting and slumbering. He used to put a glass with the bottom up, put his hands on it and rest his head on his hands. This was how he fell asleep. The inhabitants of the house used to be careful not to make any noise or racket.

Grandpa had little contact with Itshe "Lya's" sister, Meri, and her husband, Khaykel "Khazer" (pig). Meri was not a bad person. Only she had no personality and completely subordinated herself to her husband's influence, and so she became as coarse and ossified in her manner as he was.

[Page 142]

Meri was a small, broad woman whose cheeks were constantly glowing.

Due to her obesity and shapelessness, she moved sluggishly.

She liked to sit in the tavern and watch how (the guests) drank.

Her face was sweating from the constant smoke and pungent smell of beer and liquor. Due to her obesity, she puffed heavily and noisily, and in general, she looked like a piglet being roasted at that time.

Meri's husband, Khaykel, could not stand still. He was constantly in a state of restlessness. He rarely smiled and ran around puffed up and strained. Khaykel was a heavy and nasty man who never wanted to help or do anyone any favors. If someone angered him, or he just thought someone had wronged him, nothing stopped him from spending a fortune to get him back.

Khaykel litigated for years over a piece of land. It was a project to create a shortcut road to the market that cut through his property, and he opposed it.

As a result of his stubbornness, he fell out with the "balebatim" of the shtetl.

There were continuous quarrels and scandals. When the leadership of the community decided the lawsuit against him, he moved heaven and earth to challenge the court's decision. He no longer relied on the Rabbi with his demands, but only allowed proceedings in the courts of the goyim.

Almost all of Khaykel's children took after him; they were hard, angry and tense.

Itshe "Lya" was continually at odds with his sister Meri and her husband Khaykel, and although the two families lived next door to each other, they behaved in a distant and estranged manner.

Also, Yankel Bunim had no close contacts with his mother's relatives; the children of Fishke the Kalik'n. He avoided any relationship with Fishke's eldest son, Berl. Berl

Fishke's was actually a Jewish scholar and a smart man, not kind-hearted but a very authoritarian one.

Berl was a Jew, "like a flame"; tall, confident and with a long, (red) blonde beard.

[Page 143]

Almost all his children were blond. But there were no big personalities in his family.

One of his sons, Mair, was small and hunchbacked, and his head was shaped like a pumpkin. It did not seem like one head, but two. However, he was keen and very well suited for the business. Berl brought him into his forest trade and relied on him for everything.

The eldest son resembled Berl completely. He was a hard, heavy man and a miser. Like his father, he did not like to please anyone.

Berl was the "Strosto" (mayor) of Krynki, and was as cruel to his own family as he was to strangers.

Berl Fishke's had a miserable end. He got into a quarrel with his partner Shloymeke, Alter the Khoyker's son, in the forest, and Shloymeke killed him with a piece of wood.

However, Grandpa Yankel Bunim was acquainted and friends with Berl Fishke's brother-in-law, Mordekhay Shimen Grodski, a Jewish enlightener and very righteous man. He was among the most intelligent and educated people in the shtetl. He was a painter, but also carved wooden figures based on biblical themes. He and Grandpa were in very close contact and constantly invited each other home.

There were also more relatives from his father's and mother's side, but Yankel Bunim hardly maintained any contact with them.

Even when he once had to come as a supplicant to the rich relatives, he avoided the evil ones among them. He did not want to ask Khaykel "Khazer" for anything either. Grandpa used to say, "I don't want to do him that favor!"

Khaykel owned the only "lyodovnye" (a storage facility where he kept ice) in the shtetl. When Grandpa fell ill with pneumonia, Khaykel refused to give a piece of ice to save Grandpa, even though he was in mortal danger at the time.

Even to borrow some money from the well-meaning relatives, Grandpa went only when he already had "the knife on his neck." However, he used to repay the debts in small amounts afterwards.

Yankel Bunim kept his distance from Berl Fishke's. However, he went to his (family) feasts. And never did he break the tradition of baking matzah in Berl Fishke's podryat[2].

Concerning my Grandma Sime Feygl, baking matzo involved huge preparations.

[Page 144]

She did not tolerate strangers to knead the dough and did not rest until everything was exactly as she wanted. When matzo was baked for my Grandpa, it was a holiday for me! Since I was a tomboy and liked to show off, I whined for Grandma to let me pour the water into the bowl.

And she did not get rid of me so easily!

However, pouring the water did not satisfy me, I wanted to do something more flashy and spectacular. Therefore, I begged Grandma urgently to let me pour the flour.

I was placed on a little box near the flour sack. Grandma rolled up my shirt sleeves, I filled the flour into a quart (a hollow measure) and poured it into the basin. The flour had to be poured in with a measure, the size of which my Grandma determined. While kneading, she felt how much more flour had to be added.

However, I did not continue my work. I still wanted to show off to the boys outside, so I went to the porch to boast to them. When Grandma finally found me, she no longer wanted to entrust me with the work.

Translator's footnotes:

1. This time the name is written with vowel sign as "Lya", the next time without vowel sign. I now stay with "Lya".
2. matse „podryat" = the term for matzo-baking process, a Russian term literally meaning sub-contract work, probably as you needed a large number of people for short time to perform certain type of work

[Page 145]

Yankel Bunim and the Factory Owners

As a result of his cramped and uncomfortable apartments, it was not possible for Yankel Bunim to set up cabinets with religious books. My father, peace be upon him, told me that in Grandfather's house in the village there were some cupboards with hundreds of secular and religious books.

But during the pogrom, the peasants had torn them up and burned them.

Yankel Bunim, in addition to the (newspaper) "Rech" and "Ha-Tsfira", had subscribed to the "Fraynt" together with an associate, and also used to borrow books from Levin. The latter was the only one in the shtetl who sold writing utensils and lent books at 5 kopecks a week.

The grocer and librarian Levin was a relative by marriage[1] of Grandpa. Yankel Bunim's daughter-in-law and Levin's wife were sisters. Levin liked to lend my Grandpa a book, even without payment. Grandpa was a frequent guest in his store and therefore had the opportunity to read all the new Yiddish, Hebrew and Russian publications.

The first Yiddish books I read, Mendele's[2] "Di Klyatshe", "Fishke the Krumer" and "The Takse"[3] were brought to me by Grandpa Yankel Bunim. He also subscribed to booklets and newspaper supplements. He provided me with Sholem Aleykhem's books and stories, which appeared printed in booklets.

Yakev Dinezon's[4] stories, "Yosele"[5] and "Hershele"[6] illustrated human cruelty to me. My pity for the two orphan boys and the unfortunate, poor Talmud student "Hershele" tore me apart with wailing and weeping.

Grandpa Yankel Bunim had asked Levin to give me only the books he had chosen for me to read. He contributed three kopeks a week for me.

On Yankel Bunim's instruction I read the Jewish translation of Shakespeare's "King Lear".

[Page 146]

The book "Cold and Warm" made a great impression on me. Tenenboym[7] had declared himself as the author, but in reality it was Jules Verne.

The book tells the story of a sailor who is stranded on an island after a shipwreck. He makes his way to a village and then wanders to unknown and dangerous places. The sailor experiences wondrous stories, he travels and wanders until he joins an expedition to the North Pole.

The book describes in great detail the polar bears, the months-long nights, the Eskimos, the whaling with harpoons, and the dreariness of the sky and ice at the North Pole.

Besides providing me with books, Yankel Bunim insisted that I learn Russian. This was not an easy thing to do, for the teachers of the Jewish elementary schools did not want a student to go somewhere else in the middle of the day.

However, Yankel Bunim had arranged it so that I went to the "Narodni Utshilitshe" (elementary school) in the first half of the day, and to the Kheyder (elementary school) in the second half.

When in Krynki three modern "khadorim-mesukonim"[8] were established, I was sent to the "Ozheraner" for two semesters in such a reformed elementary school. I also went to modern teachers who taught reading and writing in Yiddish. However, I did not stay with them for more than one semester.

In the shtetl, my Grandpa Yankel Bunim was considered the best "bal-koyre"[9]. However, because of his shortness of breath, he could hardly do so. Nevertheless, during the mutual guest visits[10], his comrade and friend, Berl Fishke's brother-in-law Mordekhay Shimen, who was the "bal-koyre" in the Kavkazer Bes-Medresh, used to urge him to read aloud.

Grandpa taught both my father and his youngest son Mair (who was killed by a bomb in Bialystok) to read aloud. An artisan minyan[11] had asked Yankel Bunim to read for them. But when his breathing problems prevented him, one of the sons had to take over. Finally, however, he gave it up altogether, for he could not rely on his sons.

My father was seldom at home and Mair had already begun to seek out the "brothers and sisters" and to fight a battle not only against the rich and the government, but also against God.

Yankel Bunim was not someone who let himself go. He did not like it when someone dressed up, but insisted on cleanliness and could not stand it when someone was dirty. He avoided people who did not groom themselves.

[Page 147]

I still remember how he scolded his youngest son Mair violently for not keeping himself clean. Mair was perhaps ten years old at the time. Domestic hardship chased him out to the factory, and he had to help there with hard work to reduce abject poverty.

What did this little boy know? For him, his work in the factory meant that he was already an adult, and this gave him the opportunity to show off to the boys of his age who were still going to the kheyder.

To prove that he was already a "factory goer," Mair liked to rub his pants with "degre" (grease). The dried grease caused the pants to shine.

At noon, the tanners used to go home to eat. The clean ones of them changed their clothes. Mair, however, wanted to show off and flaunt himself in front of the boys, so he came to lunch with shiny, dirty pants.

Grandpa was rarely home during the noon hours.

But by chance he once arrived (at home) when Mair was just in the house. He became very angry and ordered Mair with harsh words never to dare to come home in such an outfit again.

Yankel Bunim did not like to show off his knowledge. However, he could not stand ignoramuses.

On Shabbat, it was customary for Jews to gather around a teacher in the Bes-Medresh to listen to him. They asked questions and engaged in debates. Yankel Bunim never sat down at the table with them. He usually leaned, somewhat apart, against a stand and listened to the teacher. An incorrect interpretation, however, bothered him very much, and he was then not ashamed to contradict the teacher.

Yankel Bunim had skill in writing petitions. However, he avoided dealing with it and tried to avoid it. Nevertheless, when people urged him to do it, he did it for their sake. He could speak Russian well and liked to converse in that language.

In the house of his nephew, Itshe "Lya", the colloquial language was Russian, because the pristav[12] and the naziratel[13] went in and out there. Both Itshe "Lya's" children and he himself often conversed with my Grandpa in that language.

[Page 148]

Yankel Bunim did not tolerate hostility between people. He taught his children that they should not be influenced by hatred and malice. He himself quickly became enraged and angry.

However, he also cooled down again quickly.

Grandpa did not like injustice and falsehood, and when he noticed that people were trying to deceive him, he would get upset. However, whoever won his trust, he met with warmth and deep friendship.

Yankel Bunim felt that his grudge should not be held forever. He even forgave the blacksmith and the peasants in the village for killing his father and destroying his fortune. "God has punished them with blindness, with dullness and ignorance," he used to say.

His knowledge of a few foreign languages kept him connected to the larger world and caused him to be objective and free from small-town parochialism. All this made it easier for him to endure the great and tragic change in his life.

Yankel Bunim knew that new and different times were coming. And neither did he want, nor did he try to prevent his children from behaving as they wished. For him, a noble lineage did not matter. He did not mind if his sons made friends with boys who did not belong to an exalted class.

Great events were in the offing. In the shtetl, the "Buntovshtshikes", the rebels, caused unrest and tumult. The tanners were preparing for the first strike. The factory owners were restless. They did not know exactly what was happening, but understood very well that something was being planned against them.

The balebatim and factory owners did not know how to prevent the meetings of the young people. However, they had noticed that the agitators came from middle-class homes.

When preparations for the first strike began and unity was created among the tanners, many fathers saw with concern how their own children joined forces with the "Zhulikes," as the renegade young bokherim, the boys from the lower estates, were called.

[Page 149]

The balebatim, seeing that Yankel Bunim's sons were making common cause with the gang, came to him and admonished him as to why he was allowing this to happen.

"What can I do?" replied Yankel Bunim to the balebatim, "they are grown-up young men and already bear the burden of earning their living.

They truly fulfill the word, 'bezeyes apekho tokhel lekhem'.[14]

The balebatim were angry with him. However, this did not bother Yankel Bunim. He felt that it was not his place to please the factory owners and, for their sake, to act like a gendarme against his own children.

If they joined forces with the bokherim, that was their concern.

Translator's footnotes:

1.   חותן= mekhutn, the most common meaning: close relative of the groom or bride, father of the daughter or son-in-law
2.   Mendele Moykher Sforim
3.   the Mare; Fishke the Lame; the Tax
4.   Jacob Dinesohn/ Yankev Dinezon, Yiddish author, 1856 (1836?) -1919, https://en.wikipedia.org/wiki/Jacob_Dinezon
5.   „Yosele"= 1899 novel about an abused Kheyder boy.
6.   „Hershele"= 1891 novel about a poor yeshivah student
7.   maybe   Arn   Tenenboym   http://yleksikon.blogspot.com/2016/10/arn-tenenboym.html
8.   Plural of חדר-מתוקן= kheyder-mesukn, reformed elementary school
9.   בעל קורא= balkoyre, reader, prayer leader in house of prayer or synagogue
10.   כיבוד=kibed, Hospitality in honor of a guest, the food and drink with which one entertains a guest, honor.
11.   מִנְיָן=minyen, Minimum number of participants to the common prayer (quorum)
12.   pristav: Chief officer of a shtetl, chief superintendent of police
13.   naziratel: high Russian functionary who also signed certificates.
14.   בזעת אפיך תאכל לחם= "In the sweat of thy face shalt thou eat thy bread", Bereshit 3, 19

[Page 150]

First Agitators in Krynki

Of the seventeen children that Grandma Feygl had given birth to, eight remained: six sons and two daughters.

When Sime Feygl remembered the other children who could not grow up, she was overwhelmed with pain. She did not complain or cry, because she assumed that it was fate that did not allow her children to grow up; but it hurt her very much. Once, the thought occurred to her that at least a few children would still be with her if they had all survived.

They were all gone now, scattered around the world, and she was left alone.

Every time another one of her children disappeared from the shtetl, it left a deep pain in her. Grandpa Yankel Bunim, however, felt that the children had to be let go. There was an apostasy of morals and beliefs in the shtetl, and a young person had to go out into the wide world. Sime Feygl did not want to contradict her husband.

The children did not move because they wanted to leave their parents, but the bitter poverty and the danger to their freedom and their lives chased them to foreign lands.

The eldest son, Aharon Velvel, whom Grandpa had sent to relatives in Bialystok to learn a trade, was the subject of rumors in the shtetl that he would incite the weavers there to rebellion. He rarely came to Krynki or was heard from, but suddenly, without anyone expecting him, Aharon Velvel appeared in Krynki.

The fact that he was hanging around jobless and being secretive increased the whispers that he was mixed up in a "shtashke" (uprising) of the weavers and had become involved with the "Buntovshtshikes" (the rebels) in Bialystok.

A few weeks after Aharon Velvel's arrival in Krynki, Khayim Leyzer, Yonah the Stolyer's[1], also arrived from Grodno. And as far as he was concerned, it was known for certain that he harbored dangerous thoughts concerning the rich and the government.

[Page 151]

The fact that both boys were now seen together gave rise to a strong suspicion that they were up to something that was not entirely unproblematic.

It didn't take long at all, and gossip began in the shtetl that the two boys were stirring up the young tanners. Too many young men had been spotted running down to the field and then "disappearing".

Aharon Velvel began to influence his two younger brothers, Moyshe Berl and Khayim Shloyme, who were already working as tanners, with propaganda.

Aharon Velvel used to walk down Sokolker (Sokółka) Street with them on Friday evenings. He would point out to them their poverty and the terrible situation in which the Krinker tanners found themselves.

Indeed, at that time their situation was terrible. What was being done to them was nothing but brutal and savage exploitation.

A "meistares"[2] system had been introduced into the tanneries at that time. These were a kind of "kontraktors" (contract labor companies), which can only be compared to the contract labor systems in the "Svet-shop" (sweatshop) era. In America, however, it was handled in a more moderate way.

The "meistares" offered labor to the factory owners. The "contractors" lent and paid for the labor force. The work itself was done in the tanneries owned by the factory owners. However, the balebos (boss) of the workers was the "master" (meister).

Tanners could earn at most up to two rubles a week. However, wages were not paid every week, but with delays of three, sometimes even six months.

In the meantime, the "meistares" threw down (to the workers) a few guilders (one guilder was worth 15 kopecks). And they did so only when a worker tearfully urged them. It was then the following exceptions that moved the "master":

When someone needed money for a healer, the wife was expecting childbirth, a bris (brit milah) or a wedding was coming up.

Working hours began at 5 a.m. and ended only when the "master" sent (the workers) home. Usually the workday lasted from 5 a.m. to 9 or 10 p.m.

[Page 152]

On Thursday one worked all night[3] and on Friday until noon. On Shabbat, immediately after the Havdalah, one had to go back to work. It is clear that such a situation offered favorable conditions to the agitators.

Aharon Velvel's younger brothers, impulsive, sentimental and emotional boys, were deeply and strongly influenced by the agitation and began to entrust their brother's speeches to other boys in the factory.

At home, Aharon Velvel also drew his father into conversations about the situation of the tanners. He pointed out the situation of the craftsmen and the injustice done to them by pious Jews who were only concerned about accumulating "mitsves". My Grandpa liked to discuss these things with him, and Aharon Velvel got him books, pamphlets, appeals (leaflets) and also the popular propaganda book by Eyb Kahan[4], "Rafael Neritsekh"[5].

Yankel Bunim liked the statements of Aharon Vevel and also what Kahan wanted to express through his book "Rafael Neritsekh". However, he could not accept the fact that those who were supposedly fighting for justice had also started a fight against God and religion.

He used to say, "You cannot overthrow God from His throne. If you actually fight to put an end to injustice, you cannot do so without faith in God. For God and Judaism represent the highest form of ethics, and without ethics you cannot establish a just government; for only faith in God and Judaism embody sincerity and justice."

My Grandpa did not mind that his boys were busy uniting the craftsmen, but he gave them to understand clearly that they should not turn away from God's ways.

In addition to the two agitators, my uncle Aharon Velvel and Khayim Leyzer, Yonah the Stolyer's, there were already some young people in Krynki who considered themselves socialists and therefore behaved conspiratorially.

This group of young people, which included the Bialystoker Yankel Tsales, Leyzer Harkovitsher and his sister Bashke the "Gele" (the Blond), also helped to politically enlighten the tanners.

[Page 153]

Later, they were joined by the following (agitators) who devoted themselves to the work with great devotion: Hershl Pinke the Shames's son, the daughter of Gabeytshik, Yosl Ayzik Halpern, Avrohem Partse and Itshe Grodner.

These names may have no meaning to strangers, especially now, in these hard, brutal, and cynical times. At that time, however, they were deeply idealistic young boys and girls from upper-class families who were willing to offer themselves as sacrifices to secure (or so they believed, at least) "bread, happiness, and freedom" for poor people.

They were the first in Krynki to provide political enlightenment to the depressed tanners, teaching them to fight for an easier life and against servitude.

All those involved in the "awareness and education" work divided the shtetl into districts, and each of them took on the task of integrating the young people of "their" district into the "unity movement". The agitators sought out the "yatn" (chaps), took them on a walk down to Sokolker or Shishlevitser Street and gave them "enlightenment" lessons there.

When the "enlighteners" knew that there were a hundred "Farbritshne" (factory workers) who could be relied upon, they brought them together. This was the beginning of the "skhodkes".

These gatherings took place during the day on Shabbat, in one of the forests of the shtetl, in the "Virnyen's" ("Virion's"), "Yente's" or "Rozboniker" (Robber's) forest. Beforehand, each individual had been told to come alone, and quietly, to the meeting place.

In order not to arouse suspicion among the townspeople, the young people used to walk in twos through different streets and alleys. In the forest, the tanners sat down in a semicircle. One of the "enlighteners" or a delegated agitator would then give illustrative speeches, read to the audience from books or pamphlets, and inform them about what was happening just beyond Krynki: There, in the big wide world, the workers and poor people united, formed a "Bund" (union) and fought for a better life.

After these speeches, everyone held hands, took an oath and sang fight songs taught to them by the agitators as a symbol of the common "Bund" and unity.

Translator's footnotes:

1.   Khayim Leyzer, Yonah dem/the Stolyer's= "one (Khayim Leyzer) who descends from Yonah the Stolyer (carpenter)". These formulations with the 's' after the name, which in this case indicates the profession, are very typical for Yiddish, but also for individual German dialects. It is very likely that the one so designated is the direct descendant, i.e. son or daughter, but exceptions are also conceivable.

2.   „meystares", „meistares" = This seems to have been the term for a kind of temporary employment agency grouped around its "master" („meister"), possibly a skilled worker. The master was responsible, among other things, for recruitment, providing workers and allocating their wages. However, the expressions " meistares" and "meister" are not clearly delineated in the text

3.   I assume, based on other reports from this period, that only occasionally, on special instructions, was all-night work done and at least a longer break was taken in the factory for sleep.

4.   Eyb (Abe) Kahan, Abraham Cahan (1860-1951) alias Dovid Bernshteyn = Founder   of   the   New   Yorker   socialist   Yiddish   "The   Forward". https://de.wikipedia.org/wiki/Abraham_Cahan
https://en.wikipedia.org/wiki/Abraham_Cahan

5.   רפֿאל נעריצך, "Rafael Neritsekh, Tale about a carpenter who came to his senses" , see   https://www.yiddishbookcenter.org/collections/yiddish-books/spb-nybc209680/cahan-abraham-refael-neritsekh-an-ertsehlung-vegen-a-stoyler-vos-iz-gekumen

[Page 154]

First Tanner Strike

Impressive and imposing scenes took place in the forest, where the factory workers joined together in "akhdes"[1]; they were scenes where faith and naivete (of the young people) were manifested in emotion and pathos.

The spectacular impression when taking the sacred oath remained in the memory and blood of the tanners. The scene was celebrated with such solemnity that everyone was imbued with a deep sacred feeling.

Those who were present in the forest when the oath was first taken usually recounted it later with pathos and great longing.

Even now, my uncle, Khayim Shloyme (Heyman Kohn/Cohen) still comes alive with elation when he recounts the "oath scenes." His descriptions enable me to reproduce (that scene) here.

There were only a few "enlightened" people in Krynki at that time. The Jews were deeply rooted in the customs and traditions of Jewish life, and what the agitators told them and demanded of them meant a revolt and a drastic change in their life and behavior.

The tanners, who started to be politicized in confidential conversations on walks and later in secret meetings ("skhodkes") in the forest, were still not reliable "elements".

The agitators pursued two goals:

Strengthening the sense of community ("akhdes") as well as preventing the "meistares" (temporary employment agencies) from receiving information about the "preparations." The younger ones, who were already enlightened, knew a little of the propaganda jargon at that time and were already singing the melodies and words of the "brothers and sisters" songs. For the great masses, however, these were all still strange things.

[Page 155]

When the first big secret meeting took place in the "Razboyniker" forest, which was about 5 verst (3,30 miles) away from the shtetl, the leaders, with the support of the "safe elements", made a real spectacle. While the tanners were sitting in a semicircle, suddenly a voice was heard coming from nearby, but the "baldover" (causer) could not be seen.

The voice told about the hard life and the situation in which the factory owners and "meistares" kept the tanners like slaves.

The fact that the voice came from a hidden corner and one could not see the face of the " baldarshn" (speaker) created an atmosphere of mysticism and curiosity.

The impression came up as if – lehavdl![2] – the scene with Moses, to whom God had revealed himself through his voice in the desert could be heard reinacted. Only the burning thorn bush was still missing.

When the voice ceased, everyone was asked to stand and form a circle. The voice rose again:

"Brothers," the voice cried out, "is all that I have spoken before you true?"

"Yes," was the reply.

"Do you want to create akhdes?" the voice asked again.

"We do!" replied the crowd.

"Will you all stand up for one and one for all?" "We will," they shouted.

"Will you keep all you have heard secret from the factory owners and meistares?"

"We will!"

"If so, you must swear!"

Soon, one of the group showed up with a religious book and phylacteries. He raised the sacred objects aloft, and the crowd recited the oath to the invisible voice to preserve "akhdes" and to keep everything that was spoken secret.

After this ceremony, everyone took each other by the hand, and the "enlightened" sang:

> "Brothers and sisters in work and need,
> to all who are spread and dispersed,
> come here, come together, the flag is prepared,
> it flickers with fury, it's red with blood,
> We swear the oath of life and death! "[3]

Those who were with us in the forest at that time have forever memorized these scenes. When the "akhdes" movement began to spread, the agitators (previously sent to the shtetl) went back to Bialystok. The (political) enlightenment of the Tanners was now left to the "enlightened" of the Shtetl.

[Page 156]

The main leaders at that time were Hershl Pinke the Shames's, Itshke Grodner and my uncle Moyshe Berl. In addition, my second uncle, Khayim Shloyme, was also active.

During the year that the training and preparations dragged on, the factory owners had not the slightest idea of what was actually going on among the tanners. They only sensed that there was some unrest, but they did not know anything more precise. The oath that the workers had taken on the book and the phylacteries was guarded like a sanctuary.

The workers kept their secret so strictly that even when the strike broke out, the balebatim still thought that this was nothing more than some kind of prank by the "khevre"[4], the gang.

The strike broke out by chance. A foreman of the factory owner Hershl Grosman slapped a worker, and this was the impulse that made the anger of workers in all factories boil over. The first to leave their workplaces were the tanners from Grosman's factory. The second evening, on a Tuesday, a meeting of all the tanners was held, where it was decided that no one should go to work the next day.

At first, the factory owners and the "meistares" thought it was some kind of jest. They cracked their jokes and laughed at the "statshnikes", the rebels. "Ey," they said, "they'll get hungry all right, and then they'll come back to work!" But when this wish did not come true, my Grandpa Khayim Osher's nephew[5], Ayzik Krushenaner, who was one of the very respected balebatim at that time, said:

"I see that we probably won't get anywhere with them like this; it seems that this was a put-up affair by this gang!"

The balebatim were alarmed and stirred up the shtetl. They sent shamosim[6] to the workers' homes to scout out why they had not shown up for work. As previously agreed, the answer was:

"(We demand):

Abolish the Meistares, (the system of temporary work agencies), pay wages every week, directly through the factory owners, and introduce a working time of 12 hours- from 7 a.m. to 7 p.m.!"

The demand that wages be paid directly by the factory owners was a really serious one.

(Apart from the fact that the "meistares" paid only a few rubles of wages to the poor when it was worth their while, they often cheated them out of their money, declared themselves bankrupt, or even fled with the hard-earned earnings of the wage earners, and there was no one left to take care of the hard-working).

[Page 157]

The factory owners were not prepared for such insubordination. In their meeting they decided to summon the "rebels" to the Rabbi.

The Krinker Rabbi Borekh Lavski, zts"l[7] was not very popular among the workers and the poor people.

Among the rich and noble he was very recognized and influential and they held him in high esteem. He himself was also a wealthy man, and his son, Vigder, was one of the really big factory owners.

The Rabbi after him, R' Zalmen Sender[8], in contrast, was constantly at odds with the powerful and influential, but popular with the workers. Zalmen Sender, zts"l, enjoyed a very great reputation in the Jewish world. He always stood up for the craftsmen and chastised the factory owners.

He even refused to pray in the Bes-Hamedresh where the rich prayed. He went instead to pray in the "Kavkazer" Bes-ha Medresh, which for a time was considered the prayer house of the workers. Later, when the powerful in society took the position of gaboes[9], he sought out for prayer the minyonim (prayer quorums), where the craftsmen prayed.

A narrative about Zalmen Sender, zts"l, reports that he was asked how he felt about what is written there, "Rabbi gives honor to the rich"[10]. His answer was:

"Well, that Rabbi knew who a rich man is, but I do not know!"

Rabbi R' Borekh Stavski[11] sent for Hershl Pinkes the Shames's, who was one of the leaders of the strike at that time. When Hershl arrived, the Rabbi was already sitting there, surrounded by all the factory owners. Immediately, (the Rabbi) began to sternly rebuke Hershl for allowing Jewish workers to take part in a revolt.

"I am already very surprised at you," said R' Borekh to Hershl Pinkes[12], "you are teachable, so I ask you, is this a proper way for a Jew to resolve a conflict in this way? When Jews complain about each other, they usually come to the Rabbi for a ruling according to Jewish law (the Torah), and the Rabbi will decide who is right!"

In response, Hershl Pinkes told him, "Rabbi, you wonder at me, and I wonder at you.

A judgement according to Jewish law can only be made when one has the power and the other has the right. But here we are dealing with a very different story. Because you can clearly see for yourself that we have the power.

[Page 158]

And I tell you, Rabbi, that we also have the right on our side, that's just the way it is! So I ask you, what is the need for a Jewish judgement?"

"It may indeed be that you are right," R' Borekh replied, "and presumably you have the power. But, we are now in the middle of the zman[13], so wait until the end of the zman, then you will be heard with your demands, so an agreement will be reached!"

Immediately Hershl replied: "Rabbi, how can it be that you speak like this? It is explicitly written: "Poyel khoyzer beyoyse hayom – The factory worker may withdraw from an agreement on the same day – and even in the middle of the hour!"

Hershl Pinke the Shames's asked the Rabbi why he actually kept demanding that the community leadership give him raises. He reminded him that the Rabbi before him was satisfied with very little. He also accused him of being on the side of the factory owners because he himself was a rich man and, moreover, his son Vigder was a factory owner.

This audacity astonished R' Borekh and the balebatim. The Rabbi immediately ordered Hershl to leave his house. Seeing that the workers remained obstinate and rebellious, the factory owners, with the Rabbi's consent, turned to the governor of Grodno. And after a week, a large group of gendarmes arrived in Krynki, led by their colonel, the polkovnik.

This was the first time that Krynki had such a large number of police "as guests". The gendarmes immediately began to crack down with terror and cruelty. The leaders of the strike were captured and murderously beaten.

This, however, stirred up the skilled workers even more, and the struggle, which divided the shtetl into two hostile crowds, became not only more bitter but also bloodier.

The leaders began to hide. Their homes were attacked and in dozens of Jewish houses people could not sleep through the nights; they stayed awake and in agitation because they were afraid that the gendarmes would burst into their houses. Hershl Pinke the Shames's and still others were arrested and sent to prison in Grodno.

At that time, craftsmen in Krinker houses quietly sang this song:

> "Footsteps of tyrants could be heard
> at 12 o'clock in the night,
> at that time a star dropped down at our place,
> such a one that sparkles in the night.
>
> Our tears are not yet dried
> for those sent away to Siberia,
> when suddenly we hear the news,

[Page 159]

that a new brother has already been detained.

> How sad it is and how oppressive,
> to live in such a land."[14]

The attacks on the leaders of the "Statshke" did not even stop at Grandpa. A few times heavy footsteps and loud banging on the door kept him awake for nights.

The gendarmes did not have to spend much time to search Grandpa's home. They had inspected his poor, cramped room "before you could count to three". When they had convinced themselves that whoever they were looking for was neither in nor under the bed, nor in the only closet, they were already gone. But only for a while, and the very next day they were "guests" at Grandpa's again.

Nokhem Anshel was eager to be lenient with Grandpa. He summoned him and advised him to talk his sons out of continuing to get involved with the "Buntovshtshikes" (rebels).

Grandpa assured him, however, that he could not do anything. His sons already knew what they were doing, no sermon on his part would help, and he couldn't beat them up either.

Translator's footnotes:

1.   אַחדות= Akhdes, at this point I would like to go into more detail about this Hebrew-rooted word, which I have translated before with "unity, union". For the last term, however, no Hebrew ambiguous word from the "holy" language would have been needed. It is interesting to note, however, that the word root אחד also stands for "identity" and "uniqueness" and is used in biblical usage in the Jewish credo, Sh'ma Yisroel, among others, when speaking of the "one G'd," monotheism. I think that when the text later speaks of "creating akhdes", it may also refer to a kind of (new) religious, sacred identity that is to be created and to which, with the inclusion of "old" religious objects, the oath is sworn.

2.   להבדיל= lehavdl, this Hebrew-rooted word is applied to distinguish between the holy and the worldly-profane for pietistic reasons, which is just mentioned; "not comparable with".

3.   This is the anthem of the "Bund", the "Shvue". You can listen to a version of the song here https://www.youtube.com/watch?app=desktop&v=KZg-5RBFjbA

4.   חברה= Khevre, I have so far translated this term differently, as it can have different meanings. It is composed of a word root (khaver) that means "comrade, friend". Khevre means: society, association, gang, comrades, group

5.   shvesterkind= In the Yiddish/English dictionary this term is translated as "cousin", in German it is the niece or nephew. In the present text, the relationships are often known and translated accordingly.

6.   שמשים= Plural of shames, synagogue servants. One could assume that there is a spelling mistake here and "messengers" are meant, but these would be written שליחים. In the Yizkor book "Pinkas Krynki" , page 71, where it is quoted from "Vi nekhtn geshen", it is also spoken about שמשים

7.   זצ"ל = tzadik livracha, the memory of the righteous be a blessing

8.   a photograph can be seen here https://www.ebay.com/itm/153442353777

9.   גבאות= gaboes, plural of gabe, secretarial office, synagogue employee, the same as gaboim.

10.   רבי מכבד את עשירים = "Rabbi pays honor to the rich", this refers to commentaries and accounts around, among others, Rabbi Akiva, who explicitly considered it a religiously based duty to respect and honor the rich. Rabbi Akiva was himself a very rich man and had corresponding contacts with the rich. I have translated here a little freely. (find more about here Eruvin 86:1 https://www.jewishvirtuallibrary.org/tractate-eruvin-chapter-8 .

11.   There seems to be a spelling mistake here, above it says "Lavski".

12.   The name alternates between "Pinke" and "Pinkes". It can be different grammatical forms, which is just not clear to me here

13.   zman= Semester, term of contracts, but the term is also used in the designation of different seasons

14.   Moses Beregovsky collected sound recordings of Jewish folklore and workers' songs at that time, about 1910-1930. The original song "Trit fun tiranen" was provided with a slightly modified text at that time in Krynki, listen to the song here https://www.audio.ipri.kiev.ua/CD6.html

[Page 160]

Strikers Hinder Praying

The factory owners intervened with force and the help of the gendarmes to break the strike. They brought tanners from surrounding towns (to the factories), and there was a drama in Krynki.

After all, the outrage was great: how had it become possible for Jews to act against Jews, for murders and hostility against Jewish families to occur?

The craftsmen joined together. On Shabbat, they entered the large Bes-ha Medresh, where the factory owners prayed, and stopped the reading of the Torah. Then, on the second Shabbat, the prayer house was already guarded by gendarmes. But the craftsmen with their wives and children simply broke in. This was a sacrilege!

The "Yonim" (Russian soldiers) beat the Jews and arrested a large number of them. Thereupon, a storm of protest broke out in the shtetl. The anger and the cries of lamentation exerted such pressure that all the detainees were released.

But this did not lessen the terror, nor did it stop the nightly house searches. Young people whom the gendarmes found at home were arrested.

A mood of tension and attrition spread over the shtetl. Brawls broke out between the strikebreakers and the "statshnikes", the strikers.

When the factory owners realized that they were getting nowhere with the Jews from neighboring towns, they sent messengers to Smorgon, to Romanovka, to the district around Volyn (Volhynia) and to Berdychiv to persuade tanners to come to Krynki.

When the "Statshnikes" learned about it, they decided to fight to the knife not to let the strangers reach Krynki.

In order to prevent the lured Jews from arriving in the shtetl, it was necessary for members of the movement to stop them in Bialystok.[1]

[Page 161]

For the errand, my uncle, Moyshe Berl, was chosen. He had to notify his older brother, Aharon Velvel, who led the Bialystoker "Boyevoy otryad"[2] (the movement's protective group), that the foreign workers should be stopped when they arrived at the station.

Moyshe Berl, the 15-year-old lad, with a piece of bread in his pocket, set out on foot for Bialystok, which was about 7 Russian miles or 50 verst (53,1 km) from Krynki.

For such a distance one usually had to walk for a few days, but Moyshe Berl did not walk! His passion, youth and conviction drove him and chased him. He did not pause. He hurried and strained, day and night.

On the way, peasants let him jump on their cart. After two days and nights he arrived in Bialystok.

Aharon Velvel, together with his "khevre", his gang, waited for the train, and those who could not be "convinced" by them were violently forced to turn around and go home.

Thus, the Smorgonians, Romanovks and Berditshvers did not reach Kynki at all.

When the factory owners realized that they could hardly do anything, they let the skilled workers know that they should come to work and would get everything they had asked for.

The first tanners' strike in Krynki was won!

The workers had won the strike. However, my Grandpa, Yankel Bunim, had lost. His sons learned that this strike was only a kind of exercise for the great transformation (of society); when the workers together would destroy the so-called "capitalism" and the "samoderzhav", the autocracy.

The workers were satisfied that they would now receive their wages every week, that the system of "meystares" had been abolished and that they no longer had to work longer than "from 7 to 7". But my Grandfather's sons were far from satisfied.

They began to agitate against the rich and noble as well as against the autocracy. And so it was not long before the police were once again waking up Grandpa's household in the middle of the night

His youngest son, Khayim Shloyme, had to flee to Bialystok. There he was hidden by his brother, Aharon Velvel.

However, the latter also brought him together with the Bundists there.

[Page 162]

However, in a quarter where some of the revolutionary youth had gathered, a police raid was carried out and all were detained.

On the second day, when the detainees were led to the police prefect for interrogation from the Bialystok prison, which was located on Vashlikover Street (in Russian, the "Nikolayevski Ulitsa"), Aharon Velvel, with a group, raided the guard and freed everyone.

Aharon Velvel hid Khayim Shloyme in weaving factories, where he also slept. The "Shpulyarkes" (winders) worked especially at night to provide protection for the revolutionaries who had to hide from the police.

But Khayim Shloyme could not stay in the factories for long. My Grandmother Sime Feygl went to her rich relatives, the Barishes, to raise money to send Khayim Shloyme out of Russia. He then went first to London and later to America.

Thanks to him, the whole family came to America, he brought them all over with his money.

He also caught up with his beloved, Yakhe Feygl, rest in peace. She was a great and very clever personality. He met her in the movement and one can talk about them as in romance novels; they were devoted to each other with love and dedication, as it was the case between my Grandpa Yankel Bunim and Grandma Sime Feygl.

From my uncle, Khayim Shloyme, we inherited the name "Kohn" (Cohen). A compatriot named Kohn, to whom Khayim Shloyme had gone in New York, advised him to change his name "Krinker" to "Kohn" (Cohen).

Yankel Bunim's eldest son, Aharon Velvel, served as a kind of confident between the Krinker youth who arrived in Bialystok and the movement in Bialystok.

Aharon Velvel, tall, with broad shoulders and determined face, was an extraordinary, daring and fearless hero who was afraid of nothing.

When he was the leader of the "Boyevoy otryad", both the factory owners and the police trembled.

Aharon Velvel was sent to Siberia for four years for an assassination he had committed with others on a weaver manufacturer.

[Page 163]

The factory owner Nokhem Kolner, used to fight the workers with cruelty and doggedness not only in his factory but in general.

During the great weavers' strike from 1895 to 1896 he played a bitter role. He was the leader and main spokesman for the weaver factory owners, preventing them from compromising with the workers. Warnings did not deter him. On the contrary, he only became more dogged and stubborn. In the heat of the strike, he denounced some bokherim (Jewish boys) to the police. This sealed his fate.

One evening on Shabbat, when Nokhem Kolner was coming from praying, several from the "khevre" next to his apartment on "Sarazer" Street, in the "Zaviker's yard", ambushed him and shot him. Together with Aharon Velvel, eleven (other) leaders of the "Boyevoy otryal" were arrested.

Five were convicted, and Aharon Velvel's sentence was "four years of exile to a remote village in the Irkutsk administrative district."

On the deportation he was accompanied by his girlfriend. In the Moscow "Butyrka" prison they got married. At her request, after the sentence was pronounced, she left for Siberia together with the prisoner convoy. In exile she had two children, a boy and a girl.

I still remember how the two children, Sasha and Helena, came to Krynki from Siberia with their mother.

Aharon Velvel's sweetheart, Mirtshe, an active and devoted activist in the movement, went with him to Siberia (at first) not so much out of love for him, but rather because it was in keeping with the revolutionary spirit of the times.

Mirtshe was a romantic young woman. Besides Aharon Velvel, another young bokher had fallen in love with her – Nyomke! She liked this fellow even more, so she sought his closeness.

However, Aharon Velvel's condemnation to exile resulted in Mirtshe becoming estranged from Nyomke and forming a permanent union with Aharon Velvel.

Yankel Bunim's worries about his sons would not cease. Moyshe Berl caused him particular grief.

The latter was very much involved in the preparations for the second tanners' strike in Krynki. He was already in the "Bund" at that time and participated in stirring up the tanners politically.

[Page 164]

The second strike was not so sudden and unexpected for the factory owners. They were no longer as confused and helpless as in the first strike and fought the "statshnikes" with great doggedness and cruelty.

The first activity of the police was to arrest all the (strike) leaders. Moyshe Berl was tortured for five days in the Krinker "reshotke", the prison. The beatings injured his lungs, and when he was released, he spat blood.

My Grandpa urged him to escape from Krynki. Moyshe Berl then dressed up in women's clothes and my mama, rest in peace, led him, hooked in his arm, far out of town.

At that time Aharon Velvel was already in prison. Moyshe Berl first stayed with relatives in Bialystok for a few weeks and then traveled to London.

In London, however, Moyshe Berl became very ill. The great man and humanist, Peter Kropotkin[3], then took him into his home and cared for him until Khayim Shloyme, his brother, brought him to America.

Kropotkin had met Moyshe Berl in the library that the anarchists ran in London's "Whitechapel," on Commercial Road.

The local residents, Kropotkin, Teplov, (Nikolay) Tshaykovski and Emma Goldman when she came to London, used to stay in the library.

This group of respected revolutionaries supported all Russian political refugees. Since Moyshe Berl was also ill as a result of the police torture, Kropotkin took him in.

He took care of him and literally put him "back on his feet".

Translator's footnotes:

    1.   There is still no rail connection to Krynki.
    2.   „boyevoy otryad"= from Russian literally "fighting (combat) group", Yosl Cohen refers to it in brackets as "protection group"
    3.   Pyotr Alexeyevich Kropotkin (1842- 1921), Russian anarchist, historian, scientist and philosopher who fought for a society free of violence and domination

[Page 165]

The "Kavkaz" Street

It took me a long time to get used to my father after he returned from the soldiers. I did not want to leave my Grandpa Khayim Osher and my Grandma Rive at any price, because after all they were my parents to me!

It took me a long time to accept that that man with the "Komets"[1] beard (which looked like a band-aid stuck under his lip), whom I was to call "Papa", was actually my Dad.

It took months to persuade and plead with me to move into the house where my parents lived.

The apartment that Mother had rented from Alter Milb before Papa came home was counted among the better ones.

The new furniture with the unusual cabinet that had been refined into a "shafe", a bookcase, and the large lamp with the lampshade gave the apartment an almost stately appearance.

The apartment was located in the lower part of "Kavkaz". The former inhabitants of the street had long ago been replaced by others, so the gang "Akhim" ("the brothers"), through which the street had received its bad reputation, had long since ceased to exist. Only older Jews still remembered the times when the "Akhim" ruled and frightened the whole area around Krynki.

However, nevertheless "Kavkaz" remained just "Kavkaz".

And the inhabitants of the shtetl always looked at the "Kavkazers" with some suspicion and contempt.

Kavkaz did not consist of a single street, but of a chain of several streets that formed the shape of a "Khes"[2]. Only upper-class people lived along these streets. One of the streets, however, rather a kind of dead end, was considered the "real Kavkaz".

In the upper part of "Kavkaz" lived the rich and "balebatish" families. In this part also lived Grandpa Yankel Bunim's nephew ("sister's child"), Berl Fishke's, who was the mayor of the shtetl. However, downstream, right next to a muddy passageway, there was the "Zhabe (Frog) Alley".

[Page 166]

Here, in about 15 to 20 houses, lived people of non-noble descent who were considered and treated like the "untouchables" in Hinduism. These people who were considered "unworthy" and "lepers" were called "Kapitses"[3].

The "Kapitses" were horse traders and horse thieves, but among them were also pickpockets. In a word, almost the whole Krinker "underworld" had its nest in those houses and the muddy alley in the lower part of Kavkaz.

The children of the Kapitses were loud, daring and naughty brats and were known as thugs. Both in summer and winter they ran around barefoot, dirty and unwashed, and many were "decorated" with scabbed heads.

They were the ones who broke the window panes, tore off the fruits, ran after the carts and were the terror of all the boys. At weddings they stood behind the windows, and when the bride and groom were led into the synagogue courtyard to the wedding canopy, they ran in front and set off fireworks.

At weddings they practiced pranks, pricked the guests with needles and knotted the women's dresses together.

They were at the forefront of all scandals.

Our apartment at Alter Milb was located right on the border that separated the upper Kavkaz from the muddy alley where the "Kapitses" lived.

So we were in close proximity to each other, and for such a hot-blooded, wild and temperamental boy like me, it was impossible to separate myself from the "Zhabe Alley" brats and to avoid them.

Even if I had wanted to, I couldn't have done it, because the rascals would have broken my bones. They hated it when you acted haughty and aloof towards them. Any arrogance would have cost me my life.

It was not easy for me to join the boys because I was very afraid of them at first. They usually tore the hat off my head and tried everything possible to get me into a fight.

[Page 167]

When I came home from school, I didn't walk but I ran the last part of the way to the house. They (the brats) were already sitting on wooden blocks or on entrance stairs and were lying in wait to chase me as soon as they caught sight of me. So I arrived half-dead in the house and stood at the window to look after them.

They would then grimace at me, bend down and shout, "Boo, boo!"

This could not go on for long, so I decided to make peace with them.

Once, when they were chasing me, I just stopped.

They were frozen and amazed for a moment and looked at each other. The strongest of the boys walked right up to me and growled:

"Well!"

"What, well?", I asked. Right then his words blurted out, right in my face, "Who do you think you are? There are no privileged people here, everyone is equal. You live on Kavkaz, don't you? Then you must be a Kavkazer too!"

"What do you want from me?", I wanted to know.

"A toy," he shouted. This was an allusion that I should make some kind of "contribution" so that they would keep peace with me.

When I brought him "the toy", I was allowed to sit on the wooden blocks with him, and later the boys included me in their "command".

That I made common cause with the gang, my mother learned only when she gave birth to my brother Mair.

Instead of bringing home boys from my school to recite the "Krishme"[4] for the woman in childbed, I brought the Kavkaz boy's gang. I wanted them to have all the sweets, nuts and cake that were usually distributed to the children after reciting the Krishme.

When mom saw the dirty, barefoot and disheveled urchins, it certainly put a strain on her childbed.

The brats of the "Zhabe Alley" did not completely waste their time on wild (pranks) and destructions. Like all other children, they liked to hear and tell stories and dreamed of faraway lands and strange, different people.

[Page 168]

On summer nights, the "Zhabe Alley" boys would sit down on wooden blocks or house doorways and listen curiously to the stories that a boy who was good at storytelling would relay.

Most of the tales were about demons and ghosts, devilish creatures and monsters, about hell and the sinners who roasted in it, about the corpses that came to the "cold" synagogue every night, exactly at midnight. They usually put on a prayer shawl, called for the reading of the Torah and prayed until the last star disappeared.

There were boys who testified to, themselves, hearing the voices of the corpses coming out of the "cold" synagogue. In every occurrence and apparition the rascals interpreted different meanings and clues.

A glowing red sunset was interpreted as a sign of coming wars.

The boys sang songs with words and melodies that were full of longing and mysticism. Not all the boys who gathered on the blocks were descended from the "Kapitses." Many joined the "command" (from the outside), as I did.

The leaders were boys from the other side of Kavkaz street, just not those from "Zhabe Alley".

The top leader was Yanke Katyut (why he got the surname I don't know).

Yanke's father was a teacher in the Jewish elementary school, a great poor man. His only asset was a goat. Both he, his wife and Yanke's siblings were calm and composed people. Yanke, however, was a hothead, a fiery boy.

He always went barefoot. The mud that had grown into his flesh had stained his feet. He was taller than all the other boys and had a body like bronze. He could bend and do tricks like an acrobat or those "magicians," as they were called in the little town.

The boys looked at Yanke with wide eyes and adored him. He liked to brag that he could bend and twist so well because he rubbed butter on his body every day. The boys believed everything he said.

[Page 169]

Yanke Katyut was a skillful and clever boy. He had ingenious ideas. In his wars with the boys from other streets he provided a lot of ingenuity and thoughtful strategies. He was daring, and no one could compete with him.

Yanke liked stories, he liked to listen or tell them himself, but only about demons, devils and corpses.

He asserted that if you put your ear to the threshold of the house where a corpse was lying, you could hear the dead man fighting with the angel of death to prevent the latter from carrying him away.

He organized the "command" in a truly military way; there were "soldiers, officers, generals, brigades, nations and armies".

Since he liked to listen to me telling stories and also appreciated my daring, he included me in his "staff" and made me his adjutant.

In this "staff" there were also Hershl "Boyte" (prey) and Zeydke "Kirbeses" (pumpkin). Hershl Boyte was not a spoiled boy, on the contrary, he was a good and obedient one. His father Yisroeltshke the Klezmer, was a cheerful bon vivant. He never stayed in one place and went to America about fifteen times.

Zeydke "Kirbises" was already a bold and strong boy. Zeydke liked to fight and be the leader.

He was smart, with original ideas, and liked to play tricks on others or make fun of other boys.

In winter, black "fur" hats were worn that looked like they were made of the fur of Karakul sheep, but they were made of cloth. Zeydke and I were like twins. To have fun with the other boys, we smeared our hats with soot and looked for a victim.

So, beforehand, we determined a boy whom we wanted to mock. We would go up to him, engage him in conversation, and bet him that we would guess what he had eaten today. We played such pranks only on Shabbat, when all the children were off school.

The meals on Shabbat were the same for everyone: the "cholent" stews, either with a piece of meat, steamed potatoes, with sweet vegetables or pearl barley, carrots, turnips, or even with plums and potatoes.

[Page 170]

The "guessing" went like this with us: I or Zeydke held the boy by the shoulders, and the other of us brushed his soot-prepared cap over his face, so that the boy's face was smeared.

"You ate beet stew!" It was also conceivable that it had even been carrot stew. In any case, we kept stroking the face with our hats until we "guessed the right meal."

When I and Zeydke were "done" with the boy, we would take him through our whole "command" and our gang would have fun making jokes and mocking the boy.

Yosl, five years old

Translator's footnotes:

　　1.　　komets-berdl= the קמץ is a vowel sign that denotes an "o" in Yiddish. It has the
form of a "T".
　　2.　　the eighth letter, the "Khes", Hebrew "Khet".
　　3.　　possibly, from kopite= hoof
　　4.　　קריאת-שמע= / Jewish creed, the "Sh'ma Yisroel" or „Shema"

[Page 171]

Aunty Sore's Stories

Many of the stories I told the "Kavkazer" brats on summer evenings when we sat on
the logs or front steps, I had heard from my Aunt Sore.

Although she was a few years older than me, she was terrified of me.

I used to push her and hit her. As she grew older, I couldn't stand to see her hanging
out with boys and girls of the same age.

Just as I saw her going out for a walk or spending time with her friends, I would snap and make a violent and angry scene at her. If she just caught sight of me from afar, she would run away to hide.

I terrorized and chased Sore in a terrible way. But the more she ran away from me to hide, the more my desire to chase, catch and beat her increased.

I took special pleasure in seeing how she was frightened. Once I invaded Motl Tsholne's house like a savage because I didn't like the fact that she was hanging out with Motl Tsholne's son. I drove Sore out of the house with a stick.

The stories Sore told me were interesting and extraordinary. She had heard many of them from my Grandpa. But she could also make up her own beautiful stories. When my parents went out for a visit or a walk, Sore usually came to watch over me and my younger brother Mair.

Sore loved to tell about her heroic brothers, especially the oldest, Aharon Velvel, who had been exiled to Siberia, and the other two who had escaped to America.

Her stories always ended with, "They (the brothers) are suffering and suffered because they stood up for the poor."

Sore aroused in me admiration for her brothers, since they had been expelled because of their love for the poor. In my imagination, I saw them as tall, strong, and fearless heroes who laid down their lives for the poor.

[Page 172]

From her I also learned that far away there was a tsar who was a bad man. He kept soldiers and guards to preserve the interests of the rich.

Sore taught me to sing songs, some of which she had heard adults sing. At that time, the young people performed some plays by Goldfaden[1], whose songs were very common and were often sung.

One song had the flavor of revolt and hatred for the tsar's children, it went like this:

"Ding, dong, ding, dong,
whose children are driving there,
they are the tsar's, the tsar's,
on the stove they are sitting,
under the stove they are sweating,
they are rubbing matches,

they are chasing ducks away,
without any speech they stay."[2]

At the end of the last words it was common to laugh at the top of one's lungs, "ha, ha, without any speech they stay".

Sore was passionate about teasing me. She liked to laugh at other children and even adults. I don't know from whom she had inherited this inclination, because her father, Yankel Bunim, peace be upon him, did not like to mock other people. His children were good, hearty, honest and noble people.

But this bad habit of "pulling their leg", this "oplakhn-ontsien", as they themselves called it, was something almost every one of them had.

They especially enjoyed making fun of someone and embarrassing him or her. When they had chosen a victim, they would ask him a foolish question.

They used to wink at each other, while a smile was already playing in their eyes and around their mouths, and sparkle with joy when the helpless victim could not answer the illogical question and stood there dumbfounded and perplexed.

Sore could make my life hell when she imitated how my Grandma spoke. She would stand on a bench to demonstrate how tall Rive was. Then she would grimace and mimic Rive's speech.

I would usually get angry and cry watching her mimic Rive's way of walking and talking.

Sore especially liked to imitate how Rive pronounced Grandpa Khayim Osher's name. Until the end of her days, Grandma, in her Yiddish-Polish dialect, would not say "Khayim Osher" but "Ka-em Oosher."

[Page 173]

In general, it hurt me when the difference in size between Khayim Osher and Rive was ridiculed, and additionally the fact that everyone in Yankel Bunim's family had two names.

From Dad's side, Sore teased me with Grandma Rive's dialect. And from Mom's side, my uncle, Dodye the baker, teased me that Grandpa Yankel Bunim, Grandma Sime Feygl and all their children had two names – except for one daughter, Henye.

When Uncle Dodye, the baker, wanted to provoke me, he used to quietly and calmly enumerate the names of Grandpa Yankel Bunim and his household.

To do this, he would clench his left hand into a fist and lift finger after finger from his left hand with his right hand, enumerating:

"Yankel Bunim, Sime Feygl, Aharon Velvel, Abe Yudl, Leyzer Hersh, Moyshe Berl, Khayim Shloyme, Mair Yonah, Sore Rivke."

Then when it was Henye's turn, who had only one name, he would pause for a moment.

Soon, however, he gave himself a jolt:

"Henye-Penye"[3], he exclaimed hastily, laughing himself half to death at his idea.

When my brother Mair (Meier) was born, people began to pay less attention to me. That disturbed me enormously! I was just looking for ideas that would give cause for (my family) to be worried about me.

To provoke my parents and family, I spent even more time with the "Kavkazer" boys.

I was the very first to run to a scuffle, break windows, tear off fruit or do other wild foolishness.

On the border that separated Kavkaz from the "Zhabe Alley", where the "Kapitses" lived, there was a well from which the inhabitants of the lower area of Kavkaz drew water.

The narrow path where the "Kapitses" lived was a little to the side of the alley. On the other side of the path lived about 15 to 20 non-Jewish families who had their houses and large gardens there.

Just opposite the well lived a Polish Christian, Maril, with two daughters, older, scrawny and ugly girls.

These "shiksas" ran a laundry and came to the well quite a few times to draw water.

[Page 174]

They knew me well, and I often helped them draw water and carry the buckets when they used a stick instead of a water carrier pole.

For this purpose, the stick was pulled through the wire eyelets of the buckets. One had to carry the front end of the stick, and the other the back end, and so we carried the water.

I often helped the gentiles to carry the water into the house, and in return they invited me to eat with them. At some point I was already part of the family. Old Maril liked me very much, and whenever I had the opportunity, I visited the Christians. Maril let me pick all the fruits that grew in his garden.

Maril was sick, only skin and bones and croaked dully. He was suffering from "Tshakhotke", tuberculosis, and was in a lot of pain. All day long he sat there and warmed himself in the sun.

He looked typically Polish with his "proud" nose and short-shaven hair sticking out like hedgehog spikes. His face was yellowish from the disease, his eyes were deep in their sockets, and his cheekbones stood out sharp and pointed.

Once, when I entered the Christian house, I got a great fright.

Maril was lying stretched out on a board, dressed in black clothes, with a white shirt and a small black tie.

His hands were folded together and held a cross. Next to the cross was a shimmering sheet of paper with writing framed in black.

Around the corpse sat about twenty to thirty people.

Large candles were burning on a small table, and a gentile peasant boy, a giant, was playing a harmonica beside it.

Out of sheer fright, I wanted to run away. However, one of Maril's daughters grabbed me by the hand and pulled me to her. Her bony hands were like iron. She put me between her legs so that I could not move.

After a priest had "opgebentsht", as the Christian praying is called among us, the corpse was put into a box and the crowd went to the church.

The "Shiksa", the Christian girl, still held me tightly by her hand, and thus led me into the church with her.

[Page 175]

Inside the church, terrible fear gripped me. Everything I saw inside made me feel frightened. The many pictures and portraits on the walls confused me. The "shiksa" took off my cap.

When suddenly music sounded, I was completely startled. In the huge space of the church an invisible voice rose!

The crowd moved further inward. Suddenly, everyone fell to their knees. The "shiksa" let go of me.

I put on my cap and ran to the exit.

In the anteroom, however, I bumped into a Christian woman who was obviously late. From my panic and because I had my hat on, the woman concluded that I must be a Jewish child. She chased me and then gave me a blow between the shoulders with her fist.

I was just able to run outside, then I fell, covered in blood.

The vicious woman had injured one of my lungs!

A whole series of visits to the doctors began. They gave instructions to give me lots of milk to drink and lots of sweets to eat.

This pleased me.

I was paid attention to again.

I wanted to stay sick for a very long time. After no more blood showed, I helped myself to "fabricate" it. I scratched my gums with my fingernail until they bled and spat into a handkerchief.

I took it to my mother and convinced her that I was still sick.

[Page 176]

Translator's footnotes:

1.   Avrom (Abraham) Goldfaden, 1840-1908, Jewish folk poet and composer, founder of the Yiddish theater. He was an extremely popular figure in the Jewish world. On the occasion of his funeral in New York, 50,000 Jewish mourners were expected to attend; moreover, Jewish stores closed as the funeral procession passed.

2.   The original of the text is not only somewhat longer, but differs in the last sentence. Thus it does not say "on loshn blaybn zey" but "in khaloshes blaybn zey", and this statement with the ambiguous Hebraism means among other things also: "in disgust, in   a   rotten   thing   they   remain"!   see https://archive.org/details/nybc212225/page/15/mode/1up

3.   Possibly an allusion to "Henny Penny" or also called "Chicken Little", an old folk tale of the Jewish author Joseph Jacobs.

[Page 177]

<u>Third Part</u>

The Shtetl

[Page 178]

A part of the Krinker market

[Page 179]

Krinik (Krynki)

The Krinkers were nicknamed "thieves". The surrounding towns and cities also had their nicknames, such as: "Sokolker, the "Sibirnikes"[1]; Bialystoker, the "Cake Eaters"; Vashlikover, the "Goats", Shishlevitser, the "Kozes"[2].

The Krinkers got their nickname because of the Jewish band of robbers called "Akhim" (brothers), because they were led by a couple of brothers.

These bandits used to rob transients, aristocratic residences and abandoned inns.

They also stole horses, and it was known that lost horses had to be searched for in Krynki. For many years the "Akhim" gang terrorized the whole area. It disappeared after several leaders either died, were sent to labor camps or to Siberia.

Those who remained had in the meantime "socially matured" and become quiet. They engaged in honest and decent work.

Krynki was a typical Jewish shtetl; the Jews lived in the center of town and the goyim more on the outer edge of the shtetl. Krynki was built like a kind of tire in the shape of a blossom. In the center was the marketplace, from which all the streets departed and intersected. It can be said that the shtetl and its streets were located at the feet of the marketplace.

The round built marketplace itself was in the center of three rings. In the first, (innermost) market ring lived many rich and "balebatish" people, and the hotel of the shtetl, which belonged to Itshe "Lya", the nephew of my Grandpa, stood in the first row of the market houses. Quite a few of the shtetl's inns were also located there.

In the second ring, a bit away from the houses, there were "budkes", wooden stalls that served as stores. In such a "budke" one could not hold much merchandise, and so usually only one or two items were sold.

Just behind the "budkes", in the third ring, were the stores. All the trade of the shtetl was concentrated in the stores.

[Page 180]

These sold different goods, and one could not only get in them all that the townspeople needed, but also what the surrounding farmers needed.

Twice a week, on Sunday and Thursday, farmers usually brought goods from their villages to sell, and in return they took what they themselves needed. The merchants depended on the two market days, because they meant their main sales.

Twice a year, for one or two weeks, large fairs were held, which were attended not only by peasants from remote villages, but also by Jews from the surrounding towns.

Right in the middle of the market there was the "saray", the shed. It contained all the utensils of the fire department for extinguishing a fire, the water hoses and the "batshes", that is, the water barrels on two wheels, which had to be pulled to the fire.

At the market there was also the house of Khatskel the "Sheynker" (innkeeper), where all the weddings took place. The processions to the chuppah, the wedding canopy, that did not lead to the large synagogue ("cold shul") took place in the open air[3], near the "Saray".

At the foot of the market the streets crossed. All the main streets, except for Kavkazer, which began a little detached, originated at the market.

Krynki had about ten streets, except for the side streets and paths connected to the main streets. Each name of a street expressed its characteristic, for example:

"Tepershe (Pottery) Street"; pots were made there.

"Kantselyar Street"; there was the government office.

"Gabarske (Tanners') Street"; all the big tanneries were located there, "Potsht Street" (with the post office), etc.

The soil of the shtetl was productive and fertile. Krynki got its name because of the "Krenitses", the springs of water, which rose there. Wherever one dug, one found watercourses.

Outside the city, where it went to the fields, there were many swamps. The earth around them was black and "fat", and peat was cut from it, or, as the townspeople said, "torp". This was used for heating.

It was a substitute for coal and was cheap to have, thus many houses were heated with peat.

The farmers supplied the peat. They cut the earth around the swamps into brick shapes. These bricks were dried and later brought to the city on carts for sale.

[Page 181]

In the shtetl, besides the "cold" shul, there were some bote-medroshim[4] and a few minyonim[5]. The most respected shtibl of the Hasidic people was that of the Slonimer, the other Hasidic dynasties such as the "Gerer", "Kotsker" and "Kobriner" only formed minyonim. However, they were so few that they prayed in the misnagdic bote-medroshim. Unlike the Slonimer Rabbi, their Rabbis never came to Krynki, and only a few of the "Gerer" or "Kotsker" Hasids went to see their Rabbis when needed or on occasion.

Krynki also became famous for its great Rabbinical geniuses who occupied the position of Rabbi. Their names were Rabbi Avrohem Kharef[6], also called R' Avremtshik, Rabbi Borekh Lavski, zts"l[7], Rabbi Zalmen Sender, zts"l and the famous Rabbi Shapiro.

Besides its great and famous "moyre-hoyroes"[8], the city also boasted the great "tsadek", the wise and righteous man, R' Yosele, z"l[9].

Ayzik -Benyamin Zeliks, a Jew, also came from Krynki. He pretended to be a "good yud"[10] and traveled around the Volhynia area. He was of very low descent and had hardly any schooling. However, in order to earn an income, he performed as a "good yud". In the Volhynia area he was known and famous as a Bal-Moyfes, a miracle worker.

He was exposed, however, by a man from Krynki who came to the town of Volhynia on business just as Ayzik-Benyamin Zeliks was holding a Shabbat service there.

Out of curiosity, the Krinker went to the Hasidic shtibl to see the Rabbi the shtetl boasted about. There, however, he uncovered the hoax, and the "good yud" had to leave town.

After a few years, Ayzik-Benyamin Zeliks settled back in Krynki and went about the houses there begging.

Krynki was the only shtetl in the area that had its own klezmer band. For a few years it was the custom that on Friday evenings, at Parshe Beha'atlotkha[11], the musicians would play in the shul. However, when R' Borekh Stavski became the Rabbi in Krynki, he abolished this custom because the women often came home too late for the light blessing.

The leader of the music band was Moyshe Kreynes. He played the violin as his main instrument and also taught children who wanted to learn an instrument. His lessons were usually very loud, with him tapping the beat with his foot and yelling, "One, two, three! One, two, three!"

Jewish doctors had no luck in the shtetl. For example, there was a doctor Goldberg who was called "Lupatsh"[12] because he had a cleft lip.

[Page 182]

However, he was called to see a sick person only on Shabbat because one is not allowed to handle money on that day. Thus, he was rarely paid. Eventually, he escaped from the shtetl.

In the shtetl there was also a studied obstetrician, a Polish woman named "Stefanovtshekhe", whose services were used mainly by the people who were more educated and wealthy. In the shtetl, however, it was customary to call for a delivery the Jewish midwife Miryam Rezyl, the daughter of Moyshe the Khazn (cantor). On Purim, she sent a ginger cake as shalekhmones[13] to the children she had helped into the world.

Some time ago she prevented a young Jewish woman who had studied obstetrics in Vilnius from settling in Krynki. She played such a mean trick on the daughter of Eliya the Mason that this graduate woman had to flee the city in the middle of the night and could not even take her tippet and graduate hat with her, with which she liked to dress up.

The Krinkers did not like cantors, they were considered like a fifth wheel. When a cantor did arrive in the shtetl, many of them even with fine and well-trained choirs, the Jews who wanted to hear him prayed in the first minyen and then went to the cantor just for entertainment, but not to pray with him.

However, even if the cantor had been the very best, he never got his money's worth. Usually, before he had finished his prayer chant, the Jews would contort their faces and wave their hands, peh, peh...he didn't take anything, and he was gone.[14]

The Krinkers had a special dialect. Instead of saying "s'iz do" (it's there), they said "es iz ido". They called the gum not "yasles" but "asles", the rag not "shmate" but "smate" and they did not say "shpatsirn" (walk) but "spatsirn", furthermore they said "mundzhir" instead of "mundir" to the uniform.

Parents were not called "tate-mame" but "mami-tati", grandparents were not called "bobe-zeyde" but "zeydi-bobi", and an "eh" at the end of a word was pronounced as an "i".

They could not pronounce an "h" at the beginning of a word, and so the "have" became "ave". And so on...[15]

Apart from the fact that the shtetl had the "enlightenment movement", it had its cultural and educational institutions and many "Khevres", groups that helped shape Jewish life, e.g.: "Gmiles-Khsodim"[16],

"Biker-Khoylim"[17], "Moes-Khitn"[18] and "Hakhnoses-Kale"[19]. In addition, there were many elementary schools, a Russian school and college, modernized elementary schools and a library.

Frank and free the pigs ran around (in the shtetl), they used not only to feel at home, but even considered it beneath their dignity to stretch out on the streets, so they trotted to the market to lounge around. The pigs caused great distress.

[Page 183]

Mothers used to guard their children that they should not go outside with food, because not only once it had happened that a child with food in its hand had been dragged along quite a few streets by a pig.

The Jewish community dared several times to expel them from the streets, but each time the goyim won in the courts, and the shtetl had to make peace – in "goles" (exile); and so, in addition to the suffering caused by the goyim, one had to endure constantly the suffering caused by their pigs.

The fact that there was constant spring water in Krynki helped the town to become the center of the tanning industry. The mineral water provided good leather, which was qualitatively distinguished from the tanneries of other cities.

In Krynki there was no great and bitter poverty. Only a few Krinkers went begging. However, Tevl "Vatshul" and Blumke, Mordekhay "Bedzdush's" wife, often used to go out on Shabbat to find a few pieces of challah.

Mordekhay "Bezdush"[20] and his wife Blumke were water carriers, for which they used a "Koromisle", a water carrier pole. For one kopek they would bring water from the wells. Both had asthma, and many times their shortness of breath forced them to stay in bed for several days. Blumke then walked around town collecting challah for her household.

They had two or three daughters who were extraordinary persons, and therefore there was not only one young and "balebatish" man who fell in love with one of the daughters. But, what well-to-do, middle-class man would want to marry into the family of Mordekhay "Bezdush"?

Besides Mordekhay, there were other Jews in the shtetl with "surnames", such as: "Motsh-Potsh" (mud-patch). "the Katshkes" (the ducks), "the Kugelekh" (the balls or puddings), "the Gimzhelakh", "the Bebelakh" (the beans), "the Ebelakh", "Lafonts with the Bells", "Dratsh", "Shamush" (an extra light), "Flekhtl" (lichen), "Skreytshik" (scratch?), "Itshe Malekh-Hamoves" (angel of death).

This Itshke used to always walk around with his buttons undone and his shirt open, his hair disheveled and his eyes protruding. He looked exactly as the townspeople imagined an angel of death.

There were also the nicknames "Itke-Kitke", Leyzer "Drales" and "Alter Khales".

[Page 184]

When at Simkhes Toyre[21] the processions around the Bimah started to move, schoolchildren used to sing the melody of "Ozer Dalim"[22], but for fun included the nicknames of residents (in the text of the old poem, which sounded something like this):

"Leyzer Drales, please save, Alter Khales, please succeed, Itke-Kitke, we answered the day we read it".

There were also "surnames" like "Kirbes (Pumpkin)", "Mukhalap", "Milb (Mite)", "Slabets", "the Farbrenter (Burnt)" and "Yente Kleyn-Kepele (Little Head)".

Those who did not have a funny "surname" were called either after their professional activity or after the name of their fathers or mothers. Some were also named after the name of the town they came from, such as "Itshke Grodner", "Shmuel Azhorer" and "the Lapinitser".

One young man was called "Itshke di Meydl (the Girl)."

This Itshke did not grow a beard and everyone knew that he had not been circumcised.

However, he put on men's clothes and also acted like a man. It is said that he even got married in America.

Malke from Krynki, who had converted from Judaism to Christianity, married a Polish, well-off young man, Yanek. He was a kind of amateur photographer and it was said that he had taken his wife from the Grodner brothel at that time.

His house was the meeting place of all the Krinker young people who wanted to engage in something heretical. If you saw a young man coming out of Yanek's house, you knew he had eaten pork.

Yanek and his mother, her name shall be erased, were fierce Jew haters. They, good speakers of Yiddish, did live among and associate with Jews, but they were also the source of all propaganda against Jews. When it was profitable for him, Yanek became a powerful revolutionary. But it was known all too well that he was a denunciator.

The convert was no better than he. She played the role of a pious Catholic and did not even show remnants of friendship to Jews. She, who came from the brothel, acted as the personified righteousness and as young men reported, she did not let herself be touched.

However, she did not fare well with Yanek, because when he was drunk, he used to reproach her for her Jewish ancestry.

At the market, while shopping, she was shunned by the women. She longed for a conversation with a Jewish woman, but her wish was not granted.

She had no children, and when she had sorrows that she wanted to get off her chest, she confided in the young people who came to her house to do heretical things. She was content, she said, not to have children, "because that way there are a few less goyim in the world."

Translator's footnotes:

1.   In each of the second and third lines the first letters are not printed, so it is not sure if this is really the word "sibirnik". A "sibirnik" is a criminal who was sent into exile to Siberia.
2.   koze= prison, goat, trickster, cheat
3.   It is in accordance with Jewish tradition that the ceremony around the wedding canopy, the chuppah, usually takes place outdoors. The wedding canopy symbolizes the house that the bride and groom will build, it is open on four sides to express the hospitality of the bride and groom. According to some traditions, it also symbolizes that the offspring of the bride and groom should be as numerous as the stars in the sky above the chuppah and that the bride and groom will lead a household according to "heavenly" ideals.

4.   Plural of בית-מדרש =Bes-Medresh. A Bes-(Ha)medresh is primarily a house for studying the Talmud, but it is also used as a synagogue (shul).

5.   Plural of מנין, minyen or minyan, Prayer quorum, at least 10 adult Jewish males are required for a Jewish worship service.

6.   Kharef= astute

7.   זצ״ל= may the memory of a saint be for a blessing

8.   מורה-הוראה= a moyre-hoyroe is a Rabbi, judge, a Jew who may answer inquiries to the Rabbi

9.   ז״ל= of blessed memory

10.   A"gutter (good) yud"= "good Jew", the term sometimes also stands for the Rabbi, who is consulted, among other things, to give advice or cure a disease

11.   פרשה בהעלותך= a particular section of the Torah. The reading section of the 2nd or 3rd Shabbat in the month of Siwan is read, which in the Gregorian calendar begins in the middle to end of the month of May. However, until 1918, Russia still applied the Julian calendar, which was 13 days back.

12.   lupatsh, łupacz = Haddock

13.   שלחמנות= The shalekhmones were usually small gift baskets filled with fruits or nascvhenries given by close relatives or friends on Purim

14.   Perhaps it should be mentioned at this point that there was generally a split within Judaism at the beginning of the 19th century, which affected in particular the outward form of religious practice and led to a renewal of synagogue music, which in part adapted itself more and more to Christian contemporary church music, and besides choral songs even included the organ in its repertoire. Already since the 17th century, the participation of a choir in the Jewish service was common in some Orthodox communities, although its role was very limited.

15.   The dialect contains many of the "typical" features of Lithuanian Yiddish

16.   גמילות-חסדים= Gmiles-Khsodim, Associations that granted interest-free loans, cooperative lending fund

17.   ביקור-חולים= Biker-Khoylim, charitable organization to help the poor and sick, a kind of hospital

18.   מעות-חיטין= Moes-Khitn, "Money for Wheat," a fund so that the poor could buy matzah for Passover and honor the holiday

19.   הכנסת-כלה = Hakhnoses-Kale, Aid organization for poor girls or orphan girls so they could get married

20.   The name is spelled differently each time. I think the "name" derives from the Slavic "bezdech", which means breathless.

21.   שׂמחת-תּורה= Simkhes-toyre, Simkhat-Torah, Feast on the day after the Feast of Tabernacles, feast for the completion of the annual circle of reading the Torah.

22.   עוזר דלים= Ozer Dalim, Hoshiya Na, Helper/Rescuer of the poor, an ancient 181ikipe, an ancient liturgical poem that can be recited at the opening of the Simcha Torah festival. The school children inserted the nicknames of the residents in the 181ikipe, possibly in the places where the paraphrase of the name of G'd is actually written. The original text can be seen here https://old-piyut-org-il.translate.goog/textual/181ikiped/580.html?_x_tr_sch=http&_x_tr_sl=iw&_x_tr_tl=de&_x_tr_hl=de&_x_tr_pto=sc

[Page 185]

Personalities and Remarkable Things

The Krinker youth boasted of Shimen Sikorski, one from the town who had helped in the assassination of von Plehve. Sikorski's deed confirmed that the Krinker "Khevre" was daring, heroic and idealistic.

However, the sthetl had not only heroic and brave boys and girls, who played an important and respected role in the 1905 revolution and even before, but also Jew traitors and good-for-nothings.

I remember two of them:

The first, Katshandre, was a denunciator on a grand scale, consorting with the influential authorities. He was ugly: his right eye was almost completely covered by the eyelid, with only a small opening at the lash line from which red flesh peeked out.

Katshandre was not permanently in Krynki, but spied on Krinkers who were in other cities, especially Grodno and Bialystok.

He had brought his wife, a personality! It was rumored, however, that Katshandre, just like the Pole Yanek, had taken his wife from a brothel.

The "Khevre" warned him and threatened him a few times. Later there was talk that the Krinker lads had cut out Katshandre's tongue.

The second informant was Mayrem Tsinges (Tongue), who was nicknamed for his large tongue. He never left the shtetl. The boys wanted to leave Mayrem alone, because they thought that he could save the Jews some grief given his connections to the authorities. And he was indeed useful to them – for cash in the hand.

Tsinges was always in a hurry, never walking, always running. In his haste, his hat always slipped on the back of his head and the open lapels of his caftan flapped.

[Page 186]

When he was reprimanded for his "stories," he used to argue, "Someone else could be worse!" So the shtetl tolerated him like other afflictions.

To my Grandpa Yankel Bunim, however, Tsinges caused worry and grief. The government demanded 600 rubles from Yankel Bunim because two of his sons had not enlisted. The police often visited my Grandpa to confiscate "valuable" things from his apartment to "settle the debt." Mayrem Tsinges knew when the police would come.

Grandpa paid him a usurious wage. In return, Mayrem Tsinges did him the courtesy of coming by and warning that the bedding had to be packed away.

In panic and haste, the bedding and other things that were at least thought to be valuable were then taken to a neighbor or relative.

The authorities, however, made their demands not only on Grandpa, but also on his children. When we expected the police in our apartment, there was a big commotion.

Often Mom took us children to relatives to spend the night, and our parents slept without bedding, because they were afraid that the police would invade in the middle of the night.

This was real life!

Only the great Jewish confidence helped to get through this kind of excitement, tension and fear.

Krynki had to offer not only interesting personalities, but also interesting events. There were naive Jews who did not know what they wanted. For example, one Jew used to buy a new hat, but when he had it, he wished to have back the guilder that the hat had cost.

Another curiosity was the Jewess Itke Bertshekovitsh, who distributed the mail for the Jews. Itke was an extremely capable grocer, but she let herself go and was very slovenly. It was said that she probably wore seven or eight dresses on top of each other. She was something of a prankster- liked to joke around and didn't care if people made fun of her.

There was little entertainment in the shtetl. Once a circus came to visit us. A group of four or five comedians would usually come in summer.

[Page 187]

On a cloth they had spread on the bridge, they did various tricks. They twisted, rolled, jumped on and through hoops. The townspeople marveled at their acrobatic display.

Commotion arose when Gypsies would arrive in the shtetl. They set up their camp on the "Vigon", near the river. Jewish mothers reacted with fright, they used to teach their children how to beware of the Gypsies in order not to be taken away by them.

A Gypsy child who had light hair and white skin was generally considered to be kidnapped.

The fuss about the Gypsies filled the whole shtetl. Even the rich and powerful came to the "Vigon", stopped from afar and admired the hustle and bustle and the noise of the Gypsies.

The young "Khevre" stayed in the field until late at night, listening with longing to the songs of the Gypsies around campfires.

Driving in and out of the shtetl, the Gypsies sang a loudly echoing song:

"Mi tsigani (which sounded like 'misi-ani') tshesni lyudi, gdey mi yedem, tam mi budye".

(" We Gypsies are honest people, wherever we descend, there we stay").

"Mi tsigani, vadku filu, I koni mi lovilo".

"We Gypsies drank liquor and stole horses".

Once a man and a woman appeared in the shtetl, they were street singers. The couple, actually from Ukraine, went from street to street singing with a tearful melody and sad words about the catastrophe of the Jews in the Bialystok pogrom. A few words of their dialect were not understood, but the two of them entertained the audience and made the women cry.

The man played on a bandura, the woman closed her eyes, spread her arms and sang in a hoarse, harsh voice: "Whoever read the newspaper, of the famous city of Bialystok, which met such a bad misfortune on the first, second and third day."[1]

We learned a lot of folk songs and popular tunes from them, and children and adults sang, "Goodbye, my dear bride, I will long for you more than for any others, goodbye and pray for me to God that I will not be sent to Dalny Vladyvostok".

[Page 188]

At first, the Krinkers did not understand the words spoken in the Ukrainian Yiddish dialect and, in their confusion, attributed a different meaning to the words. It took some time before they realized that "man man," as the singer pronounced it, meant only "my man."

There was a crowd when Khayim Osher's nephew, Yisroel "the Great," brought home a gramophone with a flaring horn. Hundreds gathered at the windows to listen to the songs and the cantorial singings. Those who were allowed inside considered it a great privilege.

In addition to the cantorial songs, Yisroel also played interesting popular tunes on his gramophone. The most prominent ones at that time were:

"Moyshele, my husband, under the earth you shall go, in the fire you shall burn, already long enough I have begged you to take me to you!"[2]

The second song went like this:

"Oh help, a thief, he has robbed me, stolen all my wealth, seven shirts and the cups, three with patches, four with holes. Oh help, a thief, he has robbed me!"[3]

A very extraordinary guy was Yankel Yehuda the blacksmith. He made the Rabbi's life a misery. He especially had it in for Rabbi r' Borekh Stavski (Lavski?). When the "balebatim", the rich and powerful, did not heed the opinion of the common people regarding municipal matters, such as the meat tax or funds for the midwives and the bathhouse, the "amkho"[4] objected vehemently, usually disrupting the Torah readings and making scandals.

Yankel Yehuda the blacksmith was a great scoffer and took out his protest against the behavior of the "balebatim" on the Rabbi.

Yankel Yehuda very much loved the "bitter drop". Whenever he felt like giving the Rabbi a hard time, he would do so after praying.

Immediately after the first minyen, he fortified himself with a "quarter" of liquor and ate onion or garlic with it.

Yankel Yehuda would then usually visit the Rabbi when the latter was just getting up. Sleepy as he was, the Rabbi listened to the displeasure that the blacksmith and the "amkho" harbored toward the rich and powerful.

Yankel Yehuda usually did not even want to sit down. After all, he was a healthy man, he had drunk properly, and so his voice was enough to scare the Rabbi.

[Page 189]

R' Borekh Stavski used to beg him:

"Reb Yakev Yehuda, now that's enough, please leave me alone, because otherwise I will faint before your eyes!"

However, the other did not do him this favor until he had gotten rid of all his complaints. Yankel Yehuda's son Lipe already took after his father. He did not interfere in the affairs of the Jewish community, but he drank twice as much as his father.

When Lipe was already properly drunk, he would lie down on a stone in the middle of the market, take off his boots and say:

"Well, thanks God, I'm home on the stove already!"

The introduction of street lighting made a big impression. Lamps were mounted on poles and could be pulled up and down with wires. They burned with kerosene and with wicks[5], and a goy lit them.

Later, a so-called "Iluzyon" was opened in the shtetl, and for the first time the Krinkers saw living people moving on a screen.

The spectacle this created in the early days was immense. Some of the people simply thought it was magic.

Even greater excitement than that of the "Iluzyon" was caused by the omnibus that brought passengers from Krynki to Sokolka. Carters ran to the Rabbi to forbid it, since it deprived them of their income. They went to Hasidic Rabbis, and together with the women, they put wild curses on the omnibus and its owners.

It used to happen that because of the poor condition of the roads, the omnibus gave up the ghost because the engine was defective or a wheel broke apart. This caused great joy among the carters, "You see," they boasted, "that our curses have helped!"

Among the goyim, the omnibus caused great horror. When they saw it, they would scatter in fright; they called it "Tshort Obkaike," which means "He is being chased by the devil". The school children were very happy when they saw the omnibus arrive and depart. They used to run after it to the market when it arrived, and accompany it a little way out to the main street when it left.

The older Jews and the idlers, the sons of the rich, also used to wait for its arrival.

Important Poles really came alive.

[Page 190]

They usually gathered next to the house of "Khatskel the She(y)nker", scanned the bus and admired the "seykhl"[6] of the carriage to be able to run without a horse.

In addition to the non-Jewish chauffeur, who was called "Shafyor", there was employed a conductor, named the "Farbrenter" (Burnt). The "Burnt", son of a carter, was a real good-for-nothing as a little boy, a brawler and a wild rascal. Because of his pranks he was very disliked.

The suffering he caused would have been enough for a bigger town than Krynki. (He and his) gang of rascals not only knotted the wedding guests' clothes with each other, but also threw lumps of garbage and old rags at many weddings.

A custom of this gang was also to set off fireworks at weddings. The "burned" one was the main brawler of them and did all the reprehensible deeds.

Once, at a wedding, the "Burnt" went on a rampage. He filled his mouth with kerosene, lit a sheet of paper on fire, and spat kerosene on the burning sheet of paper.

The fire exploded in his face, and the lower part of his face up to his nose, mouth and cheeks were burned.

After this accident, he began to become a civilized person. He became calm and "respectable", got married and, in his own way, led a good bourgeois life.

Nobody remembered his real name, he remained the "Burnt".

As a conductor, the "Burnt" was dressed up in a uniform, which he usually bragged about and showed off. The signal for the departure of the bus was given by a horn. The "Burnt" used to stretch himself as high as he could with great zeal, to wipe the blowpipe with a clean cloth, to take it in his mouth and to emit a reverberating sound.

The rascals vented their grudge on the "Burnt". The rich sons, the Poles and the idlers, envied his uniform and the fact that he could travel freely between Krynki and Sokolka.

Translator's footnotes:

1.	Accordingly, this was the second, terrible three-day Bialystok pogrom which took place in 1906.
2.	The text is written in a Yiddish dialect. Here, too, the Krinkers certainly did not know what they were singing at first
3.	This song was sung in many versions with different lyrics, one variant can be heard here https://www.youtube.com/watch?app=desktop&v=DfmlHhRaPgM
4.	עמך= amkho, literally "your people", Jews, Jewish craftsmen
5.	shtetkes= This word actually means "little brush". I assume that they were wicks that were cut so that their shape resembled a little brush
6.	שׂכל= seykhl, Yosl uses here (perhaps ironically) a Hebraism that primarily means prudence, understanding, but may well also stand for "idea, reason"

[Page 191]

Crazy and Disturbed People

There were a lot of "mental patients" living in Krynki, among them interesting, wild and also simply dumb people. The most interesting was Shloyme Dubrover. However, he could not be counted among the Krinkers, because his "territory" included dozens of other large and small towns in the area.

Among the people who became behaviorally disturbed in a particular season, or just seemed a bit twisted, were a few goyim who had grown up and lived well with the Jewish population.

The wildest was Motke, a coarse, rough fellow, who, besides being mentally ill, was a great fool. He lacked, however, the ingenuity that other "madmen" often displayed. His illness consisted of dealing with (and caring for) his deceased father.

Motke's mother, a small, stooped Jewish woman, but very nimble and energetic, made her living running an iron store. When Motke got upset, he would attack his mother, hitting her with rage and screaming obsessively.

As a result of their clamor, the whole shtetl usually ran together. The townspeople mustered all their courage and strength and tried to restrain Motke who would often chase those who tried to calm him with a tool made of iron.

His illness was manifested mainly in carrying food to his father's grave and yelling around, "I need a hot meal for Dad!"

Every day at a certain hour he would jump up impetuously, shrug his shoulders violently, and run to the cemetery.

Schoolchildren used to run after him, shouting:

"Where are you going, Motki?"

"I'm going to bring Dad some hot food!"

"Is he hungry?"

"He's been gone for half a day and hasn't eaten anything yet, he won't be able to lie still!"

He used to dump the meal on his father's grave, "There you go Daddy, recover well, tomorrow I'll bring you a better meal!"

If his mother had not prepared anything warm, or tried to talk him out of going to the cemetery, he fell upon her.

[Page 192]

The second mental patient, Mair "Tsitsun", was a careless person, constantly dirty and shabbily dressed. He mainly blamed his mother for weaning him too early.

The third of the already famous troika of "madmen" was Shimen "a Zhonki" (a Woman), a strong man with broad shoulders, a stern face and a thick, blond-curled beard.

He used to ask to marry him off. He could not articulate distinctly. His only clear words were, "I want a zhonki!"

People used to ask him:.

"Shimen, will you be able to feed a zhonki?"

In response, he used to enumerate that he could carry water, chop wood, and do other jobs as well to provide a living. One of his favorite sayings was, "Ikh shuge, ale shuge!" ("I'm crazy but so is everybody else!")

When a photographer from Grodno or Bialystok came to the shtetl, he set it up so that he could seek out the threesome and take their portraits. The photographer posed the three in the most bizarre and comical poses, with their coats on backwards, hats turned upside down, holding a broom or riding on a stove hook, and other similar things.

The photographer then pasted the portraits into a glass display case and set it up outside his "studio".

When the townspeople saw the "madmen" in their poses, they would stop at the showcase for hours, laughing and joking at the expense of the outlandish people.

One "insane person," Mayrem, never spoke. There were various rumors and legends about Mayrem. He was a tall and handsome man, and with his black hair and long black beard he looked more like a Russian Orthodox church leader than a Jew.

In the summer he went barefoot. He earned his living by carrying water, and slept in the large Bes-Medresh.

It was said that he was of high descent and very educated, had several university degrees and could speak many languages fluently.

However, since he did not speak, all these rumors were never confirmed.

Anyway, people would look him up to ask him to write foreign addresses.

[Page 193]

And people told that it was a pleasure to see his handwriting[1] Mayrem stood mute because of a vow he had taken to atone for a debt.

Among the virtues that the townsfolk attributed to him was that he played the violin. But no one had ever heard him play. He was not thought to be completely insane, but rather a kind of unhinged man who had made a vow and was now putting it into practice. However, he actually showed many highly peculiar characteristics, so he could sometimes, just like that, laugh himself half to death.

There was also the whimsical Itshke Kugelekh, who, whenever someone died, would run around town with glee, knocking on shutters and announcing the news. Itshke did hard labor in the tanneries, never staying long in one factory. When he started at a new factory, he always brought in hides from his previous factory, commenting, "While there is a shortage of hide here, the old factory has more than enough hide!"

There were oddballs with heretical ideas and women who were considered abnormal because they gossiped extremely much.

One of the three "insane" women was Mayte, an already elderly goye. She usually wore a robe with a train over several dresses pulled over each other. She fashioned a dolly[2] out of a ball of cloth, which she cuddled, rocked, and sang to sleep.

At some point she was found leaning against the wall of a building. In death, she still held her dolly pressed to her chest.

Yente "Little Head" was not actually "crazy," she just had a vision disorder. Her parents kept her clean and chaste and did not let her out of the house. But as soon as they just turned around, Yente would sneak out of the house.

Yente was really a tragic figure. Her body was normal and fully developed, she had a beautiful face with red cheeks.

But her head was as big as that of a one-year-old child. She spoke only half words. No one bothered her until, as a result of some misfortune that happened to her, she became the center of women's ridicule and gossip for some time.

[Page 194]

Yente "Little Head" had become pregnant! At first, no one in the shtetl wanted to believe it, but Yente had snuck away from the home supervision and her bulging belly was now impossible to miss. When the women saw her, there was excitement and commotion, "Yente Little Head is on the street!"

Once, noisy women gathered at the stoop to a house entrance and lay in wait for Yente. With cunning, they lured Yente into the house. Dozens of women joined them. They sat Yente down on a table, felt her belly, and winked at each other.

"Yente, Yente, who gave you such a big belly?"

"The Obnter," she replied, meaning that the "Burnt" had impregnated her.

But whether the "Burnt" was really the culprit could never be clarified. He denied and swore "stone and bone" that he had nothing to do with the matter. It was most likely that the enemies of the "Burnt" had persuaded Yente to make this statement.

Adotshke was a strange goye from a neighboring village. She had already worked as a maid in almost every upper-class home but never stayed long in one place.

She had even worked in our house about twenty times. She was paid with food or a dress, and once she was even given a ruble.

Adotshke was ugly with a pockmarked[3] face. Her "mental illness" was that she talked for hours without stopping, all without sense or reason. She met with the same misfortune as Yente "Little Head," and she blamed the factory's constable, who was called "Stibun"[4] by the Jews because of his tall stature.

As a pregnant woman, Adotshke would not be allowed into any house, but my mother had mercy and took her in. As a result of her situation, Adotshke became even more confused. She talked without stopping and uttered wild curses at "Stibun." .

To interrupt her pregnancy, she punched her stomach and squeezed it on the edge of the table.

[Page 195]

Suddenly she disappeared. A few months later, however, she appeared with a bright boy in her arms. But no one wanted to take her in with a child. She hung around for a while until she finally disappeared forever.

There were two people who became insane in certain seasons: Kotiel and Simkhe, the son of Rokhel Motshke and biological nephew of my grandfather, Yankel Bunim.

Kotiel was a quiet man and a great personality.

The mental illness first struck him when he was still a young man. However, he already had a large family with 7 or 8 children.

Kotiel was an immigrant and worked as a teacher from the very beginning. Suddenly, however, he interrupted this activity and became a tanner. He earned little, maybe three or four rubles a week. The reason I know is that he worked in my father's factory for a while[5].

Kotiel's insane condition began after he became a Hassid of the Kobrin dynasty. He was "normal" for a whole year, but during the time of the month of Tamuz[6], the illness gripped him. Then he ran about the streets shouting that the shtetl could wash itself clean of its sins only by ritual bathing. Barefoot, he ran to the river and had to be rescued (from drowning) there dozens of times.

Simkhe, the son of Rokhel Matshke[7], was a Jewish Talmud scholar. He had been ordained as a Rabbi, but did not manage to hold such a position, although he believed that he was entitled to the post of Rabbi in Krynki. He was also able to ritually slaughter, however, he did not receive approval for this either, which annoyed and pained him deeply.

Once a year Simkhe was stricken with a mental illness. Then he tried to prove on himself that he was able to slaughter in the Jewish kosher way. Several times he survived. Finally, however, he succeeded in slaughtering. This last time he performed it (on himself) like on a piece of cattle.

People who were possessed by a "Dybbuk"[8] were also brought to Krynki. (The sick) were led through the shtetl to the nearby village of Krushenan (Kruszniany), where Tatars were living. It was believed that their "saint"[9] could heal the possessed who were exclusively girls and young women. They crowed like roosters, barked like dogs or meowed like cats.

The sick were brought on peasant carts. Schoolchildren accompanied them out to the road to Krushenan.

Whether the "holy" Tatar could actually give them a cure is not known. The sick never drove back through the shtetl.

Translator's footnotes:

1.   the Yiddish expression „shpiglen zikh" is ambiguous. I cannot exclude the possibility that people also had the feeling of being mirrored, i.e. "looking into a kind of glass ball", when they saw his handwriting.
2.   literally "figure"
3.   „liseyt"= The vocabulary may derive from several very similar sounding Slavic words, possibly it was also a fungal infection (tinea)
4.   „stibun" = a bulb or leek plant (according to the dictionary "solid onion tube")
5.   We learn more about this factory later

6.   In the month of Tamuz two Jewish tragedies took place. On the 17th of Tamuz, Moses, on his return from Mount Sinai, seeing the Israelites dancing around the Golden Calf, smashed the first pair of the Tablets of the Covenant in anger and many years later, also on a 17th of Tamuz, the destruction of the First Temple was initiated by the Babylonians.

7.   The name is spelled differently in the text

8.   דיבוק= Dybbuk, literally "attachment", according to popular belief it is a sinful soul of a deceased person that occupies a living person

9.   The mentioned Tatars are Muslims. I think that the "saint" was a "healer" or "quack" as we have learned on page 63. About the history of the Tatars in today's Podlaskie you can learn more here https://en.wikipedia.org/wiki/Tatars

[Page 196]

Entertainments and Games

As a serious town, Krynki, with its many hard-working people, was inhabited only by a few depraved young fellows. Moreover, there was no large number of "hazenikes"[1]; and people interested exclusively in "food and fare" were unknown. Also, alcoholics were few and far between.

Especially when the revolutionary movements arose, it seemed sacrilegious to the youth to indulge in banalities. A revolutionary had to be serious. Shallow entertainment and games were interpreted as an expression of idleness and laziness, in which only the "bourgeoisie" was interested.

But this did not mean that Krynki was a "sleepy nest". The youth, while demanding to learn and expand their knowledge, did not generally spurn cultural life. Talented "enlightened" people even performed plays. In addition to the occasional play, there were jugglers and interesting characters in town who caused a sensation, entertainment and laughter.

Among them was a Jew with the nickname: "Lafonts with the bells". His sons and grandsons inherited his "surname".

I remember the first son of "Lafonts", he lived below Kavkaz, in the precinct of the " Kapitses" on the small Zhabe Alley. For a while Lafonts used to live a quiet and solid life. But when a phase of confusion overcame him, he put on original robes sewn together from brightly colored patches.

On his head he wore a little hat with bells and on his shoulders a timpani with dozens of clappers and mallets. To all these clanging and drumming accessories were added various saucers. Everything was connected with a rope, which he in turn attached to a hook on his boot. And on top of that, he held plates made of brass in his hands.

In this outfit "Lafonts" then usually went to the market, where his strange appearance attracted attention not only among the school children, but even among the "balebatim".

[Page 197]

He was usually surrounded and then gave a "concert" on all his drumming "instruments".

Lafonts bent and threw himself in the air, turned his head and produced strange sounds and a hellish noise, wild, far sounding and crazy.

The gentile chimney sweep Yakev was never seen as a washed person in clean clothes. He was always covered with soot. On his shoulders Yakev carried the sweeping broom, to which was attached a heavy iron tool.

The peasants used Yakev as a surface for advertisements. On his chest constantly hung a sign announcing, for example:

"Whoever knows someone who has a pig, tell him to bring it to the market!".

It was very common for the children to gather together for certain games. Only the boys of excessively pious fathers or even of "wild" Hasids, kept away from it.

Girls played "pilke and tseykhns" (ball and signs) with small cubes made of sheep bones. The trick was to throw the cubes up and quickly catch them again with the hand.

The boys had two games that depended on speed and skill. The most common was called "tshort" (devil). On average, up to ten boys participated in this game. Each boy had a stick that reached no higher than his belt and lined up with the other players.

One end of the stick rested on the tip of the right foot and the upper end was held with a finger. Then, at the same time, everyone began to shake their right foot and fling the stick up into the air. This was called "bugern."

The boy whose stick did not fly far enough became the "tshort".

The "thort" positioned himself in the middle of the field and had to stick a little piece of wood into a small mound of earth.

The players had to stand around a perimeter that had previously been marked with chalk. The trick was to throw the sticks so that they knocked the little piece of wood out of the mound. The "tshort" usually had to run as fast as possible to put the little piece of wood back in place and prevent the players from getting their sticks back.

[Page 198]

The players, in turn, had to avoid leaving the little piece of wood in the mound. The goal of the "tshort" was to get rid of his role as "Tshort" again.

To do this, he had to touch one of the other players with his stick and knock the stick[2] out of his hand.

The other player was not allowed to let this happen, and so a boisterous trial of skill, speed and clever strategy began between the two players.

A similar game with only minor modifications was "montshik"[3].

The boys also played with buttons and pieces of colored glass.

At Tishe-Bov[4], in addition to carving wooden swords, they used to throw "siskes"[5]. It was dangerous for girls to show themselves outside.

The more daring among them went out into the street with headscarves. True scallywags usually tore off the scarves and put burrs all over the girls' hair.

Very spoiled boys also threw the burrs into beards. And so there was not only one Jew who had to spend hours afterwards plucking the burrs out of his beard again.

Tishe-Bov was the happiest and wildest day for the rattle gangs.

The day before Passover was very boisterous. Brazen louts and snots usually did not sleep the night before Passover but ran about the shtetl collecting shavings and little pieces of wood. Very daring ones simply dragged away whole logs of wood from the carpenters and roofers and even stole barrels of "mazhe", a grease for greasing the wheels of carts, which burned long and brightly.

The gang dug a hollow in the field, filled it with woody material and set everything on fire.

Already at dawn, the rascals stood around the pit, shouting obsessively, "Burn leaven, burn Passover dumplings!"

Great pleasure was given to the louts to carry the objects contaminated with leaven for ritual purification. The pans were "white-washed", but the utensils made of tin or pewter were taken to the locksmith to be dipped in hot water.

In the summer, the gang engaged in a special sport: tearing off pea pods in the fields of the large landowner Virnye (Virion).

[Page 199]

The guards did not manage to protect the pods – and the brats caused great destruction, stamping and trampling the fields.

To tear off the pods, they went in groups, and there was a strategy associated with it. The members of the gang wrapped a rope around their upper shirts, creating a kind of sack into which they could put the pea pods.

The reason for going out in groups was to keep the guards busy and confused all the time, because they didn't know who to hunt for first. At one point, the landowner brought in Cossacks. These hid themselves and then suddenly sprang out from their hiding place to hunt for the boys.

I and a second boy were also chased by a Cossack. But he could not catch us. A pouring rain fell, and the Cossack was finally so exhausted that he gave up the chase. In the shtetl, however, they already knew what had happened to me and the other boy.

Late that night we both arrived at the shtetl tired, exhausted and completely soaked to the bone.

I was afraid to go inside the house. Below the entrance door, in the forefront of the house, I heard my mother crying. Her grief gave me courage to go inside. Guiltily, I stopped at the doorstep.

My mother looked at me in wonder for a while. – If the Cossack had grabbed me, surely his punishment would not have been worse than that!

In winter, on Shabbat evenings, the boys used to go sledding. They harnessed sleds to the horses, and the commotion, noise and laughter echoed through the streets.

The boys rode their sleds only downhill, up the hill they pulled the sleds behind them and sang: "Sunday potatoes, Monday potatoes, Tuesday potatoes, Wednesday potatoes, Thursday and Friday potatoes, on Shabbat as an exception potato "Kugl" (casserole), Sunday again potatoes!"

The rascals threw snowballs at each other, formed snowmen and placed them at the window to scare women and children.

Adult young boys and girls played "find" and "hide and seek". On Friday evenings, fruit pits and nuts were cracked. In summer, on Shabbat, people used to walk in the woods, and in winter they skated on the pond.

[Page 200]

There were wild and cruel brawls among the boys, involving wars fought from one street against the other street. The main warriors were the "Kavkazer" louts. These, however, rarely interfered in wars between streets.

The boys of all streets trembled in real mortal fear of the "Kavkazers".

Mainly stones were used as weapons, and since the wars often took place in the market, there were not a few adult passers-by who were seriously injured in the head.

Translator's footnotes:

1.　הזהניק= hazenik: a man interested only in earthly, material things and the present
2.　I think there is a small mistake here and the author means "stick" and not "little piece of wood", so I have translated it accordingly.
3.　"montshik"= very little, minute
4.　תישעה-באָב= Tishe-Bov, Ninth ("tishe") day in the month of Ov, day of mourning after destruction of the holy temple of Jerusalem in the years 586 B.C. and 70 A.D.
5.　Literally, "prickle, thorn", but I assume that burdock is meant.

[Page 201]

Nokhem Anshel, the Most Powerful Man

The most important factory owner and the most powerful man in the shtetl was Nokhem Anshel Kinishinski. Born in Kobrin, he traveled to Krinik after robbing my Great-Grandfather.

Nokhem Anshel was somewhat related to my Great-Grandpa.

He arrived at the latter's residence on the Meshenik estate just as Mair Yonah was struggling not to be evicted from his property.

Grandpa Yankel Bunim was ill at that time. Nokhem Anshel managed the business temporarily entrusted to him in such a way that he fled when Mair Yonah returned.

After arriving in Krynki, Nokhem Anshel used to bring flour to the bakeries for a miller. Shortly after, he became an accountant for the rich and powerful Dovid Marein (Dovid Todreses), who had a distillery on the estate of a Polish aristocrat, Virnye (Virion).

Dovid Todreses was a distinguished man of great importance. His stone house in the market was surrounded by a large garden and was the most beautiful residence in the shtetl. At some point, Dovid began to get worse. While he became increasingly poorer, however, Nokhem Anshel became increasingly richer.

Dovid became impoverished to such an extent that he had to sell all his possessions and moved to Grodno.

Not long after Dovid Marein left the shtetl, Nokhem Anshel opened a tannery. Years later, when Nokhem Anshel had already become a powerful man, Dovid Marein used to come to him and ask for alms.

His decline to impoverishment had hit Dovid with full force. When he came to Nokhem Anshel, he appeared haggard and subservient. Nokhem Anshel usually gave him short shrift with a few rubles to send him quickly back to Grodno.

Nokhem Anshel's tannery grew steadily.

[Page 202]

It did not take long, and the control of the entire city leather production was in his hands.

Krynki was a great center of leather tanning.

Shoes and boots were made from hides of horse leather. The main sales centers were Moscow and Warsaw.

There were different tanneries. In the "wet" tanneries the whole hide was processed and then the leather was cut into three parts: "lapes"[1], "dubkes"[2] and "shilder"[3]. "Lapes" came from thepwas or legs (of the animal), "dubkes" from the back part and "shilder" from the sides and neck.

The individual parts were tanned a second time. The coarser " lapes" and "dubkes" were exported to Moscow; the thinner, nobler "shilder" pieces were sold from Warsaw.

From the "shilder" pieces three more parts were cut: "leaves" for gaiters[4], "soyuzn"[5] for boots and "shpitskes" (laces) for children's shoes.

In the beginning, Nokhem Anshel only worked out the "lapes", "dubkes" and "shilder". Later, he concentrated on tanning the whole hide, but sold the parts to small "contractors" called "Leynketnikes"[6].

Through his business, Nokhem Anshel not only became wealthy, but also gained control over the small tanneries that depended on him.

Many of them did not have enough money, and Nokhem Anshel usually charged interest on the bills that were not paid on time. Nokhem Anshel was a "First Guild Kupets"[7], which was a great privilege at that time. This title, which elevated him to the first-rank merchant, gave him the right to travel and live in all cities outside the "Tkhum Hamoyshev"[8].

In the shtetl, Nokhem Anshel occupied a top position and had very strong influence. He was very well read and usually "learned"[9] with the Jews in the large Bes-Medresh on Shabbat, during the time between the minkhe and mayrev prayers[10].

He had a good voice and was a talented "menagen"[11]. When Nokhem Anshel prayed from the podium, people came gladly to hear him.

Just like his high, important position, his physical figure and demeanor was significant, rude and arrogant.

[Page 203]

He spoke with a sharp "r", controlled and confident. He let everyone know that he was powerful and influential; however, he was very unpopular because of his cruelty. When Nokhem Anshel wanted to achieve something, he cleared everything that hindered him out of the way. He never had pity or showed leniency. He hated the poor and made no secret of it. For him, the only thing that mattered was that people obeyed him and were subservient.

When Zalmen Sender, zts"l, became Rabbi in Krynki, Nokhem Anshel immediately had a dispute with him because Zalmen Sender sided with the workers and the poor.

Zalmen Sender was infinitely popular in the shtetl, and people boasted about him. The Krinkers glorified him especially after he refused the offer to become Rabbi in Warsaw.

"Reb Zalmen Sender said that he would rather be the Rabbi in Krynki than in the big city of Warsaw!"

When Nokhem Anshel was still working for Dovid Todreses, he became an important guest in the home of the handsome tobacconist, Shmuel Tabatshnik. His wife Henye was the sister of my great-grandfather, Yosl Pruzhanski (Yosl Tsherebukh).

Shmuel had several sons and three daughters, Roshke, Hode and Sheynke. They were small, but beautiful. All of them had the habit of sitting hunched over, with their heads sunk between their shoulders.

Nokhem Anshel began to "dress up" for the daughters. Shmuel let him know, however, that if he wanted to marry one of his daughters, it had to be the eldest, Roshke.

Shmuel Tabatshnik also married off his other two daughters; Hode to a Bialystok weaver, Nisl. Sheynke, who had previously had a love affair with Grandpa Yankel Bunim's nephew, Borekh Hersh, he married off to Yisroel Hertske, who later became a large leather manufacturer.

Nokhem Anshel did not let Roshke have much influence. However, she was no woman to simply pass over. Since Nokhem Anshel did not want to have heated arguments with her, he, in many ways, let her go her own way. In one thing there was perfect harmony between them: in wickedness.

Roshke was at odds with her two sisters; in general, she kept her distance from her family.

But she was fond of my Grandfather, Khayim Osher.

[Page 204]

The day before the holidays, she used to invite him for honey cake and schnapps.

Roshke's spite knew no bounds. After her father's death, when her mother ran out of her meager savings, Roshke used to throw her a few rubles every now and then. She didn't want to concern herself much with her mother.

(One day) old Henye Tabatshnik slipped and injured herself, whereupon she decided to go to Nokhem Anshel for the time being. But when Roshke realized that the sick woman wanted to stay with her, she told the carter to drive Henye away to Grandpa Kayim Osher.

At that time, my Grandpa lived on Kantselarye Street in a room with a corridor where bark was chopped. The dust spread and constantly hung over the whole apartment.

Grandma Rive let Aunt Henye Tabatshnik sleep in her bed and stayed overnight with the daughters. Every day, until Henye's death, Uncle Yisroel used to go to Nokhem Anshel to get a jug of milk.

The workers hated Nokhem Anshel not only because of his big belly, power and authority, all characteristics of a typical "bourgeois", but also because of the way he treated them.

In the first strike, Nokhem Anshel was the only one who would not allow any compromise with the workers. In the second strike, which incidentally failed, Nokhem Ashel encouraged the gendarmes to act brutally.

He advised the colonel of the gendarmerie on how to fight the strikers. As a result of his advice, hundreds of young boys were tortured behind Krinker prison bars and dozens were transferred to Grodner prison.

The strike was broken then as a result of the hunger of the poor and the cruelty of the gendarmes. Nokhem Anshel had wanted to teach the poor a lesson and put it into practice.

As a result of Nokhem Anshel's brutal actions, the hostility against him intensified. The townspeople cursed his name:

"May Nokhem Anshel live a miserable life, may he be sick and bedridden for a long time, where is there such a thing that while that wise Tsadek had to die, Nokhem Anshel is in perfect health?"

[Page 205]

When the revolutionary movement arose in Krynki, the consideration of what to do with Nokhem Anshel was constantly on the agenda of the central committees. There were sentiments that one should "get rid" of him. However, the very influential "Bund" did not allow this. Its members thought that Nokhem Anshel should only be made to feel a little afraid.

With regard to the anarchists, who had already found strong support among the young tanners, it was known that they had already set out to eventually "liquidate" Nokhem Anshel.

In order not to give the anarchists the credit for killing Nokhem Anshel, some young Bundists secretly and without the knowledge of their committee set out to plan and prepare an assassination attempt on Nokhem Anshel.

Translator's footnotes:

1.   "lapes" = from "lapkes", paw
2.   "dupkes"= from the Polish "dupa", butt
3.   "shilder"= I assume that this designation is derived from "shoulder"
4.   old spats that existed and exist for people and horses, as camouflage for the soldiers even in leaf form. But what is meant by "leaves" in the text, I do not know
5.   "zoyuzn" = union
6.   "leynketnik"= I interpret this sentence as meaning that the "leynketnikes" were the masters or foremen of small contract companies, and in some cases also the owners.

7.   "kupets" = A kupets was someone who had permission to run a business ("kupetshestve")
8.   permitted residential area for Jews in tsarist Russia
9.   "lernen"= means learning and teaching
10.   Afternoon and evening prayer
11.   ממגן= menagen: melody crafter, song-smith

[Page 206]

Grandpa Yankel Bunim is Arrested

For a while, the Krinkers were very upset because of a scandal that the factory owners, with Nokhem Anshel as the main culprit, had instigated.

At that time, they let the tanners, who came to pray in the great Bes-Medresh in unclean clothes and with grease (from working the hide) on their boots, know that they would be doing them, the balebatim, a great favor to find another house of prayer.

According to Nokhem Anshel's plan, they had begun to withdraw and exclude the craftsmen from all matters and activities concerning the Bes-Hamedresh, and to pass over them in calls for Torah reading ("aliye"). The tanners made a fuss about it, but it didn't help them at all. Nokhem Anshel was the Gabe and (in that capacity) did everything he could to get rid of the tanners.

Finally, the workers saw that the balebatim would prevail and at a meeting, they decided to establish their own Bes-Medresh.

Not far from the great Bes-Medresh, there was an empty hall where soldiers had once taken up quarters. This hall now became the prayer house of the tanners.

Yankel Bunim was appointed as the Gabe, administrator and responsible leader. Every Friday, in order to be able to maintain the Bes-Medresh, Grandpa went about the factories to collect weekly dues among the craftsmen.

The factory owners did not like that at all. They sent the denunciator, Mayrem Tsinges, who was the sub-Shames in the great Bes-Medresh, after my Grandpa to make his life difficult. Tsinges did not leave my Grandpa alone anymore and threatened him to reveal to the police that the Bes-Medresh of the tanners was not a real prayer house, but a meeting place of the "Buntovshtshikes" (rebels).

When Grandpa was on his way to the factories, Mayrem Tsinges and a policeman got in his way and arrested him.

[Page 207]

When this became known in the factories, the tanners stopped working. People gathered in the market and went to the "prison" to free Yankel Bunim by force. One of them ran to Nokhem Anshel to address him about it, and he caused the "Pristav" (the police chief commissioner), to free Grandpa.

After this scandal, however, the situation did not calm down at all. The tanners were full of anger against the factory owners; the balebatim, in turn, agreed to close the tanners' "Bes-Medresh". Upon their denunciation that it was not a Bes-Medresh but a revolutionary meeting center, the police sealed this "house of prayer."

This action by the factory owners added fuel to the fire. It was agreed among the leaders of the revolutionary groups to teach Nokhem Anshel a lesson as a warning to all factory owners.

Three young hot-headed revolutionary boys decided on their own to assassinate Nokhem Anshel.

However, one of the three, Shloymeke "Kirbises" (Pumpkins), the brother of my friend Zeydke, cancelled. The remaining two, Leybke Noskes and Dovid, the son of Yankel "dem Geln" (the Blond), prepared the assassination.

I remember the attack on Nokhem Anshel as if it had just happened. Grandma Rive lived on Garbarska Street right across the street from Nokhem Anshel's house.

It was on a Shabbat evening, a clear, starry night. Fresh snow clothed the surroundings in pure white and soft glow.

As was her desire, Grandma sat by the window, swaying in the darkness. Her daughter Yente asked her to light the lamp.

Rive rose and walked to the table. Suddenly, from outside, screams and great noise entered the parlor.

Yente ran out and immediately came back in trembling; "Nokhem Anshel has been stabbed with a knife! Leybke Noskes stabbed him with a knife!" Grandma gave a jerk to go outside, but stopped.

She walked quietly to the window and looked out at the people who had come running. Nokhem Anshel was thrust, but not stabbed (killed)!

[Page 208]

However, as Leybke Noskes, now named Louis Sheyn, reported to me, he was not the one who had knifed Nokhem Anshel.

In the planning of the assassination, Dovid, the son of Yankel the Blond, was supposed to shoot; in case he missed, Leybke was supposed to come along and stab Nokhem Anshel.

Leybke was responsible for letting Dovid know when the prayers ended in the great Bes-Medresh.

Afterwards, Nokhem Anshel had walked down Garbarska Street, surrounded by factory owners. His son Berl, himself a great factory owner, walked arm in arm with him. A few steps from Nokhem Anshel's house, Dovid, the son of Yankel the Blond, fired a shot and then hastily chased a knife into Nokhem Anshel's body. However, because of his thick belly and the coarse fur coat he wore, the knife did not penetrate deeply.

Nokhem Anshel was only slightly injured.

Leybke Noskes was convinced that it was only in Nokhem Anshel's house that they (came up with the idea) to connect him with the assassination, because they remembered to have seen him in the great Bes-Medresh before the attack. However, they did not know, who the second assailant was.

While they were sitting at Nokhem Anshel's trying to figure out who might be the second culprit, Dovid, son of Yankel the Blond, was sitting in the inn calmly drinking one cup after another.

Along with Leybke Noskes, an innocent Pole, a devout Catholic, who was the bell ringer of the Polish church, was also arrested.

When Leybke was arrested, he was perhaps 16 years old. At a very young age he joined the revolutionary movement. He was the only one in his family who got involved in revolutionary actions and went to the "skhodkes" (meetings) while still a boy. He had received his first political education ("agitation") from craftsmen who worked in his father's turnery.

At a very young age, Leybke already occupied an important place in the "Bund" movement; when he was imprisoned, he already enjoyed the prestige of the Central Committee of the Bund. Leybke spent several days behind bars in Krynki. On a freezing cold day he was led in a prisoner transport to the Grodner prison with his hands tied behind his back.

[Page 209]

As Leybke was led through the streets of Krynki, the tanners stood silently and watched him and the innocent Christian being driven forward, surrounded by rural policemen with bare swords.

From the "Bund" they let it be known to Nokhem Anshel that his entire family would be dealt with if he testified as a witness against Leybke. Nokhem Anshel immediately began to campaign for Leybke's release.

He himself drove to Grodno and managed to get Leybke and the Christian released on bail. When Leybke arrived in Krynki, Nokhem Anshel invited him and asked what he could do for him.

"See that I am acquitted," Leybke demanded.

Nokhem Anshel hired the best advocates, and through his intervention Leybke and the Christian were acquitted.

[Page 210]

Anarchists in Krynki

In Krynki, the class struggle was not just a theory written in agitational brochures. It is true that the surrounding towns, which had no industry, regarded socialism at that time as a kind of trinket for a few intellectuals and enlightened people. However, in Krynki the idea of social revolution was considered the goal of almost the entire youth.

It was mainly the tanners who stood up and fought, and they deserve the top place in the history of the labor struggle. However, it is also a fact that the mob joined in, and very young lads did not really understand what and why something had to be done.

And yet the latter, too, were an important part of the crowd that prodded Russia to free itself from autocracy.

The great leaders and theoreticians of the revolutionary groups knew well about the psychology of the "masses" and adapted their slogans to the level of knowledge and desires of the working people.

Lenin's appeal, "Rob the robbers," was not simply a stormy slogan in one of his speeches, but a well-thought-out method of achieving the aim. The Krinker tanners considered first and foremost the rich as their enemies; only later did they realize that it was also necessary to fight against the system, against the autocracy.

Zionism did not affect the Krinkers, only a small number of upper-class youths were engaged in it.

A few Zionist boys gathered around the Jewish pharmacist, but had no influence at all.

A Poale-Zion[1] group was formed, but it was hardly noticed and was limited to a few members.

Even before the "Bund"[2] became established, there were boys and girls in Krynki who had connections with Russian Social Democracy.

Among them were very capable and devoted idealists.

[Page 211]

When my uncle Aharon Velvel came from Bialystok to organize the tanners (in Krynki), he already had support from a class-conscious group of social democrats. The seriousness and naivete of the young people caused them to perform senseless but heroic deeds.

Menakhem, Motl Arye's son, symbolized the type of I revolutionary lad of that time. He was one of the first socialists in Krynki and was said to have spoken the oath to the tanners in the "Rozboniker Forest", which was prepared for the first strike.

It was sworn on a holy book and a few phylacteries, and after the ceremony the "class conscious ones" had sung the "Shvue of the Bund".[3]

At that time there were two different bundistic oath chants, once the already known, " brider un shvester fun arbet un noyt, tsu ale vos zaynen tsezeyt un tseshpreyt, tsuzamen, tsuzamen di fon iz greyt, zi flatert fun tsorn, fun bloyt iz zi royt, mir shvern a shvue oyf leben un toyt"[4], and second, the very first, "Sacred is nature in her robes of freedom".

After the first strike, Menakhem went to military service, but did not stay there long. He fled and arrived in Krynki just at the time when the second strike was beginning. At the market, he split the head of a policeman who was beating a striker and then fled to his sister in England. There he tried to organize the workers in her furniture factory, whereupon she chased him away. Menakhem then traveled to America.

In Chicago, Menakhem found it very difficult to fit into American life. He committed suicide for just this reason (quote): "…because the Capitalism in America is growing and strengthening. And it will be difficult to carry out a social revolution."

There were many fellows of this type in Krynki. A large number of them were not satisfied with the moderate nature of the "Bund." Hot-blooded chaps wanted "direct action."

The hot-headed fellows began to increase the anarchist influence among the young tanners. Yankel "Tsheyni" had given them the first anarchist agitation (lessons). He received this nickname from his relative, a former soldier, who gave him the Russian pet name "Tshorni" (The Black), which the children bastardized into "Tsheyni".

[Page 212]

Yisroel Iser, the son of the shoykhet (kosher slaughterer), brought Yankel to Bialystok to work there. Yankel used to join a group of the "Bund", which at that time gathered in the "Factory Alley". There, someone gave him a booklet, "The ABC of Anarchism."[5]

One day, however, the police stormed the meeting place. A policeman beat Yankel exceedingly brutally because he was a Krinker.

"Hey," he said, "you're one of those Krinker rebels!"

A vicious anger flared up in Yankel against the police supervisor, and he looked for ways to get even. However, when the Bund advised him against taking revenge on the policeman, he sought out the anarchists.

At that time Yakev Kreplyak, rest in peace, was considered a (savy) anarchist intellectual and theorist. Because of his role as an anarchist teacher and educator of youth in Bialystok, he was called "Professor."

Kreplyak supported Yankel Tsheyni, and so together they planned an assassination attempt on the police supervisor. Actually, he was to be shot, but with regard to the noise caused by a shot, it was decided to stab him with a dagger.

Two young boys distracted the police supervisor by pretending to ask something, and from behind Yankel plunged a dagger into the policeman's neck. Yankel's daring raised his prestige among the anarchists. They began to entrust him with conspiratorial tasks. Yankel especially liked the fact that he was now allowed to carry a revolver.

When Yankel Tsheyni returned to Krynki, he told some boys about the Bialystok anarchists, who acted differently from the Bundists. "The Bund," he told them, "cannot produce a revolution. Nothing will ever come of it the way the Bund is behaving. There is only one remedy: terror!"

Yankel's words made a great impression on the boys, and they recruited a few others as well. One Shabbat, in Virnyen's (Virion) forest, they collected among themselves twelve rubles.

[Page 213]

With the money, Yankel Tsheyni went to Bialystok. Kreplyak had procured for him two revolvers and a package of anarchist pamphlets. Both Yankel Tsheyni and Kreplyak then went to Krynki to organize an anarchist group there.

Two vyorst (2.1 km) away from the shtetl, Kreplyak, however, as a precaution, remained in a field near the "Parofke", the mill where tree bark was chopped. Yankel got into the shtetl and announced to some boys there that he had brought an intellectual, an agitator from Bialystok, called "Professor".

Kreplyak slept in the field that night. The next morning, a Shabbat, the boys gathered in Virnyen's forest. Kreplyak gave his first anarchist agitation speech before them. That was the beginning of the anarchist movement in Krynki.

This beginning caused important events in the shtetl. The youth was torn into two hostile camps. The power struggles between the Bundists and anarchists for influence over the Krinker youth were bitter and nasty.

In the shtetl there were also other revolutionary parties, the "Pe-Pe-Pe", the "Iskrovtses", the "Socialist Revolutionaries", the "Social Democrats" and "Poale Zion". However, in comparison with the Bund and the anarchists, their popularity was low.

For a time, the anarchists had the strongest influence on the Krinker youth. Direct action, carrying a revolver and heroic deeds had a great meaning for them. Romantic and hot-headed boys and girls were fascinated by the bravado that the anarchist movement provided. There were frequent physical confrontations between Bundists and anarchists which were particularly sharp and hostile during the 1905 revolution.

For both groups the desire to disparage the other through song was characteristic.

Bundists sang:

"The anarchists, communists, they are provocateurs, they mess up the meeting, and quickly run away!"

The Krinker anarchists produced great heroes. The majority of the boys and girls who courageously went forward and sacrificed themselves for the revolution with great enthusiasm were Krinker anarchists.

Translator's footnotes:

1. פּועלי-ציון= poyale-tsien, Poale-Zion: "Workers of Zion", name of the Zionist-Socialist movement, founded in 1906
2. Bund: Founded in 1897, its goal was to unite all (Jewish) workers of the Russian tsarist empire. The organization was a socialist, or social democratic party that rejected Zionism. You can learn more e.g. here https://www.iemj.org/en/the-bund-and-yiddish-revolutionary-songs/
3. di „bundishe shvue": the sacred oath of the Bund, later this term became the name of the anthem of the Jewish socialist workers' movement (Bund)
4. The text of the "Shvue" has already been quoted and also translated, see pages 154-155.
5. „Der Alef-Beys fun anarkhizm"= A book by Nestor Makhno (Machno), you can read more about him and his movement, Machnowschtschina, for example here https://en.wikipedia.org/wiki/Nestor_Makhno . His book mentioned in the text is still available in well-stocked bookstores.

[Page 214]

The Great Fire

Jewish houses in Krynki, apart from brick houses, were built of wood and had shingled roofs. Only the houses of the goyim, located on the outer edge of the shtel, had thatched roofs. Therefore, the greatest number of fires occurred in goyim houses and barns. The peasants extinguished them themselves, but often Jews from the shtetl came to help.

Before a volunteer fire brigade was created, the "Volne Pozhorne", noisy youngsters had their fun running with water buckets to put out fires. Especially the good-for-nothings among them got very involved, because they were able to show off in the excitement.

The boys even really came alive; they ran across the streets shouting, "Fire! Fire!"

Outside the market there were several barrels filled with water in case of fire. The water was filled in buckets only when these barrels were dragged to the burning building.

Since the barrels were constantly outside, they were rotted through from the rain and snow. Often the wheels no longer had tires, and when trying to pull the barrel away, the wheels would burst completely apart. No one in the shtetl thought of organizing a group of firemen.

Only when the "Haskala" and the revolutionary movement took root among the tanners did the idea of training young people in fire extinguishing arise.

This endeavor to establish a firefighting squad was taken up by Gamliel, the only assimilated Jew in the shtetl. Gamliel was held in high esteem among the Jews; he was said to have given up a career as a great opera singer in Petersburg because he refused to convert.

He spoke little Yiddish, and when he did, it had a pronounced Russian accent.

[Page 215]

Gamliel, a short-set man, was a funny figure with his big belly, which he pushed in front of him, and his small fat body, on which his big head was enthroned. He was no Krinker by birth. However, he had a relative, called Eliya Kopl's, who had a son, Kopl Zalkin; and the latter was a famous leather manufacturer in Bialystok.

Gamliel (also) had a leather factory and lived in a two-story stone house on the market. His apartment was among the most beautiful in the shtetl. He conducted himself in a truly suave manner. Gamliel created a fire brigade and became its main leader.

Being from Petersburg, he organized the Krinker "Pozharne Komande" (the fire department) on a metropolitan level. He divided the brigade into groups and not only provided them with special military-looking clothes, but also led them in a semi-military way.

Gamliel divided the brigade into two groups; he called the younger men "Tukhenikes", and the older ones, who had already done their military service, "Ladoshnikes". The "Tukhenikes" had to haul the water barrels and fill the buckets with water. The "Ladoshnikes" would take over the firefighting work with the fire hoses and would rescue people and objects from burning buildings.

"Tukhenikes" wore cloth hats, "Ladoshnikes" wore hats of brass with two visors, in addition, at the right hip, a hoe, which looked there like a sword. Alexander, a huge, wide-grown goy, used to blow his horn in the middle of the market to summon the fire extinguishers for drills.

There, in the market, the "pozharnikes" gathered in their semi-military uniforms and lined up in rows to march in military step, chanting soldiers, down to Shishlevitser Street.

In Yente's forest, they then received a few hours of instruction in the "Torah" of putting out fires, after which they strode back to the shtetl with the same military bustle.

[Page 216]

Gamliel, decked out in the uniform of a "chief commander," distinguished by a large eagle stamped on his brass hat, used to stand on the porch of his house during parades. When the firemen marched past him, their heads turned toward him, he would call out to them, "Zdoray malatsi!" ("Hello/be healthy, fine young men!") And the men answered, "Zhorov mi zhelayem vashe blagorodye!" ("Hello/we wish your noble-ship good health!")

Gamliel enforced an important achievement: He caused a fire house, a "sarey ", to be erected in the market, which was kept in order by the hunky goy Alexander. In the "sarey", the equipment of the fire department was kept from heat, wetness and rain.

The great fire, which destroyed over a third of the shtetl, put an end to the mere "play" of the fire department. I remember very clearly the fire that ignited on Friday morning.

At that time I studied with the teacher Tsalke Dubrover, "Tsalke with the goatee", as his students called him. He was a good and decent man who never beat his students. Tsalke had some tanner sons and two mute daughters; the eldest was a great beauty.

Tsalke lived in the upper area of Kavkaz, directly on Sokolker Street. A little apart from his home, about two houses away, lived the teacher Shmuel Avreml from Alinke. It must have been around 10 o'clock in the morning when Tsalke's daughter came in, pulled Tsalke by the sleeve of his caftan and pointed outside.

Tsalke, however, did not look around, only waved his hand and wanted to scare her away. But she clung to him and pulled him outside.

Shortly after, Tsalke came back in excitedly, "Go home, there is a fire at Shmuel Avreml's!"

That Friday it was very hot. When I came out of the school, I could already see the flames coming out of Avreml's apartment. A little further away Shloyme Kirbises was standing on his roof, scooping water from a barrel with a bucket and pouring it on the ground. Shmuel Avreml's wife stood weeping, confused and wringing her hands. Shmuel

Avreml himself ran around his burning house with his caftan flowing and his head uncovered, shouting, "Pozhar (fire)! Pozhar! Pozhar! It's burning!"

[Page 217]

As if the devil were at work, no one helped to put out the fire. In addition, as if guided by a secret hand, wind arose and blew sparks onto the neighboring houses. In a few minutes several houses were on fire. Excitement arose, helpless people ran around shouting, quite beside themselves: "Pozhar! Pozhar! It's burning!"

Furniture and bedding were dragged out of the houses. From one moment to the next, the fire spread from Kavkaz to the neighboring streets. Krynki began to go up in flames! The fire chased from house to house, people were gripped by despair and hopelessness.

Nobody came to extinguish the fire, they just let it burn.

None of the trained and militarily organized " pozharne komande" was there. Yente's forest had caught fire, and Gamliel, the "main commander", had run out with his "pozharnikes" to extinguish the forest. The shtetl had been abandoned.

The fire had already spread far beyond the borders of Kavkaz. Around the burning houses there was tumult and chaos. The people were in each other's way. Those who lived far from Kavkaz and were sure that the fire would not reach them, and those who had already become victims of the fire, came to the aid of their relatives to rescue items from the houses.

My uncles Yisroel and Perets also came rushing to us, and even some of the "Tsherebukhes". They immediately began to throw our furniture and bedding through a window into the garden.

There was a hellish noise outside, crying, shouting and tumult; "Pozhar! Pozhar! Fire! The market is on fire!"

Those who lived right by the market and had come to the aid of their relatives in Kavkaz now rushed for the market.

Grandpa Khayim Osher rushed to save the Torah scrolls from the Kavkaz Bes-Hamedresh.

Distraught Jews and weeping women ran with belongings from the burning houses.

[Page 218]

Children were standing around in the way, shouting joyfully, "A fire, a fire!"

Down from Kavkaz came running a Jew without a caftan, in a large tales-kotn[1]; it looked as if he was about to wrap himself in a garment. He pushed a fire barrel ahead of him, its iron tires rumbling on the pavement. The Jew ran hastily and excitedly and suddenly disappeared down a side street.

When the "pozharnikes" learned what was going on in the shtetl, they let the forest burn. They arrived at the shtetl when a third was already consumed by the fire.

When my father, also a "pozharnik", returned, our house was nothing but rubble and ashes. When towards evening the fire began to subside a little, the victims of the fire went to the fields. They spread on two sides of the city; on the Vigon field, which was reached from Kavkaz, from Mill Street and from the beginning of Sokolker Street, and on the Jewish cemetery.

It is a Friday, the Jews had already prepared everything for Shabbat!

Many succeeded in saving some challah, cholent and candles. Women sat around their poor possessions and lamented, not far from the river of the town. Just as in those days by the rivers of Babylon, so now the Jews were sitting there weeping and lamenting.[2]

Before night fell, the belongings that had been thrown out of the window were dragged to the Vigon; but it was not until our poor belongings were gathered up that it was noticed that my two brothers, Mair and Velvel had been lost.

Lamenting, Mother began to search the field with Father, asking about the whereabouts of the missing children.

My father received a hint that he should search among the victims of the fire in the cemetery.

"But how could they have gotten there?" lamented Mother, "the children are no longer here, burned and perished they will be, my children, my everything!"

Dad and Mom went to the burned house, maybe they would find something in the remains? But the fire wouldn't let them get close, the flames chased them away from the ruin.

[Page 219]

The last choice was the cemetery. I was left behind to guard the few belongings. Suddenly I felt very important; into my care they had put the furniture and bedding to guard!

I preened myself with Dad's fireman's uniform. The suit jacket completely enveloped me, the hat slipped down my face. Children gathered around me, and I boasted to them, "I am a pozharnik!"

A few hours later, Mom and Dad returned with their children in their arms. They had made their way through the ruins and flames to the cemetery where they found their children!

Meri (from the "Tsherebukhes") and Khaye Sore, Yisroel's wife, had taken the children to the cemetery after they had rescued the belongings from our apartment. They tried to bring the children back, but the flames prevented them from getting to Kavkaz.

Night had fallen. Women lit candles, and a bright glow rose over the whole field, for the flames of the Shabbat candles blazed to God's heaven. The Jews stood in the middle of the field to receive the Shabbat; and from dozens of nooks and crannies resounded over God's naked world and over fields and forests:

"Come my bride, come my bride, let us receive the Shabbat!"[3] Above the flames, still not extinguished but blazing to the clouds, rose the Jewish chant from the Vigon by the Krinker River, "Come in peace!"

From the very moment the Jews sang their first song, God's Shabbat had arrived, descended down upon the wide field, "Shalom Aleichem, Mal'achei hasharet, peace be upon you!"

Gentiles and rude peasant boys stood aloof at the side, looking frozen; there the shtetl burns, and the Jews light candles and chant prayers; "o, subota, subota, zhidovski praznik!"[4]

Rabbi Zalmen Sender, zts"l, immediately explained the exemption for this Shabbat: "Jews must eat and the Sabbath may be broken when life is at stake!"[5]

The very pious, however, would not hear of any of this, so the Rabbi had to give them an injunction. Perhaps for the first time in their lives, Jews had to desecrate Shabbat!

Solemn ceremonies were postponed until the next day, Shabbat, and those who had been able to save their cholent cooked it up.

[Page 220]

At "Zhabe" (Frog) Alley I saw a Jewish woman putting a cooking pot on a still smoldering fire of a burned house to warm food.

She scuffed burning pieces of wood under the pot for this purpose, and while wailing and crying, she prayed in a loud voice, "God, forgive me!"

To the side, women sat and supervised the cooking. In the middle of the field stood Jews, wrapped in their taleysim (prayer shawls), praying; and through a saved Torah scroll they had spread on a table in the middle of the field, they let God know that they still held fast to their covenant with Him.

Translator's footnotes:

1. טלית-קטן= tales-kotn: ritually fringed undershirt.
2. see psalm 137, "By the rivers of Babylon, there we sat down, we wept..."
3. "Come my bride, let us receive the Shabbat!". A line from the mystical-liturgical poem (piyyut) "Lecha Dodi, Come my friend", in which the "Queen Shabbat" is greeted. According to a kabbalistic interpretation, the "bride" is not to be equated with the "Shabbat" but with the divine presence, Shechina.
4. субота, субота, жидовскі празник!: Oh, Saturday, Saturday, Jewish holiday!
5. פקוח נפש דוחה שבת= Concept of Halacha: "An open mind rejects Shabbat" (it is permissible to desecrate Shabbat in order to save human lives)

[Page 221]

Dad Escapes from Russian-Japanese War

For two days and nights we camped on the Vigon after the fire. Those who had suffered no loss brought food, clothing and bedding to the victims of the fire. On Sunday morning, Jews from surrounding towns arrived to help us.

Many from the shtetl shared their homes with families who had been victims of the fire.

The family of Khayim Osher quartered at the "Tsherebukhes". My Dad and Grandpa Yankel Bunim were running around looking for a place to live. The Jews did not remain idle.

On Sunday, they already started building. Tents made of linen were erected where the stores had been. Goods were brought from the surrounding towns to our merchants and shopkeepers, and so trade picked up again as if nothing had happened.

Miraculously, Gabarska Street, where the factories were located, was spared from the disaster. The factories were therefore in operation; Jews were earning and setting about building a new town. However, the fire disaster could not be forgotten so easily. Shmuel Avreml, the teacher, was subjected to savage curses by the women, because it was from his house that the fire had broken out.

The women took out all their anger and resentment on Shmuel Avreml's family; no one wanted to have anything to do with them anymore, which made them feel as if they were under a kind of ban. Finally, when Shmuel Avreml could no longer bear the hostility and malice, he left town. Women ran after his cart and sent curses after him.

Various versions circulated about how the fire had started; one of the versions resembled the story of the Chicago fire[1].

"Shmuel Avreml had a cow, there was straw in the barn. Someone from the household had gone into the barn at dawn with a lantern, the cow knocked over the lantern and the straw caught fire".

[Page 222]

The apartment that Grandpa Yankel Bunim got on New Street was far from the center, opposite the Polish Church; and very few Krinkers knew where the street was.

Two roads led to the New Street; either through Mill Street, on a path that crossed from the church, or through Gabarska Street and on a narrow footbridge that crossed swamps and fields. Only Goyim, Poles and Tatars lived along the road. The latter had close relations with Jews and almost every one of them spoke Yiddish.

Most of the Tatars worked in the "wet" tannery and kept close together. They had their own houses and gardens in the New Street, and lived with their own traditions, separated from the Christians.

Externally, the street was completely different from other urban streets. Entering the street, one absolutely did not want to believe that it was a part of Krynki. The street was also different from those on the outskirts of the city, where the goyim lived.

New Street looked like a village; small houses with thatched roofs, and around them large gardens and barns. Opposite the houses were fields. In the middle of the street were two wells; and even the water was drawn differently than in the shtetl.

Both the buckets and the way they were lowered down the well were the same as those that are common practice in a village. The buckets were very large, and they were lowered (by rope) with a wheel. The filled buckets were brought back up in the same way.

Our apartment with a Polish family was a small room that barely had room for two beds, let alone other furniture. The room had no window, so it was virtually always night.

In this dark and unhappy room lived, ate and slept ten people: Grandpa, Grandma, Great Grandma Reyne Gitl, the two children, Mair and Sore, my Dad, my Mom, me and my two little brothers, Mair and Velvel.

[Page 223]

Grandpa and his family slept in the one bed, at the foot end and the head end, and our family in the second bed. The nights passed constantly in restlessness and noise; Grandpa could not sleep because of the confinement and the exhalations of all the people. He spent the nights sitting in the field. His getting up used to wake everyone up again.

When we rose from this agony and restlessness, the heavy smell that had formed in the room during the night hit our noses. This immediately drove everyone outdoors.

We had to cook with the Christians; and my Great-Grandma Reyne Gitl refused to touch food that was cooked on a goyish stove. She began to get weaker and weaker, until my Grandpa ran to the Rabbi to order her to eat the food.

But she would not follow the Rabbi either.

"I don't want to eat from an oven where the cooking is not kosher!" She was stubborn and actually got sick, so they had to take her to the Jewish "hospital."

Soon after her admission there, her daughter, i.e. my Grandmother, also became ill and had to go to the "hospital", which was actually the municipal poorhouse at that time. After the fire, many victims of the fire had been quartered there.

Since there was no one to care for the sick, my grandfather and his two children also moved into the "hospital". So now five of them lived there in one room; we, however, got more space in the goyish chamber.

During the few months we lived there, I really came alive; I played with the goyish rascals in the big garden, and often one of the sons, Semyon, would take me out into the fields where he tended sheep and cattle. He taught me various games and also told me wonderful stories.

He taught me to carve pipes out of willow and to play on them. However, I did not have too much time with him, because a Jewish boy has to go to the kheyder!

Like probably all children, I also asked various questions that an adult cannot answer right away. I really wanted to know why one person is called "Dad" and the other "Mom", and why it is not the other way around.

In general, I wanted to get behind the mystery of what distinguishes a man from a woman, but both Mom and Dad drove me away every time I bothered them with my stupid questions.

[Page 224]

The way into the house led through a garden. Once, when I came home from school, my eyes fell on a shikse (a Christian girl), sleeping under a tree; she had completely uncovered herself. My eyes lingered on her body, and the sight shook me! Crying, I ran to my mom to tell her that the Shikse was a "mum"![2]

Mom's laughter left me excited, amazed and confused.

In the kheyder I confided my "discovery" to a boy; "why are you surprised?" he said, "everything is different among the goyim!" I childhood! Innocent Jewish boys!

Together with Grandma Rive we moved from the apartment with the Christians to the "Sholker" melamed[3] on the Mill Street.

Not long after the fire, Krynki was struck by another calamity; scarlet fever! Moreover, some time before the Great Fire, there was an epidemic in the shtetl, chicken pox, from which hundreds of children died. Fear and terror reigned in the homes. Children were taken from schools and amulets were tied around them.[4]

Misnagdim laughed about it, but the women didn't care. With my amulet on the red ribbon, I knew that a "good spirit" was watching over me. That is why I sneaked out of the house and was not afraid to go into houses where people with chickenpox were lying.

At my friend Zeydke Kirbeses I saw his sister Dobe lying with high fever; the chickenpox had inflamed her face.

Yanke Katyuts' brother also died of chickenpox.

I saw Tevl Vatshul wrap the little body in a linen cloth, take it under his arm and bring it to the funeral.

Yanke's mom pulled out her hair and wailed. She accompanied the body to the porch. Tevl would not allow her to go with him to the cemetery. Yanke Katyut ran outside at that time and bragged that his little brother had died.

The scarlet fever did not steer clear of me.

[Page 225]

I became deathly ill, and before my two brothers could be taken to relatives, they too fell ill. I still remember the two younger children lying in their cradles; and me in bed.

Mom and Grandma took care of us. In fact, we owed our healing to the Jewish doctor "Lupatsh" (so called because of his cleft lip).

He was a good and very pious doctor. However, the Jews preferred to call for the Polish doctor Dzhitkovski, so the Jewish doctor left Krynki.

While a plague was raging in the shtetl; riots and upheavals were raging in the country; it was a very troubled time. The war with Japan was already reaching our Krinker homeland. The crying of women and children whose husbands and fathers had been drafted could be heard in the streets.

One early morning I was awakened by a great wailing; everyone in the parlor was crying! Grandpa Yankel Bunim had come, Papa was running around the apartment excitedly and restlessly; he could neither sit nor stand. Now it was his turn; he had received the news from Grodno that he had to leave his wife and children behind and go far away from all his dearest and nearest to fight with the Japanese, for the Tsar and for "Mother Russia".

The turmoil and commotion lasted for a whole day. Next day, Mama packed Papa's clothes, his prayer shawl and his tfiln[5] in a straw basket. Grandma prepared rusks.

During the day they kept the door locked. If someone wanted to enter, he would be asked, "Who's there?"

Late that night there was a loud knock on the door and a firm voice called out, "Open up!" Dad quickly ran to us, gave me and his other two children a kiss on the forehead and, with his basket in hand, jumped out the window, into the darkness. Again he left his wife and children; he ran away to save himself and begin anew somewhere, far away, in a new land and on foreign soil.

Again I was left without a father; but this time together with my two little brothers.

Translator's footnotes:

1.   For the Chicago fire disaster of October 1871, which broke out in a barn, see https://en.wikipedia.org/wiki/Great_Chicago_Fire
2.   מום= (spoken "moom"), blemish, defect, deformity. As a little boy, Yosl saw a woman for the first time, and did not know how to express it better.
3.   מלמד= melamed, teacher in a kheyder, the Jewish elementary school

4. קמיעות = kameyes, especially a piece of paper with a holy saying or holy name as protection against bad luck or evil spirits

5. תפילין = tfil(i)n, capsules of black leather, from which hang black leather straps, the "retsues", and in which lie pieces of parchment with prayers or verses. The "tfiln" are worn by adult men on their heads and on their left arms.

[Page 226]

Workers Rule Krynki

Stormy times had dawned. In the shtetl, people began to hear and talk about names and places that were previously unknown; "Stesl"[1], "Makarov"[2], "Kropotkin"[3], "Port-Artur"[4], the "Yapontshikes"[5] with their "General Nogi".[6]

The conversations in the Bote-Medroshim and in the market were perhaps still a little far from reality, but in many homes such conversations were already filled with grief and lamentation.

Hundreds of Krinkers had been picked up and put on transports to Grodno, to be sent from there to military junctions and to the front, far away, to "that side of the Sambatyen"[7].

The war with the "Yapontshikes" had already reached its end, however, unrest began in the country.

Krynki no longer needed to be stirred up; the Krinker tanners not only got up with the illusion of a "social revolution," but they lived and went to sleep with it.

Krinkers no longer needed any preparation for it; a call, a strong word were already enough to drive the tanners immediately into the streets and set about creating a system of "workers' power."

The naïve Krinker boys and girls, who already knew from appropriate books all the ways and methods to lead not only a revolution, but also a world "in the dawn after the revolution", actually believed that the only thing that had to be done was to take the guns of the policemen, tear the portrait of the tsar and proclaim the "rule of the proletariat".

Almost every year, continuous waves of strikes erupted in the shtetl; heroic resistance and the experience that the factory owners could be taught their lesson created a foundation of security and self-confidence among the tanners.

The younger ones, who already belonged to the "Bund" or the anarchists, knew "with certainty" that it was only up to them, and the world would be built on a society of "liberty, equality, fraternity".

[Page 227]

The only thing that remained to be done was to eliminate the autocracy and the "bourgeoisie".

When the news of the march to the tsar's palace in Petersburg with its bloody end, led by the provocative priest Gapon[8], reached the shtetl, along with the news of the subsequent strike called by the railroad workers, the tanners perceived this as a sign of the times that their hour had now struck; "the social revolution had arrived!"

A little over a week after the events in Petersburg, when (Mother) Russia was still snuggling big and lazy in her fur coats and the little huts, the Krinker youth were already beginning to revolt.

The "Bund" and the anarchists had decided to gather the tanners and lead them in a demonstration of solidarity with the Petersburger railroaders. On the agreed day, January 17, 1905, at 12 o'clock, the tanners stopped work, marching in lines from each factory to the "cold" synagogue.

There, from the podium, speakers – Jews and goyim – called on workers to join the ranks of the striking Petersburger railroad workers and resist the autocracy.

The speeches and heated words called for revolution. The leaders of the "Bund" themselves didn't intend to incite the workers to revolt. They thought that it would be enough to stir up the tanners a little with revolutionary enthusiasm in order to sharpen their "revolutionary consciousness".

After that they would disperse and go home, and had fulfilled their duty to "demonstrate". But when the tanners heard that the revolution had already broken out in Petersburg and the speakers called for their own uprising, eager and heated participants demanded that one should immediately go out into the street, take possession of the Shtetl and proclaim the "rule of the proletariat".

Voices echoed through the synagogue:

"Long live workers' power!"; and in closed ranks, with red and black flags, they sang the Marseillaise and marched outside through the shtetl. Some fellows ran ahead and ordered the stores to close. In fright, the shopkeepers hastily retreated into their houses.

It was a leaden day; sleet softened the shtetl. The streets, however, were filled with the singing and determination of the youth, who walked through the market with fluttering flags to abolish the autocracy and the bourgeoisie.

[Page 228]

Meanwhile, the noise from outside had reached the inside of the houses, as had the sleet that penetrated the windows, and it was lukewarm in the parlor. Grandma Rive sat worried, thinking of her son Meyshke, who was surely out there with the others. "The yatn, the young people have banded together!" someone shouted yanking open the door.

(By "yatn" we did not mean the louts, as the term was later bastardized, but the fellows and the youth. A "yat" was a lad and a "yatl" was a little boy).

From house to house the news spread that "the youth is rebelling". Krynki had already become accustomed to frequent riots of the tanners. Krinker revolts were absolutely nothing new for the townspeople. But they knew immediately that this rebellion was now a completely different one; it was directed not only against the rich, but also against the government!

The Krinkers began to feel that the "end of the world" was now approaching. Everything would be " head down and feet up". Neighbors gathered at our house;

"What will be, what will be? The 'yatn' will abolish everything, not only the tsar, but also money. There will be no more money!"

A horror befell us- "no more money!"

The great poor and have-nots, the bitter destitute trembled. Mom remained seated in worry and anxiety.

"How can we live without money?!"

Mom took out a wallet from under a pillow, got on the table and jammed the wallet in the ceiling of the room; "Whatever comes," she said, "let's hide the few rubles first!"

She hurried to protect not only "the few rubles" but also her other "capital."

Without having discussed beforehand, without certain plans, the youth set about disarming the few policemen. The police chief and a few guards fled to "Yente's forest"; the shtetl passed into the hands of the "proletariat".

Some anarchist youth carried small pistols and became the "armed force".

[Page 229]

The young people spread out over the shtetl. Some of them went to the administration office, others to the government buildings. The goal was to destroy and eliminate everything that symbolized self-rule.

In the tumult mingled also suspicious and dark figures, robbers and good-for-nothings, who ran with the crowd and took advantage of the unrest to rob and plunder for themselves.

Two of the gang took all the money found in the administration office and fled the shtetl the next day. The following day, the "expropriators were dispossessed".

Yankel Tsheyni, who had created the first anarchist group in Krynki, was carrying a little over 40 rubles, which he just managed to snatch from the administration office before the two from that group robbed all the remaining money. The next day, however, a couple of heavily drunk and armed "yatn" came and ordered him to hand over the money.

The youths also made their way to the post office. They broke every piece of furniture there; the portrait of the tsar they hung on a tree and shot through it. While doing so, they sang:

"Sisters and brothers, let's leave aside the formal you and let's shorten Nikolai's life, Sisters and brothers, they already talk through the telegraph, we don't need a tsar, we don't need a God!

Sisters and brothers, let's take over the world, away with the bourgeoisie, we don't need any gelt."

Persons from that gang also went to the "Monopol", (the government pub), to rob it. Many stowed liquor bottles in their pockets or started drinking.

The "enlightened" forcibly ended the robberies, took the bottles out of the pockets and broke them.

Some people went berserk and started killing the policemen and their families. Leybke Noskes saved the lives of the police chief and his family. The prayers of his wife, who was scared to death, did not help, only Leybke's intervention saved them all.

[Page 230]

Voices and revolver shots carried through the shtetl, and fathers and mothers sat in the houses, filled with sorrow and worry. It was not until late at night that things became quiet. The revolution had succeeded – Krynki had passed into the power of the "proletariat".

At home everyone was awake. My uncle Meyshke came in in a good mood but completely drenched. He reported everything that had happened outside, including that the "yatn" had cut the wire of the telegraph.

Meyshke had brought "looted goods" into the parlor; two silver spoons. Grandma Rive was furious and insisted that he should hand over the "robbery" immediately. Meyshke then left the house and did not return that night.

During the night it stopped raining and snowing. The shtetl lay melancholy and sodden, the stores were closed; the doors of the rich people's houses were locked and the shutters were clamped shut.

The "yatn" appointed patrols from among them to guard the shtetl.

Few residents went out at that time; only the "yatn" filled the streets.

Red and black flags were fluttering. Chants went through the streets and the words from the "Shvue of the Bund" mingled with the anarchist songs. Groups chanted: "Brider and shvester fun arbet un noyt, tsu ale vos zaynen tsezeyt un tseshprayt"[9].

Anarchist young people wearing black shirts sang Edelstadt's "oh how long, oh how long, will you remain slaves and carry these shameful chains, how long will you create shining riches, for those who rob your bread."

A chant rose above it:

"Let's shorten Nikolai's life, we don't need a tsar, we don't need a God!"

At that time we lived in the house of the Sholker teacher on Mill Street, and when I looked out of the window, I saw the drunken Yoshke walking outside, equipped with a sword, which he held at his side like a real policeman. He ran up to the Polish church, was he going to arrest the priest?

Translator's footnotes:

1.   General   Anatoly   Mikhaylovich   St(o)essel,   see https://en.wikipedia.org/wiki/Anatoly_Stessel
2.   vice-admiral   Stepan   Osipovich   Makarov, https://en.wikipedia.org/wiki/Stepan_Makarov
3.   Pjotr Alexejewitsch Kropotkin, he was already mentioned before, see https://en.wikipedia.org/wiki/Peter_Kropotkin
4.   Port-Arthur: On 08.02.1904 Japan attacked the Russian fleet lying off Port Arthur, which marked the beginning of the Russo-Japanese War
5.   Yapontshikes= Japanese

6. Nogi Maruseke: Count Nogi Maresuke, a Japanese general in the Imperial Japanese War, see https://en.wikipedia.org/wiki/Nogi_Maresuke

7. Sambatyen= the mythical Sambatyon River, which was already mentioned before, see https://en.wikipedia.org/wiki/Sambation

8. Georgy Apollonowitsh Gapon (1870-1906), a Russian Orthodox priest converted from Judaism, who played a tragic and dubious dual role within the revolutionary workers' movement. He believed in the success of a peaceful protest while maintaining the tsarist regime and wanted, in January 1905, to present a petition to the tsar on the so-called "Bloody Sunday," when tens of thousands of workers took part in a protest march in Petersburg. However, on the part of the tsarist regime, the peaceful demonstrators were fired upon and hundreds of them were shot.

9. This song has been recited several times, see page 155 for translation and links to sound samples.

[Page 231]

A group of Krinker revolutionaries
in the courtyard of Grodner Prison, 1905
On the right is the great hero – Nyomke Fridman (Nyomke, Hershl the
"Kretsikn's"); on the left behind the bars is Leybke Noskes (Louis Sheyn)

[Page 232]

Soldiers in Krynki

For two days and nights the Krinker "yatn" held the shtetl under the rule of the "proletariat". After Petersburg, Krynki was the second city to rise in revolt against autocracy. But Krynki was the first city ever within the great Russian Empire where a "Rabotshya Sovet" (Workers' Council) was established.

On the third day of the "Rabotshi Vlast" (The Workers' Rule), news made the rounds that soldiers were being sent from Sokolka to Krynki. The police chief had been able to reach Sokolka and told what had happened in the shtetl.

The entire youth ran to meet the soldiers. Some of them had a few weapons with them, others carried iron tools; the girls were collecting stones in their aprons. They met the first troop of soldiers on Sokolker Street, on the road leading to the market.

The two groups stood face to face, one against the other; the soldiers held the lances (bayonets) on their rifles pointed at the faces of the heated and I youth. From the revolutionary crowd emerged a non-Jewish peasant boy; Fyodor Derushke (Doroshke), who later played a sad role as a traitor and informer.

He was a good speaker of Yiddish, a member of the "Bund" and began to address the soldiers. He called on them to show solidarity with the workers and join them. When asked by the commander if this was a mutiny, he replied, "no, this is a revolution!"

After him, another Christian who was active in the " Bund ", Aleksander Kishkel, began to address the soldiers. A very dramatic moment took place when Fyodor unbuttoned his shirt and asked the soldiers to shoot at him.

However, the commander, who had apparently been ordered to shoot, did not do so. Later, he was removed from the shtetl for that, demoted and punished. The commander began to ask the youth to let him enter the shtetl peacefully. He assured them that he would not cause any bloodshed and would not harm anyone.

[Page 233]

When the soldiers entered the city and positioned themselves in the market, the commander proclaimed a state of war. Immediately, the hunt began for those who had participated in the uprising.

A bitter and evil terror arose in the shtetl; hundreds of young men were arrested and, tied together and with their hands behind their backs, driven through the city for transport to Grodno.

The first victim of the state of war was an innocent Jew, Yankel Tsalel, the baker. He had gone to the stable at dawn to fetch wood. Due to the wind, and because he was hard of hearing, he had not heard the order to stop; and the guard soldier shot him.

Nothing could be done against the Krinker fellows; the terror aggravated their anger and resistance. In addition to the soldiers, the government had to send Cossacks and Circassians to the shtetl.

The soldiers were quartered in "Yente's Bes-Hamedresh"; and for the Cossacks and Circassians were prepared a camp in Yente's forest.

Some of the boys who were able to hide escaped from Krynki; among them Leybke Noskes and Yankel Tsheyni. Yankel Tsheyni left Krynki in a very extraordinary way.

On the night of the revolution, when Grandma sent Meyshke away to return the two stolen silver spoons he went to Yankel Tsheyni to sleep there.

In the middle of the night, Meyshke and Yankel were awakened by two young men from the neighboring shtetl of Horodok.

Having heard about the revolution in Krynki (so they said), they had come to ask Meyshke and Yankel to visit their town "in order to carry out a revolution there as well".

A sleigh was already waiting outside to take them to Horodok (Gródek). On the way, Meyshke and Yankel learned that Yankel "Professor" (Keplyak) had sent for them.

In Horodok the Krinker group met Yakev Kreplyak, peace be upon him, and German youths working in the weaving mills of the neighboring town of Badke. The leaders immediately divided committees and gave instructions to start shrilling the factory whistles.

[Page 234]

The townspeople thought that a fire had broken out and ran to the marketplace. Yankel Tsheyni unveiled a black flag that read in Russian letters:

"Workers of all countries unite- long live anarchy!"

Yankel Kreplyak spoke to the people from a platform. The essence of his speech was:

"While the rich eat chocolate, we poor do not even have bread!"

When Kreplyak finished his speech, the "conscious ones" exclaimed, "Long live anarchy!"

Suddenly a commotion arose, "Police are coming!". The people ran apart in fright.

Nothing came of the revolution. Later, the (Krinker) youths found out that a tax collector had made off with the money he carried from the "Monopol". On the way back to Krynki, Meyshke and Yankel learned that the shtetl had been completely taken by the soldiers. They separated from each other.

My uncle Meyshke was immediately arrested at that time; Yankel Tsheyni returned to his home. Through the window he saw the informer Mayrem Tsinges walking in front of a group of soldiers. Mayrem wiped his finger over his nose, which meant: "Get lost!"

Consequently, Yankel left Krynki after a few days. Leybke Noskes also fled the shtetl. He stayed in Bialystok for some time until he was told that he could come back to Krynki. This, however, was a kind of trap! Leybke arrived in the shtetl on Thursday; on Friday morning, while still in bed, he sensed in his sleep that he was being threatened. He jumped up and saw quite a few Cossacks and "Circassians" with drawn weapons pointed at him.

The hundreds of Krinker "bokherim" who were imprisoned in Grodner Prison brought tumult and turmoil there. They did not follow the rules of the prison, broke benches and provoked with hunger strikes.

In Krynki itself, things were not quiet either. Neither the soldiers nor the Kozaks could quell the anger of the Krinker yatn.

[Page 235]

The youth met as before and held meetings in their own manner.

The main gatherings took place in the woods; but several times the strong Cossack guards tracked down the meetings and dragged boys and girls with them through the Krinker streets.

Revolutionary meetings were held in the Bote-Medroshim. On Shabbat, before the Torah reading, yatn used to enter with weapons, a speaker would jump on the bime (bimah, platform) and give flaming agitational speeches.

Many gatherings in the Bote-Medroshim were held on Shabbat after the Tsholent meal, when the Jews were in their homes and the houses of prayer were empty.

Since I used to run after the "big guys," I witnessed a debate between anarchists and bundists in the Kavkazer Bes-Medresh. The discussion was bitter and nasty; the shouting and heckling from both parties was venomous and threatening.

I remember that it almost came to a brawl. A girl stood on the ledge by a window and shouted down the opposing speaker with hysterical interjections. They provoked some Cossacks who were sitting close to the shuttered stores and demonstratively showed their weapons.

The Krinker yatn often used to tease the Cossacks. When the latter showed themselves at the market, yatn immediately appeared, shouted out slogans and yelled (in Russian): "Hey Cossacks, you fools, you attack like dogs!" The Cossacks immediately took up the chase, the yatn ran away, shouting slogans and singing workers' songs.

From the very beginning, the Cossacks caused great grief. The Kalmyks[1] behaved particularly savagely. These were an "unbridled Mongolian gang" that frightened the inhabitants.

They once taught my Aunt Dvoyre a lesson that lingered for months. There were loaves of bread in the front of the wooden shack where Dvoyre traded. Two Kalmyk Cossacks spiked some of their loaves with their lances. Dvoyre ran after them.

[Page 236]

But they turned back and hurt her hand with a nageike (leather whip). Dvoyre then went to the "elder" and complained. Thereupon all the Kalmyk Cossacks were brought before her for identification; and she pointed to the two who had attacked her.

The "elder" assured her that the two would be punished. It was hard for the inhabitants to bear the savagery of the Cossacks. The Cossacks became calmer only when the "balebatim" (the rich and powerful) mediated.

Rumors circulated that their commander sympathized with the socialists.

The interventions of the "balebatim" often prevented bloodshed and great tragedies.

Translator's footnote:

1.   The Kalmyks are a western Mongolian people who were allowed to settle in the Lower Volga region in the 17th century after the Russian tsar was promised service in his army.

[Page 237]

Uncle Mair (Meier)

Of all my uncles, I especially loved Mama's brother Meyshke, with whom I grew up at home and who was like a brother to me; also Papa's brother Mair (Meier). Both of them I thought were brave boys who did heroic deeds.

Dad was also a hero to me; after all, during a tanners' strike, the police were looking for him and he had to hide in the stable for a few days.

When the strike was over, Papa returned from Sokolka, where he had been hiding. The tanners waited for him in the "Profitke"[1], about two vyorst (2.1 km) from Krynki, and then led him in a parade across the "Vigon" into the shtetl.

I remember Mair when he was still at school and later at the factory. Mair took pleasure in teasing and frightening me. Once he gave me such a fright that I burst into hysterical screams. Grandma Sime Feygl, like her mother, R' Velvele's daughter, was careful not to get angry or upset.

At that time, however, she was actually angry with Mair and reprimanded him, "Just take care that this doesn't have a bad ending!"

And this was already considered a curse by her.

The story Mair had told me was about a dead man who appears to someone in a dream and "demands his liver back". The trick was to draw the listener into the story and scare him with a sudden cry: "Give me your liver!"

Mair received his first agitation "lessons" in the factory, from the "Bund". During the three months he spent in the Grodner prison, he became an anarchist. In Krynki all the anarchist groups were represented: "Anarcho-Syndicalists", "Anarcho-Communists", "Ethical Anarchists" and the "Philosophical".

Mair's comrades were very young boys.

Obviously, they did not enjoy a respected status, which I infer because Mama's brother Meyshke, who was also an anarchist, had little contact with Mair and his comrades.

[Page 238]

Meyshke's close comrades were Yankel Tsheyni, Nyomke Yonah "the Stolyer's (carpenter's)" and Anshel Avreml "the Schmid's (blacksmith's)".

Mair's comrades were Nyomke Hershl "the Kretsikns"[2] (who became a great revolutionary hero that the Krinkers boast about) and Khaykel Muts, who was also a fearless fellow. By the way, it is worth mentioning that during the period of German occupation Khaykel Muts spat directly in the face of the Nazi commander, may his name be erased, and died an agonizing martyr's death.

After all, what did Mair know back then? He was a 13 or 14-year-old boy, naïve, gullible, running after those who promised to rid the world of poverty.

Mair caused my grandfather a lot of grief. Yankel Bunim thought that there were simply too many revolutionaries in a single family. Therefore, he tried to send Mair to America as soon as possible.

Mair would not hear of it; he was in the movement with far too much heart. He, a hot-tempered boy, wanted to make his mark and gain exposure. He ran along everywhere and wanted to participate in all activities.

I loved him very much!

Because of Mair, the boys allowed me to run after them. They even entrusted me with proclamations that I was allowed to carry. I was especially favored by Khaykel Muts, who was perhaps ten or eleven years older than me.

I still remember how Mair took me to a demonstration. That demonstration was scary. The anarchists wore clothes that served as a sort of uniform; black "dress shirts", black pants, black "burkes" (which were sort of short jackets like the sailors wear in our country), black peaked caps or "tuft" hats, and a black elastic mask on their faces.

The demonstrators walked in rows, like soldiers, down Mill Street to the Polish Church. They sang Jewish and Russian revolutionary songs. One of the songs remained in my memory; "March of the Anarchists".

[Page 239]

The song was truly in the style of marching music, and everyone walked to the beat of the chant and words. The singing began when the leader exclaimed:

"Let us sing the march of the Anarchists!"; and everyone started like a well-rehearsed choir:

"Let us sing the song that shall rumble like thunder, that shall explode like volleys of bullets, shall flare up like flames, under the black flag to the gigantic struggle, with firm steps to the echo of call".

From the crowd a voice shouted, "Long live Anarchy!" And the crowd roared, "Hurrah! Hooray! Hooray! Hoo-rah-a-a!"

Cossacks gathered in the market. The Jews hastily retreated to their parlors, the stores closed. Jewish hearts were seized with fear; and from Jewish homes the weeping of mothers penetrated to the outside.

The rich and powerful, with Nokhem Anshel and the Rabbi at their head, went to the head of the Cossacks and asked them not to attack; let there be no blood of Jewish children on the Krinker pavement. The Jewish pleas were successful. The Cossacks stopped in the market; and only from afar sounded to them:

"Down with autocracy! Long live anarchy! Hooray! Hoo-rah-a-a!"

A fateful turn in Mair's life was brought about by a precarious incident that set the shtetl abuzz. One Friday morning, Mair, Khaykel Muts and Nyomke, Hershl the Kretsikns, went to Nokhem Anshel to perform a "dispossession".

They entered his office and instructed Nokhem Anshel to give them money.

"What do you need money for, kiddies?" asked Nokhem Anshel.

" As a price not to kill you!"

"So that's how it is! How much money do you kiddies need not to kill me?"

"Five thousand rubles!"

"Just wait a little while, I'll go and bring it to you right away!"

Several goyim with sticks and iron tools took the weapon from the three boys. They beat them severely and threw them out.

Nokhem Anshel immediately sent a messenger to deliver the "good news" to my grandpa, Yankel Bunim.

[Page 240]

With pain and great sorrow, Grandpa received the message of what had happened to his son and vowed not to let him back into his apartment.

Mair, the innocent-I boy, would never have suspected that what he was about to do would cause such alarm in the shtetl.

It was long after the prayer when Mair returned to his father's apartment. The latter lived with Pinke the Shames, the "caller to the synagogue."

On Friday evenings before sunset, Pinke used to stand in the middle of the market, raise his head, place his right hand on his right cheek and call out:

"Come into the shul! Into the shul!"

Grandpa's apartment was entered through the back door or through Pinke's apartment. The back door was locked. So Mair went into Pinke's apartment; but before he had even opened the door, Pinke chased him out with a stick.

From then on, Mair was on his own and homeless. He was a drifter. On Shabbat morning, however, while my grandfather was at prayer, he used to sneak into the apartment. My grandma would provide him with food, comb his hair and give him a change of clothes.

It was one Shabbat. My grandpa was sick and had to pray alone (at home). Since my grandma was expecting Mair's visit, she was afraid that my grandpa would get upset when he saw him and throw him out of the house in disgrace. Grandma therefore sent me to let Mair know that he should not come until Grandpa stood for "Shmone-Esre"[3].

Certainly my grandpa never stood to the "Shmone-Esre" as long as this time.

Mair began to go under. No one wanted to realize what was happening to him. Everyone left him alone with his pain and his fate. Once I met him, weakened and dirty; he was sleeping on a bench in the Kavkazer Bes-Medresh.

Crying, I ran to my mother to tell her about it. She brought him home. Mair lived with us for a very long time after that.

We both slept in a folding bedstead. From the bed, Mair used to give agitation speeches to my mother, describing to her exactly what the happy future created by the revolution would look like. Mair's life came to a tragic end. He could no longer gain a foothold in Krynki.

[Page 241]

He did not get a job. It seems that the "movement" considered the event around Nokhem Anshel as a mere "private initiative of three yatn". Mair went to Bialystok offended.

A few weeks after Mair had gone to Bialystok a ship ticket (to America) arrived for him. However, nothing came of it; a few days before Mair's planned departure for America, he died from a bomb transported by a group (of the movement) to be thrown (later) into a meeting of top officials.

Some are of the opinion that Mair was not intended to transport the bomb (for the assassination). I think that this is a hypothesis of people who want to deny Mair's contribution in that tragic incident. They say that Mair only (by chance) saw the carriage driving with known anarchists, and asked them to give him a ride. However, there are no witnesses who could confirm this, because all those involved were killed by the bomb: and so the statement that he jumped on the cab lacks any foundation.

How could it be possible that he met the carriage with the boys at exactly the right time and that they, although they knew that they were carrying out a secret and dangerous mission, let him, an uninitiated person, ride along? Incidentally, Mair was the only one who was torn to pieces.

On the way to the meeting place the carriage drove over a stone; all of them were torn apart. Together with Mair died another Krinker, Yisroel Iser the Shoykhet's (the son of the ritual slaughterer).

The last time I saw Mair was when the police brought a picture to my grandmother – on a spread linen cloth lay only a head; Mair's head.

Translator's footnotes:

1. "profitke"= I guess it was the name of a tavern
2. Nyomke, whose surname is given under the photo as "Fridmann", was obviously the son of "the Kretsikn": obviously his father was ill with scabies
3. שמונה עשרה= Shmone-Esre, "Eighteen prayer", a very old prayer with originally 18 petitions (now 19 petitions), in which one stands up and prays silently. The prayer is then repeated aloud by the Khazn

[Page 242]

Nyomke, the Hero of the Revolution

When news of the Bialystok pogrom reached the shtetl, the Krinker Jews trembled with fear. Wild rumors spread. Every day they expected that soon the same thing would happen as in Bialystok.

The market days, for which the Jews were already waiting and which were the source of income for the grocers, were now looked forward to with fear and uncertainty.

Every gathering of peasants aroused suspicion and terror. The unrest spread and passed from the big to the small. A harmless brawl, an argument between a Jew and a goy built up into a panic.

The Krinker youth prepared to lead resistance against the attackers. When a market day ended and the last peasants left the shtetl, the Jews felt relieved and safer.

Gentile processions or funeral processions, which were otherwise habitually observed with equanimity, now drove overanxious mothers to hide their children and lock the windows.

Children who enjoyed watching the spectacle of colorful gentile processions were driven away from the windows by their mothers. Rumors arose that Ilyodor, the "black monk"[1] was preparing to visit Krynki.

The goyim of the shtetl livened up. They erected gates decorated with flowers from Sokolker Street to the Russian church. The powerful and influential ("balebatim") went to the Russian clergyman and asked him to make sure that the goyim calmed down and that the "black monarch" did not come to the shtetl.

This Russian Orthodox clergyman enjoyed a good reputation among the Jews; he was considered a friend of the Jews. He and his children behaved modestly and kindly to Jews. In contrast, the Polish priest, before whom the Jews lifted their hats and their children took them off completely, was a great enemy of Jews.

[Page 243]

Whether the clergyman actually intervened or whether it had another cause – in any case, instead of the monk, another great Orthodox clergyman came; and everything went peacefully.

At that time the governor also came to visit the shtetl. Everywhere there were gates decorated with flowers, yellow sand on the street pavements, freshly whitewashed and decorated houses. When the governor arrived, the Russian flag, the appearance and colors of which the townspeople did not know, was flying on several houses.

The most influential preened themselves with a top hat and holiday attire and, with the Rabbi in the lead, went to the first flower gate on Sokolker Street to present the governor with a Torah scroll and bread with salt.

The governor had come to inquire why Krynki was not at rest.

Life in the shtetl was heated; fear, tension and strain kept the Jews in turmoil. Hatred and bitterness between the youth, the rich and the powerful, grew even more.

The struggle among them was vicious and bitter. The cruel police terror did not stop the turmoil in the shtetl.

Every day Krinker youths were brought for the ride to Grodner prison with their hands tied behind their backs. Those who remained free kept up the resistance. Terror did not deter the Krinker "yatn".

Krinkers who went away to other cities also risked their lives there for the movement and the revolution.

The fear of raids and pogroms by the peasants in no way diminished the nasty relationship between the youth and the factory owners.

Both sides constantly measured their forces.

The "balebatim" had the police, soldiers and Cossacks on their side.

In turn, the young people had enthusiasm, willingness and idealism.

They also had pistols and bombs with which they responded to the terror. The rulers knew that the Krinker "yatn" were difficult to deal with.

[Page 244]

Therefore, after the governor's visit, they sent a whole crowd of police harassers.

The cruelest among them was a "uradnik" (Russian constable), called "the little one". The small-sized uradnik was nimble, impetuous and fearless. He was not afraid of anything or anyone. He ran dangerous errands all by himself; without the help of guards, he used to bring prisoners from Krynki to Sokolka.

The savagery and brutality of the Cossacks and the police did not lessen the concern and fear of the factory owners. Anarchist fellows kept them in permanent fear. "Expropriations" increased. On Nokhem Anshel's initiative, the factory owners decided to hold a meeting in the great Bes-Medresh to discuss means of teaching the "wild gang" a lesson.

The anarchists knew about these preparations and decided to throw a bomb into the meeting; this would get rid of all the "bourgeois rabble" at once. The Krinker anarchists had learned how to build bombs from Yankel Kreplyak.

The "Macedonian bombs", as they were called, could be made in a simple way; nails and pieces of iron were placed in a tin can, dynamite was added and a wick was fixed to the "bomb" and lit. As soon as it burned well, the tin can was thrown.

I remember very well the day when the factory owners held their meeting. It was Sunday and I was studying at the "Tshekhonovtser" teacher. The school was just opposite the big Bes-Medresh. From the window I could see the women's section.

On Gabarska Street, by the doors to the main entrance of the Bes-Medresh, Cossacks stood guard. From the window of the school we saw "the little one", the uradnik, walking back and forth.

Suddenly we heard a bang and a loud noise. The house shook, the whole school was full of smoke and shattered glass.

[Page 245]

The children ran outside, frightened. A few steps away from the school I saw the small uradnik chasing a person up to the market with a naked sword.

I ran after him. The uradnik caught up with the person and hit him with his sword on the shoulder. The man fell down and remained lying on the asphalt; dislocated, his head pushed under his arm.

At first I thought it was my uncle Mair; he was of the same stature and had his black-curled hair. I bent over him and shook him, "Mair! Mair!"; he looked at me from the side, and then I recognized him – it was Nyomke, Hershl the Kretsikn's, Mair's friend!

Cossacks began to surround the market and would not let anyone in or out. Nyomke was driven away on a farm cart.

Nyomke grew up in a household full of hardship and hunger. His father, a tailor and patch cobbler, was a great pauper. At a very young age, Nyomke was drawn into the revolutionary movement. He belonged to the same anarchist group as Mair. He, Mair, Khaykel Muts and Yisroel Iser the Shoykhet's were devoted comrades to each other.

The bomb had been thrown by Meyshke Sidrer; but instead of hurling it, he had let it scrape the ground. The bomb exploded; none of the factory owners was hurt.

Nyomke had been standing guard at the Bes-Medresh. When he heard the explosion, he ran away, chased by the uradnik. He was supposed to run through a side street to Kantselarye Street; but in the commotion he took the way to the market.

At first it was thought that the blow with the sword had wounded Nyomke. However, in the Jewish "hospital" it was found out that he was uninjured. Nyomke "the little one", as he was called, is considered one of the great heroes with whom the history of the struggle for freedom in Russia is richly blessed. Nyomke's special heroism is probably incomparable.

Nyomke was sentenced to eight years in prison in Slonim. On the way to Grodno he and the other seven prisoners were handed loaves of bread with revolvers in them. They shot the guards. Nyomke fled to Krynki, where he was immediately arrested and taken to the Grodno prison.

[Page 246]

It was on a Friday when Nyomke was brought in for a hearing. In the prison office, he attacked six guards, snatched their weapons and shot them all.

Not far from the prison, he barricaded himself in the house of a tailor. From the window he shot at the soldiers and police who had surrounded the house, killing several more of them.

When he saw that he was running out of bullets, he cut his hand and, with his blood, wrote on the wall:

"You won't take me alive! Long live anarchy!"

With the last bullet, he shot himself.

The end had also come for the small uradnik. He was shot in Sokolka, in Kapelyushnik's inn, where Krinkers liked to stay.

Before he died, he testified that the shooter was Afroitshik, the son of Yosl Moyshe the cobbler.

However, it was said it was Meyshke Sidrer who shot the uradnik, the one who had also thrown the bomb at the meeting of the factory owners in the great Bes-Medresh. The uradnik himself did not know who had shot him. He only wanted to get even with Afroitshik because he had threatened him once.

Afroitshik's trial took place in Warsaw before a Field Court. The testimonies that Afroitshik had been in Kynki at the time of the uradnik's assassination did not help. He was sentenced to death on the gallows.

His mother went to Petersburg to submit a petition to the tsar; and he changed the death sentence to 20 years in jail.

It was reported that Afoitshik was freed during the revolution of 1917; he was seen in Moscow.

Translator's footnote:

    1.   I assume that the black monk was the anti-Jewish monk Sergei M. Trufanov, formerly "Hieromonk Iliodor", see https://en.wikipedia.org/wiki/Sergei_Trufanov

[Page 247]

My Teachers – I Call a Strike at School

Three of my teachers were really brutal people. Besides them, the teacher at the Russian elementary school was also wild and disturbed, inflicting pain and suffering on the students.

At the same time, the evil teachers were actually interesting Jews. The emergence of reformed and semi-modern elementary schools had no influence on them.

Even such an old-fashioned teacher as Avrohem Shmuel "of the Kugelekh" taught Yiddish reading and writing. The truly modern classes, however, favored a system where boys and girls learned together; and one teacher there, Merke, the daughter of Moyshe Pinkhes, even used to let her students play outside in the field during the summer.

Of the three Hebrew teachers, Einshtein was the most stubborn. He was somewhat related to us; his wife was the sister of my aunt Etel. He forbade Etel's children to speak Yiddish and made sure that they spoke only Hebrew among themselves.

Aunt Etel also made sure that her children did not speak a word of Yiddish; and in order to alienate them from the language, she did not allow them to go visit Grandpa and Grandma either.

The "Azhiraner" teacher, however, taught Yiddish in addition to the "holy" language Hebrew. At the "Azhiraner", where I and also the currently well-known activist of the Poyale-Tsien[1], Yisroel Stolarski, studied, the subject matter was taught in the same way as in the Russian elementary schools. He also taught arithmetic and recited Hebrew chants.

The Russian teacher Levenson, whom the boys called "Shloyme Dubrover", which was the name of a local madman, was a real ruffian.

He and the second teacher Kanevski, from the public school[2], were assimilated Jews who did not know a word of Yiddish.

[Page 248]

In the Russian school they taught three lessons a day with the following order: one day a class had two lessons in arithmetic and one in Russian, and the next day it was the other way around. Levenson was the Russian teacher, and he thought I was a very good student.

Arithmetic was absolutely not my thing; but I was good at spelling, composition, and memorizing songs, poems, and stories.

But apart from these "virtues", Levenson did not like me at all. In addition to his passion for poking and whipping students, he especially bullied me with viciousness.

My lessons at the Russian school came to an end after Levenson gave me the task of memorizing Pushkin's Balade, "The Little Golden Fish[3]" in two days.

Early in the morning in the classroom I opened the ballad and left the book "Ruski retsh treti tshast"[4] open in the student desk.

The day was frosty, and in the classroom it was freezing cold. But I was feverish with exertion and anxiety.

Levenson came in, wrapped in malice and cold. The students stood up and all chorused, "Good morning, teacher!" After reciting the usual prayers for the Czar and his family, Levenson hastily turned to me, as if driven by someone, "Do you know the lesson?"; and without waiting for my answer, he immediately commanded me, "Read!"[5]

I lifted up the small flap of the desk and began to read from the open book.

Suddenly he ran towards me full of rage and shouted in my ear, "Scoundrel!"

He grabbed my book and started beating me wildly on the head with the book.

I was startled and confused. He hastily grabbed me by the collar and pushed me out into the corridor. After a few minutes, he flung my coat and books out through the half-open door.

I had a teacher, Leybe Matshes; he was a Kotsker Hasid[6] and seemed like melancholy personified. He was constantly walking around depressed and saddened, and often he would even fall into a short slumber in the middle of class. When he woke up, he would ask, "Well, where did we just go?"

[Page 249]

But essentially he was a Jew who liked to joke around. Twice a year he would get into a little mischief; on Purim and on Simkhe-Toyre. He would pretend to be drunk, put on his caftan inside out, put on a hat, stand on a small stall ("budke") and shout, "Come to the shul!".

On the feast days, he used to visit the Rabbi with the "balebatim" and give them answers to certain questions in an instructive manner. When he came out of the Rabbi's house, he would gather behind him dozens of boys and walk with them through the streets to the market. There he would stand in front of them a few steps away, put his hand to his cheek, raise his head and call out, "Tson Kodoshim![7]"

The children replied, "Baa, baa!"

When he saw too many children approaching, he would hastily turn to them and shout; "Dear children, good children, throw stones at me!" The children used to be so confused and ashamed that they would run away in fright.

The "Sholker", one of the vicious teachers, had the desire to beat naked bodies; but not because someone had committed a misdeed, but simply because he felt like tormenting the naked buttocks of a young body.

Suddenly and without any reason the wild greed used to attack the Sholker. His eyes then became restless, his gaze fell inquiringly over all the children until he had chosen his victim.

He told the boy to drop his pants and lie down on the table. One hand the sholker held on the naked body, and with the second he struck. Pupils did not use to stay long with him. Apparently, later he gave up the profession of a teacher.

Shaye Leyb, the Kalike (cripple), had another passion; pinching buttocks and slapping shoulders.

[Page 250]

Shaye Leyb was a teacher in the "talmetoyre", (the community school for the poor). I wanted to study with him because almost all my friends whose parents could not pay school fees were sent to Shaye Leyb.

About a hundred children studied in the "talmetoyre"; there was always a great commotion there. Shaye Leyb had to be made of iron to endure all these wild brats.

Shaye Leyb could rarely sit still while teaching. He had to keep running around to quiet the children who were scurrying around or fighting, constantly having to hold the bundle of straw on which, fastened with straps, his paralyzed foot rested.

Shaye Leyb had it in for me; all the wild things that happened in the kheyder (cheder) he blamed on me. He thought that I had my hands in all the misdeeds.

He made life difficult for me until I resolved to pay him back.

I bought a letter of pins for a kopek and fastened it under my jacket with threads I pulled through the paper.

During class, I provoked Shaye Leyb to anger him. Finally, I upset him so much that he came over to me. Apparently to protect myself, I turned my shoulder toward him. Shaye Leyb struck my shoulder violently with his hand and immediately jumped back with a wild scream.

The "Tkatsh" (weaver), a Gerer[8] Hasid, was counted among the really good teachers. His school was the only one in the shtetl where the students said the morning prayer, "Shakhres", in their own minyen. Every day a different boy was designated as the prayer leader.

The "Tkatsh" got upset quickly and at every little thing struck with the whip, walloping with fury all over the body (of a child), indiscriminately; wherever the whip only reached, the blows flew down.

I was the first to think of resisting the "Tkatsh". For this purpose I discussed with other boys, and we decided to declare a strike!

[Page 251]

My "staff", with whom I worked out all the plans for the revolt, included: Sholem, the son of Avrohem Moyshe the "mirror-folder" and Yankel, the son of Dovid the "ladies tailor".

One day before the strike, early in the morning we instructed all the boys of the minyen to swear on a Torah scroll that they would keep everything secret. Sholem had very beautiful handwriting. The evening before the strike, I dictated special versions for three announcements to him: One to be pasted in the Kavkazer Bes-Medresh where the "Tkatsh" prayed, the second for the large Bes-Medresh where the respected "balebatim" prayed, and the third for the Rabbi.

On the day of the strike, Sholem and I went at dawn, before the first prayer in the minyen, to paste the notices in both Bote-Medroshim. After the prayer in the school, we pasted the announcement for the Rabbi on the table.

We planned to all go away together to Virnyen's (Virion) forest. But before we even left, the whole shtetl already knew what the boys from "Tkatsh's" school were up to.

Instantly, the boys' fathers appeared and dragged them home by force. Dovid the ladies' tailor dragged his son, who tried to break away, to the Rabbi. The "Tkatsh" and the fathers pressed the lad to confess who had cooked up the whole commotion. Yankel revealed everything.

When we saw that the strike was "broken", Sholem and I fled the shtetl. We hid in a field near the barns of the goyim. We picked fruits to have something to eat.

People from the shtetl began to look for us. But when we couldn't stand the hunger anymore, we went back home by ourselves.

Translator's footnotes:

1. פּועלי־ציון= Poyale-Tsien, Workers of Zion, name of the Zionist-socialist movement.
2. „Dvukh klasny, trokh odelenii narodni utshilishtshy"=literally "two grades of the three departments national school"
3. Original title: Skazka o rybake I rybke, it can be assumed that Pushkin's ballad in verse form, "Tale of the Fisherman and the Fish", is based on the Grimm Brothers' fairy tale, "The Fisherman and his Wife".
4. Russian textbook for 3rd grade
5. Although he misstated it, Levenson obviously expected Yosl to recite the ballad from memory, not read it off
6. In the tradition of Rabbi Menachem Mendel of Kotzk
7. צאן קדשים= tson kodoshim, "holy sheep", designation for Jewish children
8. Ger= Hasidic dynasty, the origin of which is the Polish town of Gora Kalwaria

[Page 252]

Wild Deeds

The wildest deeds I hatched together with the naughty rascals, but also at home.

It was dangerous to leave me alone in our house, because I used to sweep everything from the bottom to the top and cause great damage. I threw pillows around, jumped from a table to the bed and "just like that" broke a little bench or a chair.

It was simply impossible to keep myself clean and tidy.

My mother just made sure that I should be dressed like the "balebatish" children; she sewed for me pants and shirts made of plush or velvet. Often a relative or neighbor who went to Bialystok or Warsaw would bring me a suit.

But it didn't look new for long. On the second day it was already unrecognizable.

Friday evening I was usually dressed up in a new suit. On Shabbat, after cholent stew, I went fruit picking with the "Kavkazer Kommando" and climbed fences and trees. By the time I got home, I was already dirty and my clothes were torn.

Mama's punishment was to lock me up in the house; she then took all my clothes and hid them, leaving me only one shirt. But she soon regretted it, because keeping me at home was even worse; she just had no idea what to do with me.

My wildness often put my life in danger. Boys used to pull out the horses' tail hairs and make strings out of them. One end of a horse's hair was held between the teeth, pulled long and made to sound with the thumbnail (of the other hand).

When the rascals saw a tethered horse, they would sneak up, lift its tail and quickly pluck out a hair.

Once I too had it in for a horse. However, it gave me such a push with its hind leg that I was flung far away and, for several hours, remained lying with great pain in my stomach, unable to move.

[Page 253]

In fact, (at that time) "a skhus had been assisting me"[1], as Grandma Rive used to say. The blow could have hit me in my face and could even have killed me. Once I performed a rather strange wild deed.

Papa had sent me to the attic to bring down an old garment. I pulled it over my head and wanted to see if I could find the ladder, blind as I was.

As a result of my fall down, I didn't have any broken bones, but I was brown, blue and swollen for weeks.

After the fire, when we lived on Mill Street, I joined a boy; his name was Yosl from the "Parofke"[2], his father ran a steam mill where bark was pounded and flour was ground. He was older, taller and wilder than me, so he was called "big Yosl", and I "little Yosl".

The two of us did the wildest and cruelest things. The boys from Mill Street trembled before us. A boy from our command had to obey both of us.

If one was unruly, he was banned by us, and none of the other boys dared to play with him or even talk to him.

Not far from us lived a leather manufacturer. His boy, a bashful and refined one, had no luck in dealing with the "big" Yosl. The latter refused to let him join our gang and was always chasing him.

Unhappy, ashamed and depressed, the boy used to stand and longingly watch us play from afar. Once he plucked up courage and approached the blocks on which the rascals usually sat in the summer evenings telling each other stories.

Yosl from the "Parofke" rose from his log, blocked his way and began to drive him away. "Get lost, you!"

"Let me play with you", begged the other tearfully.

"Get lost, why should we let you play with us? You're nothing!"

"Like hell I'm not a nothing at all", the other blurted out, "I don't have a shmekele![3]"

"Really?" wondered Yosl, "let's see! Guys, come on everybody, Zundl has no shmekl! Well, show us!"

[Page 254]

The boys surrounded the fellow, he lowered his pants and showed- that he had a golden little tube.

The goyish funerals made a tremendous impression on us. We liked the colorful parades of the boys with the white coats; the flags (the Jews called them "rags") that were carried and the singing of the Christian clergyman.

Once Yosl said to me, "Let's have a goy funeral, too!"

We grabbed a cat, turned her feet up, I held her, and Yosl strangled her by the neck. For a while she was still squawking, wriggling and trying to bite Yosl's hand with her teeth, then she died with her mouth open.

We put the dead cat in a yard next to a stable and covered it with a rag. The next day, the whole "commando" with me and Yosl in the lead, imitated the "tearful speeches" of the clergyman and buried the cat by the stable.

A quarrel was brewing between the Kavkaz rascals and those from Mill Street. Yanke Katyut, the "commander" of the Kavkaz rascals, didn't like it at all that the boys from Mill Street were imitating the Kavkazers.

He was especially angry with me for leaving the Kavkazers and associating with the boys of Mill Street.

Yosl from the "Parofke" and Yanke Katyut despised each other very much. If a Kavkaz boy came to Mill Street, they did not let him pass, but chased after him.

On the other hand, the boys from Mill Street trembled when they had to go through Kavkaz. The price to be let through one of the streets was a "toy".

Once a crying boy came and told that the Kavkaz gang had beaten him severely.

"We will wage war with them!" professed Yosl to the boys of Mill Street, and he assured them in a commander's way, "If the Kavkaz boys hit one of us again, we'll have a fight!"

We let Yanke know through a boy from another street that if he bothered a boy from Mill Street again, there would be war.

Yanke replied that he was not afraid of the Mill Street boys. If they wanted beatings, there would be beatings!

[Page 255]

How did the small-town boys know about all those customs of warfare?

The "staffs" of both streets met on the Vigon. The leaders with their "entourage" stood apart from each other. "We will break your bones if you molest a Kavkaz lad!" shouted Yanke.

"A Kavkazer must not go through the Mill Street again!" we assured Yanke.

"My people are strong", Yanke said.

"Our people are even stronger!" replied Yosl and me.

"We'll see about that! We'll see!" "The day after tomorrow we will come to you!" announced Yanke.

When the boys of Mill Street saw that the matter was really serious, they were frightened. "What should we do?" we asked each other. How stupid that we could not rely on the boys of the Mill Street!

Yosl and I went to the goyish boys whose fathers worked in the "Parofke" and tried to persuade them to help us in the war against the "Kavkazers".

We were afraid to hit each other on the Mill Street, so we let Yanke know that he would meet us not far from the "Parofke".

We gathered on the road that led to Virnyen's (Virion's) forest and then kept close to the "Parofke". In case of an emergency, we could flee there and find shelter.

The goyish lads and the few brave boys of the Mill Street armed themselves with stones and slings made of leather, with sticks, knives and whips; and we positioned ourselves by a hill to wait for the "Kavkazers".

Yanke actually knew all the arts in the field of warfare. He divided his army into two groups. One he sent through Kavkaz to the Vigon. He himself went through the Mill Street with his "main army" with loud fanfare.

We saw from a distance how Yanke and his group marched like real soldiers. They walked straight, firmly and confidently.

[Page 256]

When the "Kavkazers" were already very close to us, Yanke stepped a little away from his group and began to drum on a metal sheet with two sticks. This was the signal: the Kavkazers burst out of their ranks and ran with "Hurrah! Hurrah!"[4] – shouting towards us. Shortly after, the group from the Kavkaz side also arrived and surrounded us.

The goyish boys became frightened and fled. Only Yosl and I stayed, together with a few more bold boys from Mill Street, who had simply stayed with us out of fear of Yosl and me.

When the mothers from Mill Street saw the parade of Kavkaz brats, they realized that something was wrong. Noisily the mothers came running, scattered on the Vigon and drove away the Kavkaz rascals.

The worries I caused my mother simply began to take over. Not only did I hang out with wild brats who were thugs and window breakers, but also with those who persuaded me to steal money from my mother.

I became close friends with Sholem, Simkhe the feldsher's son. He persuaded me not only to steal money and buy nibbles with it, but also to skip the kheyder.

Sholem was an interesting boy. His father, Simkhe the feldsher, had already come to all the surrounding towns; to Shereshov, Skidel, Lune and Bodke. But he could not stay anywhere for long and came back to Krynki.

Since Sholem had been to so many small towns, he thought he was smarter and more understanding than other boys. I was very envious of Sholem because he had had a piece of bone operated out of his right leg. He used to pull up his pants, point to the wound and brag about his injury[5].

I too wanted to suffer in pain. So I bandaged my cheek and complained of toothache.

Mom used to keep her saved coins in the beaded purse that the converted soldier had given her. I found out that she hid this money in the straw mattress.

Every day I stole a coin from it.

[Page 257]

Sholem was already waiting for me. From the money we bought "kvas" (must) and "tshastes" (pastries). We used to walk down Sokolker Street to the field and have our feast there. Towards evening, when the children usually came out of school, we would go home.

When the Rabbi saw that I was missing from the kheyder, he sent a boy to inquire about me. At the same time, Mama noticed that she was missing money, and when she went to repay debts, the theft was discovered.

When I came home that evening, I could hardly bear Mama's warmth and love. Calmly she inquired what I had learned during the day. She gave me a meal to eat, which I loved very much; noodle pancakes with milk!

"Yosele, you must have studied hard today, just go out to the yard and play a little!" I did not like her excessive kindness. I went out, but I couldn't play because her calmness and over-caring worried me.

To sleep, Mama made up my sleeping bench for me. She had not done this since I went to school.

My first thought was to run away. For a while I pondered whether it would be better to run away or to stay.

As soon as I lay in the sleeping bench, Mom pulled up the covers from the foot end and began to beat me with a rod. She hit me with all her strength, screaming and crying.

"Are you going to steal again, hey? Are you going to skip school again, hey? Tell me, you thief, you scoundrel, will you go on doing it? Tell me!"

At that time, she vented all her anger and (wounded), bitter heart on me. At first I shouted, but when I kept silent, it enraged her even more. Exhausted, she sat down tiredly and broke out into a great wailing.

I did not go to the kheyder for a whole month. My body had been so whipped that I could not sit. During the time I spent at home, I rarely went outside.

I became more serious, thoughtful and silent

Translator's footnotes:

1. זכות= Skhus= merit. This expression is based on the belief that ancestors have accumulated moral or religious merit that can save a descendant from a misfortune or disaster. Therefore, there is also the supplication: "Zayn zkhus zol mir bayshteyn!", "May his merit stand by me!".
2. Parofke= The word is derived from "parove", meaning driven by steam.
3. shmekl= Penis
4. hura, hura (ouhrah, ouhrah): (Russian) battle cry
5. original "mum"= spoken "moom", defect; deformity

[Page 258]

Beginning of Adulthood

Krinker children wanted to imitate the adult boys, who were engaged in new "games". Every boy wanted to provoke the Cossacks just like the young men, run across the market and shout: "Doloy mamoderzhave- Down with autocracy!!"

Boys envied the lads who were led through the market with their hands tied behind them, surrounded by Cossacks or police constables.

A state of war prevailed in the shtetl. More than two people were not allowed to meet and talk to each other. Young men and girls used to go individually to the forest to hold a "skhodke".

Women sang a lullaby that the tsar's wife supposedly sang while cradling her son:

"Sleep, Alekseyki, my heir,
sleep, my noble person,
sleep, my only son,
sleep and do not cry.
When you grow older
you will be a great one,
you will have sums of money,
you will be the emperor of cities and villages,
one in the whole world!
The socialists will burst,
who think that they will be something.
They will shoot the anarchists,
so that not a single one of them will be left.
Now sleep, Alekseyki, my heir,
sleep and do not cry!"

In silence and in secret "skhodkes" the boys and girls sang:

"Brothers, we have concluded
by life and death a bond,
we stand in battle as comrades,
with red flags in our hands!
Should a bullet hit you, my loyal friend,
from the enemy, the hound,
I'll take you out of the flames
and heal with kisses your wounds!
You have been carried over all the roads,
which are drenched now with your blood.
You were carried into the hospital,
but after some minutes you died."

Since my uncles, Meyshke and Mair were anarchists, I used to sneak away to anarchist "skhodkes".

I became a useful boy for the big ones. I helped to carry proclamations and also hid them in our "kotakh"[1].

Often they instructed me to stand outside and let them know when police came.

[Page 259]

Because of the speeches I had heard about the "bourgeoisie," I began to harbor enmity against every factory owner. I was envious of my uncles and, like them, wanted to do something that harmed the rich and powerful.

I absolutely disliked the factory owner Paltyel. His appearance alone was enough for me to recognize in him the true bourgeois: a small man with an ample belly, with a black, neat beard, polished boots and beautiful clothes. His every movement testified to his saturation and fullness; and he walked and acted thoughtfully and decisively.

As soon as I saw him, I felt like throwing a stone at his head. Until now, I have no explanation as to why I never did. Paltyel's leather factory was on the other side of Mill Street.

Part of the factory jutted into a narrow alley and was adjacent to the Slonimer Shtibl, which was separated from the factory by a high fence.

I learned at the "Tshekhonovtser". In the winter evenings the children walked home from the kheyder with lanterns. The shortest way home was through the market, there it was always bustling and lit. However, I preferred to go through a small side alley where the factory was.

This way was dark, and I had to go through quite a few more streets; crossing "Bath" Street and a side walkway that led to "Yente's" Bes-Medresh.

Before I turned into the alley, I put stones in my pockets. Just as I entered the alley, I started running and throwing stones into the windows of the factory. I repeated this once a week.

Once, just as I was running through the alley, a huge figure came at me from a hiding place. I immediately ran back; but they started chasing me from the other side as well. I threw my lantern at the person, jumped onto the fence and from there down into the yard of the Slonimer Shtibl.

From the other side I could still hear shouting: "Stoy! Stoy! Karlaul, karlaul, razboynik! – Stop! Stop! Guard, Guard, Robber!"

I began to involve other boys for the struggle against the bourgeoisie. On Shabbat, after prayers, I gathered a few dozen of them in the Kavkazer Bes-Medresh and made speeches to them from the podium.

My words were in fact copies of the speeches I had heard from the "big ones."

[Page 260]

I often organized "skhodkes" in the woods for the boys. I wanted to get involved in any urban hustle and bustle. When goyim knocked down "pegs", I would stand next, singing along with the "Dubinushka"[2].

During a fire, I ran to help put it out. I pulled the water barrels out of the fire shed and filled the water into buckets. When people tried to revive the "volunteer fire department," I wrote a letter to Zeydke the locksmith explaining how useful boys could be in a fire.

Zeydke told (everyone) about my letter, and for a long time the young people made fun of me.

Zeydke the locksmith was one of the strong Jews in the shtetl; he was vicious, and therefore everyone was afraid of him. He used to supply and repair weapons for the revolutionary group; that is why he was held in high esteem by the "yatn". Zeydke had cold eyes, and his look alone instilled fear. He had several daughters and a son. He was not fond of his wife and daughters; all his love belonged to his only son.

We lived in his neighborhood, and I used to play with his boy.

However, I could not stand him. I didn't like that he was spoiled and that his father protected him with great care.

When my father came back from America, we moved to another apartment. However, the boy also came there to play with me. Since I didn't like him, I chased him away, whereupon he complained about me to his father.

Once a goy acquaintance, who usually brought flour to my uncle Dodye the baker, took me with his cart. He had to drive past the locksmith's house.

Zeydke saw me from the window of his establishment, came out, grabbed the horse by the bridle, pulled me down from the cart, and gave me such a fist blow that I bled profusely. The goy fled in fright.

Covered in blood, I ran home. Dad took me by the hand and we went to Zeydke.

When the latter saw us, he came out to us with a revolver and announced to my father that he would shoot if we did not leave.

[Page 261]

When Dad left for America for the second time, I now completely escaped all supervision and control. I began to make friends with older boys and often went with them to Sokolka and Bialystok. Many times days would go by without Mom knowing where I was.

At home I became calmer; I was a sensitive and romantic boy who took everything seriously and mindfully. I began to become thoughtful, and there were many things that were not clear to me and worried me.

We lived not far from the Jewish slaughterhouse; and I had watched a few times how the cattle was tied and thrown down and how immediately after the shechitaing the skin was peeled off and the warm meat was cut into pieces. After that I simply could not eat meat.

Once a murdered goy was found not far from the shtetl. At that time it was a holiday, and almost the whole town set out to look at the murder victim.

The dead man was lying in a pit, not far from the mountain where clay and sand were mined. He was lying on his side, with his arms spread out and his head crushed, and dried blood showed around a hole in his forehead.

Before night fell, a "sledovatl" (investigator) and a doctor arrived. The murdered man was transported with ropes to the top. Peasants brought tables and several wash tubs with boiling hot water outside. While some peasants shone lanterns, the dead man was dissected and examined in front of everyone in the field.

For a very long time I could no longer eat meat. Just seeing it made me nauseous and sick. The idea used to occur to me that the meat was from people.

Very early on, I began to understand the meaning of romance. It had no physical meaning for me, but I knew both from my books and from the conversations I picked up from older boys that romance had something to do with desire and thoughts of girls you wanted to be close to. I had no explanation for what that closeness meant.

[Page 262]

From the novels I only learned that romance was connected with longing and tenderness. But I did not know the meaning of both expressions. I could only guess what the grown-ups were doing. Next to us lived a family with many children. One of the girls used to sing love songs incessantly.

Her singing was soft, because in this way she wanted to express her "longing" even more strongly. I sat for hours at the window and listened to her. However, she only sang when she was at work; for example, darning or sewing.

While her hands were working, she usually held her head high and sang with half-closed eyes and a sigh:

> "Oh woe Mama, my head hurts,
> send for a doctor, or two;
> a doctor can cure man's sickness,
> but not me, Mama, and not the longing for the one I'm thinking of."

"Now get up, daughter. The sun is already rising;
if you don't follow your mother, it won't end well";

"Alas, Mama, you are right.
You are a mother who sees no evil in me.

There's a wind blowing across the open field;
over the open field.
Oh woe, Mama, I have gambled away my world;
I've gambled away my world;
I didn't ponder.
I thought it was day, in the end it's night.!"[3]

At that time I had a kind of childish romance with a girl of the same age. Her name was Perl and she was Alter Mukhalop's daughter.

Our love consisted of sitting on blocks together and singing songs.

[Page 263]

Later, I was targeted by Tanye, the daughter of Nokhem Anshel's younger daughter, Roshke. She went to the high school in Grodno. During the summer vacations she came home. At that time we lived in the neighborhood of her father, Shamshonovitsh, who owned a large leather factory.

However, Shamshonovitsh was no important personality. His father-in-law, Nokhem Anshel, did not have much pleasure with him. At one point, Shamshonovitsh had to hide outside Krynki because he had issued forged bills of exchange in the name of Grandpa Khayim Osher's brother, Yisroel Toivye.

Yisroel Toivye wanted to have him locked up. Shamshonovitsh, however, fled only after Nokhem Anshel declared with his sharp "r": "Let him go to hell; and no matter how great a fuss he makes, I will not help the crook with a penny!"

Shamshonvitsh's[4] wife Rokhke[4], however, tearfully urged Yisroel Toivye to help, and the latter made up for the damage with the counterfeit bills.

Tanye was much older than me. She already knew how to kiss and hug. She used to sing continuously the part of a Russian song: "akh zatshem eto notsh".[5] She used to snuggle up to me and stroke my head. When she left, I longed for her. But I did not see her again.

Translator's footnotes:

1. kotakh= A kind of small basement room near the oven.
2. Dubinushka= title of a Russian working song, see: https://www.youtube.com/watch?app=desktop&v=7eoZ5rsinfw
3. Possibly it is the well-known Yiddish song "Oy Mamenyu, Mamenyu, a gutinke nakht", which contains some text elements, respectively a whole verse of this song mentioned here and from which we learn a little more in terms of content. See https://ruthrubin.yivo.org/items/show/5037
4. His name and also that of "Roshke" are spelled differently here.
5. I think that he means the Russian song "Ах, зачем эта ночь" (Ah, zachem eta nochj) "Ah, why this night". See https://www.youtube.com/watch?app=desktop&v=0sZQLqlgGd8

[Page 264]

Dad Arrives and Leaves again

Two years had passed since Dad had left for a country thousands of miles away to establish an existence there. The sea prevented us from seeing each other physically, but the ships that passed it brought hot and longing letters. Every day I ran to Itke Bertsokovitsh and waited until she brought us the letters from the post office.

The postillion usually drove a "britshke", a two-wheeled carriage, through Sokolker Street and passed right by our house. We knew exactly at what hour his "droshky" would appear heading for the post office. Mom would then stand on the porch and watch as the postillion sat wedged in with his sword at his side, guarding the letter her husband had sent her from overseas.

Dad used to satisfy our longing by putting a photo of himself in almost every letter; portraits in various poses; sometimes standing, sometimes sitting; hands in the pockets of his pants, with the lap of his jacket folded over and a gold watch chain shining from his vest pocket.

The money which arrived almost every week from Dad, was always accompanied by a request to Mom to pack everything and come to him in the distant and foreign country.

My Grandma Rive, with whom we lived, read every letter from Dad and dictated the answers. She insisted that Mom would not leave her.

In the letters to Dad, Mom had to make it clear, at the behest of Grandma Rive, that she had no intention of ever leaving for the faraway land, that was separated from us by such a mysterious and evil sea.

Rive used to argue to Mom, "Who do you want to go to there? You have no one there; no brother, no sister, not a single relative. You will feel as miserable and displaced as I do. If Leyzer Hersch wants his wife and children with him, let him come to them!"

[Page 265]

That afternoon we, Grandma, me and Mama's sister Yente, Grandpa Yankel Bunim and my Aunt Sore, were standing on the Sokolker road waiting for the coachmen.

About a kilometer from the shtetl, Dad got off the cart. The wagoner sat on the coachman's seat, leaning on his whip, his head tilted to one side, watching as the women pushed each other so that they could get to Leyzer Hersh more quickly; to hug, kiss and cry.

At our house, dozens of people were already standing and waiting to receive the greetings of their near ones from the far country.

An old woman, who could not keep her head still because of her old age, just wanted to know if my father had brought her a greeting from her son. "What do you mean you haven't seen him? That can't be!" After all, her son had written to her that he lived next door to the Bes-Medresh!

But Dad didn't walk around for long dressed up as he was, with his gold watch on his chain, his foreign clothes and shoes that looked like the snouts of pigs. At some point we also stopped wondering about the strange words he used when he spoke. Everyone already knew that "no" means "no", and does not mean ordering the horse to trot off.

In addition to glasses, small pieces of tin-plates and strange cans, Dad also brought a few hundred rubles, which he had exchanged for American money in Bialystok.

We separated physically from Grandma and moved to Kavkaz, to Motl Spadviler. In the house next door, at Motl Tsholnes, Dad rented a cellar where he set up a small factory. He tanned the "shield" leather (what was cut from the sides and necks of animals) for making gaiters and boots.

A strange factory it was! With no windows or air, lit by gas lamps. It smelled damp and musty all the time, and from the walls the steam crept into your bones and settled on your lungs.

No worker wanted to come here, into this "sepulchral pit", although Dad, with a lot of patience, urgently asked for a co-worker. As a last choice, a skilled worker finally agreed to come to work for a few rubles.

A few months after Dad's arrival, his older brother also returned from America. This one, Abe Yudel, was completely different from Dad.

[Page 266]

He was very capable of managing business, but showed no willingness to do physical labor. In contrast, Papa was a hard worker who would have been lost and helpless without a factory. Since Abe Yudel had not yet decided on a business venture, Yankel Bunim came up with the idea that both of them could start a "shutfes", a business in partnership.

Abe Yudel said that he had no money (as a contribution). Grandpa, however, convinced my father that a shutfes would be worthwhile; Abe Yudel was a businessman, and with his expertise he would bring good luck and blessings, "you'll see the work will go well and the factory will grow!"

Mom didn't like the whole thing at all; she tried to dissuade Dad. However, it did not help; the shutfes was established. In order to enable him to "shield" tannery, Abe Yudel was taught the "tailor" craft.

This was a highly skilled job. Such a craftsman had to cut the fur through models made of sheet metal so that no waste remained. A bad "tailor" could even ruin a rich factory owner.

Abe Yudel did not just cause one harm.

Dad was a "folder"; this work consisted of making the fur thinner and finer with large knives.

My father was already at work at four o'clock in the morning; when Abe Yudel appeared, which was never earlier than 10 o'clock, Dad virtually began "the second day of work."

Abe Yudel was never in a hurry; quietly and calmly, he took off his jacket and set about "cutting". He was a bad "tailor", but an influential authority.

Abe Yudel usually worked for an hour or two. He was the businessman; bought the leather parts and outside conducted the negotiations with merchants who came from Warsaw as middlemen ("commissioner", as they were called) to buy finished leather for gaiters and boots.

The partnership did not last long. Mom did everything possible to annul it, with Grandma Rive supporting her. Grandpa Yankel Bunim, however, tried to placate her.

Finally, it was Abe Yudel who was fed up with the whole thing. He still hadn't brought in any money, and business was going from bad to worse. So what do you think had been bothering him?

[Page 267]

Without telling anyone, Abe Yudel stopped coming to the factory. Dad was worried; maybe Abe Yudel was sick? Perhaps, God forbid, some misfortune had happened at his home?

Dad couldn't bring himself to stop working, at least for half an hour, so he sent me to find out what had happened to Abe Yudel.

In his quiet, calm way, Abe Yudel instructed me to tell Dad that he was not coming back. A few days later it came out that Abe Yudel had set up his own little factory in the attic all the time he was a shutfes partner. The merchants he was supposed to bring to the shutfes for the purpose of doing business, he had brought to himself.

When he saw that his factory was doing well, he dissolved the partnership.

Mama ran to Grandpa Yankel Bunim, "he has brought us misfortune," she lamented. "He has taken all the merchants away from us!"

Grandpa assured her that he himself had not known about it. Abe Yudel consolidated his small factory and estimated a large loan on his leather and leather grease.[1]

Silently, he sold everything. Without telling anyone, he drove away. It was said that he had gone to Bialystok on business. Only after he had crossed the border was the secret revealed: Abe Yudel had gone back to America.

My father, too, was now struggling to get back to America. However, Grandma Rive and, of course, Mama, insisted that they would not allow it.

To cause dad to stay in Krynki, Grandma Rive set him up with a new partner; a relative of Grandpa Khayim Osher. The latter's nephew, Ayzik Krushenaner, had a son-in-law who came from Shishlevitsh.

This young man, Khayim Hershl, obviously could not find work. He was not a tanner, but tried to get a foothold in trade, which did not work.

Khayim Hershl's father-in-law, Ayzik, was one of the first leather manufacturers in Krynki. He, a great "balebos", lived in the village of "Krushenan" (Kruszyniany) all his life and ran large forest and grain businesses. Being very fond of his daughter, Rokhel, whom he had married to Khayim Hershl, he did everything to get the son-in-law a job.

[Page 268]

Grandma Rive connected my father with Khayim Hershl; and so a new shutfes was established.

Khayim Hershl contributed several hundred rubles to it and also provided a small factory; this, a dowry from his father-in-law, was attached to his house.

Dad first had to teach Khayim Hershl the craft of "folding".

The factory was far away from the city center. We therefore moved and now lived in the same house with Khayim Hershl. It was pleasant in the tannery, it had many windows, was airy and spacious. Khayim Hershl did not become a great craftsman; but he was hardworking.

In the beginning, the partnership business was a successful thing. Many traders came to buy, and the work there got a good reputation. The workers earned well and were always in high spirits. All day long the factory was filled with singing and laughter.

The gang of skilled workers was playing their "little jokes".

They would choose a victim and attach a piece of lit paper to his apron from behind with a broomstick. The victim was usually surrounded by flames, and when he ran away in fright to extinguish them, the workers burst out laughing.

Suddenly, my father fell ill with jaundice. Whatever was done, nothing helped him. He was given varying advice to get rid of the disease; one of them was that he should look into a brass bowl, ("mednitse"). The advisors assured him that the yellowing of the face would immediately disappear as soon as the yellow color of the face was reflected in the yellow brass bowl.

Finally, Dad had to go to Warsaw to see a doctor. The business was now completely run by Khayim Hershl.

I really hated Khayim Hershl. I couldn't stand his yellowish appearance, nor his disheveled blond hair sticking out in spiky strands, nor his small eyes that always shone cunningly.

For two months Papa stayed in Warsaw to cure his illness. When he came home, Khayim Hershl suddenly demanded that the balances in the books be checked, to find out how the business was going.

Since we had a common front door, I kept coming to Khayim Hershl's apartment.

[Page 269]

Both business partners sat there over the books. Dad was exhausted and overworked. From time to time he would come over to us, say something to Mom, and then go back inside to Khayim Hershl.

At home, Mama could no longer find peace. She went back and forth, wringing her hands, crying and lamenting; "woe, woe, the books show that we have to pay Khayim Hershl a lot of money. Oh, he will take everything from us, even the bedding!"

This went on for several days and nights. The mess was getting bigger and bigger. Since Papa could not find an explanation for all this, he asked the "tailor" David, "Reb Papa", to help him. David "Reb Papa" was not only the "tailor" in the factory; he had received his nickname because he had left the Krinker Talmud School and had become a "Bundist" agitator.

The workers had respect for him and his word was always respected. Both Papa and Khayim Hershl had great confidence in him. Dovid eventually discovered that during the time that Papa was not there, Khayim Hershl had falsified the balance sheets; he had increased the expenses and decreased the income. When Dovid found this out, my father fainted from his bench.

Immediately after this incident, the partners abandoned the factory. Obviously, however, Papa and Khayim Hershl still had to balance the books, so they did contract work in other factories in partnership.

With Yisroel Hertske, Nokhem Anshel's brother-in-law, we lived in harmony and frequently visited each other. Yisroel offered Dad an opportunity to work for him. Once, when I came out of school, I went to Yisroel Hertske's tannery to check on Papa. When I saw Khayim Hershl there, standing calmly as if the matter of the falsified numbers had not happened at all, I was seized with evil hatred against him.

I was a daring boy and tried to provoke him. I went to Dad and asked him, "How come you are still leading a partnership with a swindler?"

When Khayim Hershl heard this, he became enraged; he turned to me, "Hey, you little bitch! Snot nose! You impudent fellow! You! I'm going to spank you!"

[Page 270]

Khayim Hershl began to chase me. Like a cat, I jumped on a pile of leather skins, grabbed a piece of leather and started swinging it around. Khayim, however, was not deterred and immediately attacked me.

Holding the leather folded up with both hands, I began to thrash him. The blows fell on his face, on his hands, on his shoulders, on his belly. Whole scraps of skin were hanging off his face.

After that, Khayim Hershl was sick for several weeks. However, neither his wife nor he himself dared to bother me.

Not long after this event, we moved away from Khayim Hershl's apartment.

After giving up the partnership with Khayim Hershl, Dad could not bring himself to do anything.

The situation at home became difficult. The household had grown even more with the addition of two more children.

Dad said, "once and for all, I'm going to America, and no one is going to stop me!"

This time he was really persistent.

Even Grandma Rive could no longer stop him. Sunday morning, we accompanied Papa just as we had welcomed him before, to the Sokolker Road; to the path that would take him back to the vast, foreign land, separated from us by a mysterious and evil sea.

For the third time I was left without a father; but now there were four other children besides me. Friday night, after praying, Mom said to me, "Yosl, you are the oldest now, say the blessing prayers, make kiddush!"

Translator's footnote:

    1.   This sentence is ambiguous in my view. Previously, however, it had been said that, due to monopoly positions, merchants were forced to take out a loan from the merchant in order to be able to pay the high prices for the raw materials they needed

[Page 271]

The Dream-America

Whenever we were left at home without our father, we lived together with Grandma Rive. But this time, when Dad went away, we took an apartment just for us.

Mom didn't really want to live separately, but Grandma had already moved into the garret she had built on top of her son-in-law Dodye's house.

Apart from that, the household had also become bigger. Mom, however, made sure that our apartment was close to Grandma's.

Living separately did not mean that Grandma Rive gave up her supervision of us. Before we were even really awake, the house was already occupied by Rive's tall figure. She did not speak loudly, but her voice penetrated every corner of the apartment. She helped Mama with the younger children; she especially loved the little girl of the family.

My little sister was a "cry baby," as women used to say. Mom had four boys, and they all longed for a girl. However, my sister, Perl, was born weak. The boys, on the other hand, were active and restless; not to mention me.

Even my younger brother Mair was a very active boy, although he was the quietest and most attentive of all the children.

The little sister was spoiled and pampered. She was downright smothered with tenderness. Especially Grandma Rive was involved in this, for "she did not let the smallest speck of dust fall on her." The girl was so spoiled that she used to faint if one did not give in to her wishes.

I loved my little sister very much and looked after her a few times. Once Mom went out shopping and I stayed alone in the house with my sister.

She asked for something and I didn't give it to her fast enough. When she realized that she didn't get what she wanted right away, she fainted.

[Page 272]

At that very moment, Grandma Rive arrived. When Rive saw the "apple of her eye", her favorite grandchild lying so unconscious, she immediately tried to wake her up and shake her; but me she just wanted to kill. I saw that things were bad for me and I could not slip away from her, so I took the last chance and jumped out of the window.

Rive increased her vigilance over us. She was afraid that her daughter would leave her and go to her husband in the far country. She did everything she could to talk her daughter out of the idea of going to America.

Mama listened to her and gave father various excuses why she could not come to him.

Rive wanted father to return to the shtetl.

Quietly and without Mom's knowledge, I informed Dad about it in a letter.

I didn't even have to exaggerate, because Dad knew only too well how Grandma ruled over her children.

I was very angry with Grandma for keeping Mom away and talking her out of going. I began to resist and contradict her; she could not tolerate such insolence. The result was that her former affection for me dissolved into nothing

She just couldn't stand me anymore and told my mother to give up hope in me; "Let him go," she used to say, "you won't make a decent man out of him anyway!" Mom, however, very much wanted to make a "respectable" man out of me; she wanted me to behave more "balebatically" and also to achieve a higher education.

When a "gorodskoy utshileshtshe"[1] opened in the shtetl as a substitute for a gymnasium, Mama hired Baylke, the ladies tailor's daughter, who was a graduate of the Grodner Gymnasium, to prepare me for the communal "utshilishtshe".

Baylke took one ruble for a lesson. But this did not stop Mama from making sure that I received two lessons a week.

The money was, however, thrown out; although I really wanted to make it to the "gorodskoy utshileshtshe", not to learn there, but because I had a desire for the blue uniform with the shiny crest on the little hat. I really lusted after dressing up in this flashy attire.

[Page 273]

Maybe I would have made it through the (entrance) exam, but Grandma Rive interfered. She began to make it clear to my mother that my studying would lead to absolutely nothing.

Apparently, my teacher Baylke saw it that way too, because she let Mom know that she would have to tighten her belt if she still insisted that I get into the "gorodskoy utshileshtshe".

In general, I didn't want to study anymore; I had my mind set on going to America. However much Mom resisted, she finally realized that it would be better for both of us to send me to Dad.

There were important reasons why Mom had to let me go. Not only did I no longer feel like preparing for the "gorodskoy utshilishtshe", but I also generally did not want to go to the kheyder.

But letting such a wild boy like me hang around was dangerous. In fact, I was already making friends with grown-up boys, but at home I was causing worry and suffering.

I lost my fear of punishment and began to defy Grandma Rive and Grandpa Yankel Bunim.

Mom was afraid that my behavior would make me a person without morals. Moreover, I had it in for my third brother Velvel. I tormented him mercilessly. For every little thing I gave him a severe beating; I literally caused him hell.

Velvel was an interesting boy. He was also restless and hot-tempered, completely different from my second brother Mair, who was quiet and obedient and liked to learn. The teachers "fought" over him; they wanted to keep him in the schools without paying school fees, simply as an example for other children. He had an extraordinary mind; and everyone liked him for his modesty and quietness.

Velvel didn't have much desire to learn. He was always playing games, but he wasn't as wild as I was. He liked only one game; "Salesmen and Customers". Other children's games did not interest him. He didn't chase along in "Tshort"[2] or sled in the winter; he just wanted to have a "store".

[Page 274]

He kneaded himself different kinds of "goods" from clay, put them on a small box and traded with them. His pockets were constantly stuffed with porcelain, his symbol of money.

However small Velvel was, he understood that a salesman had to be neatly and cleanly dressed; and so he used to pull about ten ties on top of each other, plus two or three dress shirts and as many collars. I just couldn't stand it!

I could not bear this rigor and fastidious cleanliness. Velvel was constantly washing himself and brushing off his clothes. As soon as I saw that, I went wild. In him, I saw the rich and powerful budding, in a word; the "bourgeois!" (Now Velvel is a big retailer in Newark, New Jersey).

Mom was very worried because I kept beating Velvel. She therefore began to send Dad pleading requests to take me to him as soon as possible; if not, I would beat the boy to death.

My camaraderie with the adult boys also became a danger. Mom was afraid that I would ally myself with what she jokingly called the " akharistn un tsitsilistn"[3].

(After all), this was already happening in our family; boys who were still very young were involved in the circles of "brothers and sisters." In general, Krinker boys began their revolutionary activity in very early youth.

But the most important reason was that Mom knew it would be easier for her to break away from her mother if I were already in America. In the correspondence, Dad, who usually did not have a firm opinion, insisted that Mom come to him. He was very firm in letting us know that he would not return to Krynki.

A big part in this firm decision was played by Grandpa Yankel Bunim. He advised my father not to be influenced by sentimentalities and by Grandma Rive's objections. My very wise Grandpa Yankel Bunim knew that Dad would succeed if he remained firm.

Apparently it was also my father's reasoning that it would be easier to get my Mom over to him if I was with him first.

Right after Passover, in a registered letter, half a ship's ticket arrived for me!

Translator's footnotes:

1.   A kind of high school ; In the following text, this term, which obviously originates from Russian, is spelled differently
2.   Tshort= An old boys game with sticks where speed and skill are important, it is explained beforehand in the book
3.   I assume that these were nicknames for "anarchists and socialists".

[Page 275]

Yosl, 10 years old, before going to America

[Page 276]

Serious Comrades

The few months before leaving for America, I was burning with impatience. It constantly seemed to me that time was not passing fast enough and I wished that the day would not last long. Early in the morning I was already waiting for the night.

In the last months I became calmer and more relaxed. The approach of the great change in my life filled me with deep seriousness.

I stopped playing pranks and committing wild, counterproductive acts that only frightened other people and didn't earn me much affection from them.

So I loved to cause confusion and scare the girls in Pinke the Shames' son's house.

Pinke the Shames' daughters, Itke and Mashe, had a small tailoring workshop. My aunt Sore was apprenticed there.

When I saw the girls engrossed in their work, I would rush in screaming, wild, disheveled and seemingly quite out of breath, "It's on fire!"

The girls would immediately tear themselves away from their work and run to the door, terrified; "Where is the fire? Where?!"

"There's a fire at Yampele's!", I blurted out.

With a "Go to the devil!" they used to chase after me; but I escaped laughing

It was strange that I repeated this prank a few times, but each time the girls were frightened again.

I used to play strange jokes on strangers who came to the shtetl. When the carters dropped their passengers off at the market, they would stand there with their cloth sacks over their shoulders "as if being dropped in nowhere by a trickster".

Lost, they looked around. When, as usual, they had already circled the area and had come to terms with the geographical location, they inquired about the people they were going to visit.

[Page 277]

When I stood by, I offered to show people the way to their relatives or friends. With their cloth sack, they trailed behind me to the end of the shtetl; for what I showed was- the municipal bathhouse.

Shortly before my departure, I broke away from my childhood comrades and no longer met with them. I only kept in touch with Sholem, the son of Simkhe, the Barber Surgeon. I became friendly with adult boys who were perhaps six or eight years older than me.

I was particularly close friends with one fellow who was about eighteen years old.

He, a Sokolker, had opened a barbershop in Krynki in the hotel of Grandpa Yankel Bunim's nephew, Itshe "Lya". In his barbershop the intellectuals and aristocrats of the shtetl had their hair cut and were shaved.

This young man kept himself very clean; every thing was neatly arranged with him. The salon was tidy and airy. Often during the day he sprayed a perfume in the salon.

He was a tailor- but with a physical handicap; his right foot was crippled, and when he walked he tried to compensate for his disability with his healthy left foot. This acted as if the healthy foot wanted to overtake the sick one and flee from it.

We got to know each other in Itshe "Lya's" house, where I was already almost part of the family. Itshe the Kaliker (Cripple) considered himself a "Bundist", which did not stop him from scurrying around the police chief commissioner, who was his customer, with great pleasure.

I liked the way Itshe did his work. I made myself useful and often soaped up the customers. He showed me how to shave and cut. Itshe took his work very seriously. When he shaved someone, he stepped back a little so as not to breathe in the customer's face.

To learn how to shave people, I chose "mental patients". However, I was not successful with it. My first victim was Motke; at my very first movement the razor got stuck in his cheek! Motke jumped up with such ferocity, that he pulled the chair behind him. Who knows what would have happened if I had not fled! Itshke the Kaliker entrusted everything to me. He considered me a friend of the same age, so I felt a strong bond with him.

[Page 278]

Itshke was very much in love with a girl and consulted with me about what he should do to approach her. The girl was a tall dark-haired beauty and came from the neighboring town of Shishlovitsh. Her brother, Fishl Gets, worked in a tannery and had brought his whole family to Krynki.

Itshke had met the girl through her brother Fishl, who was also a "Bundist". He had immediately confided in me that he liked the girl.

I advised him to write a letter. He bought a book with sample letters, and I brought the girl "fiery love letters" freshly copied from the book. Even then I could compose poems and wrote rhymes full of love. Itshke had me bring them to the girl right away.

Itshke's love inspired me a little, and so I also had a romance. However, I did not know what it all meant.

I only understood that a romantic relationship had to be between a boy and a girl.

My romance came about in a strange way. Two orphans, a brother with his sister, had come from Bialystok to stay with relatives; these were respected "Kapitses" from the "Zhabe" Alley[1]. The boy had still been a thief in Bialystok and boasted that he was the most well-bred of the "Maravikhers".

The girl Frumke was exceptionally beautiful and a few years older than me. I don't remember how I introduced myself to her. But I still remember what an impression it made on me that Frumke "formally addressed" me! She was the very first one to call me "Sie"; and this brought about a tremendous change in me. I suddenly felt big, grown-up and very important.

I actually made friends with the big ones, but I knew very well, that I was still a brat.

[Page 279]

An adult had quite special characteristics: one of them was the hair under the arm, which showed on the older boys when they rolled up their sleeves from their shirts. The second one was that you were called "Sie".

Frumke rose in my esteem, as I was already a "Sie" for her.

Frumke could not read and write. I became her teacher; we used to go to the field, I sang songs for her and told her bizarre stories.

It gave me special pleasure to see her cry when I sang the song, "I have a little boy" by Morris Rozenfeld.

She herself also knew many songs that the Bialystok good-for-nothings sang. She gladly sang some of them to me. One of her favorite songs was a gypsy love song. She brought it to Krynki, and through her it became popular.

She sang it with a particularly sad undertone. The melody and the words told of a gypsy's love and longing. Her face always became very serious before she sang wistfully:

> "The sky, a pale one without a star,
> the sun had just gone down;
> There flew a melody so softly
> as if it rose from the lawn.
>
> I go by the sound through the wood,
> which is covered with thick twigs,
> there stands a white linen tent,
> a small gypsy tent.
>
> But no one is inside the tent,
> they have all gone to anywhere,
> only a gypsy woman sits lonely,
> and sings a sad song to me.

Her hair is tossed on her shoulder,
her head is leaning against a bush,
her face is burned by the sun,
and with longing quivers her chest."

[Page 280]

My aunt Sore, who was already a revolutionary and a Bundist at that time, could not stand the fact that I was dating a girl from the "Zhabe" Alley, a relative of the "Kapitses".

She set out to expose the girl for hanging out with a "little boy who was still wet behind the ears, a little rascal".

During the summer before the trip to America, I became friends with Avrohem (Abraham) Shmuel Zuts, the main leader of the "Bund". Abraham Shmuel, the son of Moyshe Aharon the Katsev (Butcher), was an interesting character.

In his very early youth, his eyesight weakened. During the revolution he was beaten so severely in the Grodner prison that he almost went blind.

He could hardly see. In his house was the shtetl's library, and in the movement he was known as "Eternal Light".

He was a close friend of Borekh Vladek[2], and when Vladek visited Europe in 1936; he together with his brother, the poet Daniel Tsharny, went specially to Krynki to visit him.

Abraham Shmuel brought me books, and I often came to his home, down on the Shishlovitser Street, near the cemetery. He used to teach me politics, explaining the meaning of socialism and the goal of the poor and oppressed to build a world where justice and joy reign. Abraham Shmuel had a great influence on me. Through him, I learned for the first time in a very concrete way what socialism meant.

In my childhood imagination it seemed to me like a doctrine of justice; I particularly internalized one of his phrases, it accompanied me constantly and later shaped my activities as an adult:

"With the pious you must first die to arrive in paradise, but we want to create a paradise already for the living!"

My frequent walks with Abraham Shmuel gave me importance and prestige among the boys who were my previous friends.

One evening I was walking with Abraham Shmuel in the market. By chance we passed close to Goland's wine store.

There the "officials and authorities" of the city used to spend their evenings.

[Page 281]

I had linked arms with Abraham Shmuel.

All of a sudden I saw the police chief come out of Goland's store and hastily approach us. First he grabbed me and pushed me away from Abraham Shmuel. Furious, he began to pat down his pockets; when he was done with him, he searched me.

This scene and the search, filled me with a strange wild joy; I began to feel exalted and was suddenly adult, respected and important in my eyes.

Translator's footnotes:

> 1.　We learned more about the "Kapitses" and the "Zhabe (Frog) Alley" on page 166 of this book
> 2.　Borekh Nakhmen Vladek-Tsharny alias Vladeck Charney

[Page 282]

Without Farewell

It didn't bother Mom that I began to behave like an adult. On the contrary, she liked that I had become quiet and "well-mannered". However, she worried because I had begun to befriend Khaykel Muts, my Uncle Mair's comrade. Mama did not think he was a decent person.

Grandma Rive was enraged every time she was told that I had been seen walking with Khaykel to the "Profitke". Whether Grandma had incited my Mama, or whether Mama alone had decided to tear apart my friendship with Khaykel, I do not know. One evening, when I was waiting for him on Sokolker Street next to the bridge by the gentile houses, Khaykel came up to me without a word and started to wallop me.

I was less unsettled by the blows than by the pain that Khaykel, whom I loved and revered, and for whom I felt respect, since he had been my older comrade and, moreover, a friend of my Uncle Mair, beat me for no reason. Actually, I wanted to give it back to him; however, I ran away instead.

That night, I lay there in agitation and felt very hurt. I shrank and became tiny like the little finger. My view of already considering myself a "big boy" burst. No, I was still a little boy, because if Khaykel had considered me an adult, he would have talked to me, explained everything to me and demanded an answer from me.

What had happened filled me with great sadness. I changed completely and began to pester Mama to send me to America even faster.

Mama would not let me go alone. Besides, I had only half a ship's ticket so far. But it just happened that my Aunt Etel was preparing for a crossing to America and promised my mother to take me with her.

Aunt Etel, a fierce egomaniac, used to exploit all relatives (for her advantage and) for her pleasure. She knew no leniency for her parents and relatives, not even for her husband and children.

[Page 283]

To keep everyone chained to her, she used to pretend to be sick. She could stay in bed for weeks and be waited on. She was lazy; never once did she wash the dishes. She always used to boss around those who let themselves become slaves as a result of their pity for her and her feigned illnesses.

Her husband, Abe Yudel, was devoted and very loyal to her. She took advantage of this by extinguishing every spark of his own will and independence.

Both families knew Etel very well. Her parents, who came from the circle of the very "balebatic" families of the town, ran the store "Brom", which was located at the annex, or passageway between both sides of the market. Her father Yosl was a Jewish scholar; both he and his wife were very energetic people.

They had three or four daughters and one son. All the daughters celebrated weddings, as they were reserved for distinguished young people. One son-in-law, Levin, spoke several languages. He was the only one in the shtetl who sold stationery and books; but also lent books for reading.

A second son-in-law, Hebrew teacher Einshtein, was the main leader of the Zionist movement in Krynki and a respected member of the community's town council.

All of Aunt Etel's sisters were hardworking and energetic women. It may be that Etel would not have sunk into such laziness and torpor if she had had a man with more assertiveness than my uncle exhibited.

A joke circulated in the family about Uncle Abe Yudel's submissiveness to his wife.

He used to clean up, cook and shop for her. Since she was always in bed, he wanted to prove his devotion to her.

She once feigned an attempt to get out of bed to prepare food for herself. My uncle, however, did not want her to exert herself and said to her, "lie still, Etelke, I will get it for you!"

He meant, of course, "make dinner." But in the family this became a joke with an ambiguous innuendo.

Etel's promise to take me with her was worthless. Her heart would not allow her to do anyone a favor.

[Page 284]

Suddenly she let it be known that she was leaving. The preparations for my trip were not yet complete and she refused to wait any longer until I was also ready. However, she promised to wait for me in Antwerp.

My naïve Mom! I told her right then that Etel would not wait for me in Antwerp; if she did not wait for me in Krynki, I argued to Mama, she would certainly not wait for me in a foreign country.

Mama, however, was confident.

The preparations for departure were now hasty. Mom went with me to Bialystok to meet an agent who would guide me across the border. She also wanted to have her eyes examined by the famous ophthalmologist Pines.

I was to go to Krynki afterwards to say goodbye to my own family, close ones, comrades, friends, wider family and the streets of the wonderful shtetl where I lived, was brought up and frolicked.

Yente, my mother's sister, lived in a shtetl not far from Bialystok, and Mama told me to say goodbye to her sister. She herself went back to Krynki. She could no longer stay in Bialystok because she had left her younger children at home.

After about a day and a night on the cart, I saw my Aunt Yente again. I was raised with her and she is like a sister to me.

The shtetl where Yente's husband had taken her after the wedding is gray and muddy.

The small store connected to the apartment stands there in tears, protruding into the mud that lies swollen on the market.

Next to the shop stand the wheels of a wagon sunk into the mud, on which unplaned boards are lying. A Jew in a corduroy caftan stands leaning against the boards, chewing a straw and staring dully into space.

Simplicity and rottenness waft from Aunt Yente's shop. From all corners, from the sacks of flour and sugar and from the half-empty shelves, exhaustion, the smell of kerosene and desolate melancholy strike one. Only when the little bell that hangs by the entrance door of the store begins to ring does the rusty torpor stir a little.

The dull sound of the bell sent my aunt out to greet me.

[Page 285]

She carried her pregnant belly and sleepy steps towards me. It seemed to touch her very little that I had come and that I was going far away across the sea. Neither of us seemed to have understood that I was visiting her to take with me the sight of Yente's figure, which I would never see again.

I don't remember how long I was in the Narev shtetl. What I do remember, however, is the joy I felt when I sat down on the cart that was to take me back to Bialystok.

There was a telegram waiting in Bialystok; Mama let me know that I was not to go to Krynki, but she would come to Bialystok. Mama brought the news that Etel's parents had received a message from her, according to which she was already on the ship. Etel had made fools of us again.

The fact that Etel was on her way to America completely changed the arrangements for my trip. Mom suggested that I should go back to Krynki and wait until they could send me with someone who was also going to America.

I did not want to go to Krynki; I was afraid that Mama would delay the trip. I threatened her that I would run away and never be heard from again if I did not travel immediately. Mama knew that I would indeed do this.

I stayed in Bialystok; I did not say goodbye to anyone in Krynki; I missed the opportunity to take a last look at my family; my grandpas and grandmas, to whom I had caused so much pain, sorrow and suffering; my brothers and sisters, my aunts, uncles, cousins, nieces and nephews; my comrades with whom I had played, made mischief and fought; the stones from the pavement; at all that and all those for whom I later longed so painfully.

Mom told Dad about the whole mess by telegraph. He got me a whole ship's ticket and let it be known that he had had to enter me at a higher age.

The period in Bialystok was a real punishment for me and Mom. She wanted me to leave as early as possible, because the children at home did not give her any peace, they were alone and she felt as if she had abandoned them.

Besides, I kept her in fear all the time;

[Page 286]

I couldn't sit still and drifted around in every corner of Bialystok.

She trembled that I might have an accident.

The last day had come; at night I would go to Grajewo, where the agent would meet me and lead me across the border.

I went to say goodbye to all my acquaintances and relatives in Bialystok. I came to the hostel where the Krinkers were stopping, and there I met Khaykel Muts. I urged him to tell me the reason why he had beaten me. He, however, did not feel like it.

But I did not let up: "You will not see me again, and I will not have peace if you do not tell me why you hit me!"

He hesitated for a while, then revealed it.

My mother had come to punish him for consorting with me. She had said (about me), "he is a young lad, he will blab something to the police one day!"

As a result, Khaykel decided to turn his back on me. The best way out was to beat me up; it seemed to him a good way to get rid of me.

When I learned this, I almost choked with anger at my mother. As soon as I had the papers, I wanted to run away from her without saying goodbye.

When I met Mama, I was very irritated; she did not understand what demon had gotten into me.

When the hackney cab that was to take us to the station arrived, I demanded that she not accompany me.

She pushed me into the hackney with fury and held me angrily, for she was afraid I would jump off and run away.

When we arrived at the station, I grabbed the small basket and ran to the front gate.

For a while she ran after me. But just before the gate that separated the station building from the tracks, she stopped.

Silently and with folded hands, she watched as I tore open the iron door of the entrance gate.

For a brief moment, I looked around; Mom stood frozen, her eyes glued to my back, which was moving farther and farther away to be engulfed by the night and the smoke billowing from the chimney of the steam locomotive.

[Page 287]

"Mother" Yente, Uncle Osher and their children

[Page 288]

To the New, Strange World

Even a train cannot leave the place where it stands quietly; it must give a jolt by force. Even a train leaves with longing those who have come to say goodbye to it. But I did not give myself a jolt; I virtually went up in smoke.

I left my mother standing dejectedly on the other side of the entrance to the Bialystok train station. Later she told me that she stood there for a long time, confused, looking into the void; she could no longer find the thread that connected the two of us.

She searched for a similarity between me and each of her family members and could not locate any figure that resembled me. "Incited dogs pull his body," she concluded.

The pain about a child, actually a child, going out into the wide world alone and without supervision did not bother Mom. She was not crying because her child left her, but out of self-pity; why had she been punished by having such a child.

I too was not bothered by the fact that Mom had stopped at the Bialystok train station, broken and confused. Instead of sorrow and pain, longing and love, an anger burned in me toward her for turning Khaykel Muts against me.

My poor Mom, she wanted to protect me; she wanted me to walk in ways that fit a "balebatic" boy. But instead, she aroused anger and hatred in me.

My mother, peace be upon her, possessed the great virtue of not falling into hysteria; outwardly she could remain calm and composed. She was completely different from my father, peace be upon him, who was heated and quick-tempered. She could still remain calm when there was commotion around her, giving the impression that anger and rage did not bother her.

When she saw that the anger was growing and she could not calm it down, she would withdraw and let the irascible person come to his senses and cool down on his own.

[Page 289]

On the way to the station she paid absolutely no attention to my anger and rage. Calmly and composedly she instructed me how to behave towards the agent in Grajewo and calmly she put the envelope with all the papers into a bag, telling me where to go in Antwerp for my ship ticket that Papa had gotten for me; after all, because Aunt Etel had left without me, half the ship's ticket had to be exchanged for a whole one.

At dawn the train arrived in Grajewo. The city was still asleep. The passengers, still disheveled and exhausted, dragged themselves, carelessly dressed, down the stairs of the train with their suitcases. In seconds the crowd had dispersed; it parted like torn limbs from a body; and each individual limb the coachmen tried to capture for themselves.

My knock on the agent's door shattered the silence on the other side. Footsteps were heard, walking with unwillingness; and a harsh voice wanted to know angrily:

"Who's there?"

The watchword was, "The hunchback fell down!"

An evil Jewess with a crooked face hastily pulled me into the house and quickly locked the door. Hopscotching a bit, she ordered me to follow her. In a corner of the third room, she yanked open a door that was built into the floor and instructed me to descend the stairs. A faint flame and several dozen strained and frightened eyes welcomed me.

The cellar was rusted and lay there in melancholy, no bright ray found its way in there. The few iron black beds looked like leftover rotten teeth in an empty mouth.

On the beds some people lay awake with frightened faces and widened eyes. The basket in my hand reassured them; it was the assurance that a new roommate had arrived, not a gendarme.

[Page 290]

After about an hour, a swaying Jewish woman with a huge belly, which showed under her dress like risen dough, carried in a jug of boiled water and black bread on a dirty tray.

After breakfast, she instructed three residents of the basement to get dressed and follow her.

The agent did not operate the smuggling across the border on foot. She provided her clients with false passports and let them pass by train the short distance from Grajewo to Proskin (Prostken), which was already on the other side of the border.

My name on the passport would be "Itshke Lavende".

With great doggedness, the Jewish woman instructed me to constantly repeat (the name and reason for my trip): "Itshke Lavende, you are going to Germany to get well. Do not forget it! Don't forget it! Itshke Lavende! Itshke Lavende! Don't be frightened, answer immediately; you are going to Germany to get well!"

At dawn of the third day, after breakfast of hot water and black bread, the Jewess led me outside.

I had not seen daylight for over two days. The morning light made me squint my eyes.

The agent did not allow (me to get used to the light first) to drive away the blindness. In great haste, she nudged me to walk faster.

A walk of several minutes brought us to a small side street where a coachman let us know with a wave of his hand that we should hurry to him.

In the station we were met by a confident and calm woman; she was very neatly dressed and behaved with dignity and composure.

"That's your mother, don't forget it," the agent told me. Quick as an arrow from a bow the minutes passed; "there, where you see the white stones, there is the border!"

Beyond the white stones a different world is beginning already. The few white stones separated two worlds! It is not more than a few white stones, but neat little houses with red and green colored roofs come towards you; and people – others, dressed up, they even move a little differently; yet there are only a few white stones in between!

My "Mom" led me to a house that was just down by the railroad. She pointed to a wooden building, "there is the bathroom".

In the "bath" we felt like a flock of scratchy sheep, as the people on the other side of the white stones treated us with such disgust and anger.

[Page 291]

Quite a few people walked around with white jackets and treated the border crossers with terrible disgust.

With every movement they let it be known, brutally and in all clarity, that they were disgusted and nauseated by all those people; but even those who wore gloves dragged the clothes we had to take off with two fingers.

In the "bath" the cold bit into the naked bodies; the austerity and contempt instilled terror in the "unfortunate lucky ones"; yet they were willing to endure all the shame to move on over stretches of land separated and divided by white stones and over raging waves.

After the procedure in the "bath" was over, Germans with big bellies, blue uniforms with conspicuous brass buttons, hats "with two cap visors" or soldier's caps and small swords on the sides began to chase us into the wagons.

They were wagons for transporting cattle. One had to sit on the floor; near the roof was a small opening that served as a kind of ventilator. Such a wagon was crammed with over fifty men and women and their luggage; there was not even enough room to stand, the people lay huddled together; it was impossible for them to stretch out their legs.

But who was bothered by the narrowness and discomfort? Nobody! Almost all of them were young boys and girls. Their songs and laughter drowned out the rattle of the train wheels. They all liked each other and felt close to each other; the joy spread from one to another and made the narrowness fade into oblivion.

At the station, something flew into my eye. When we arrived in Berlin, the eye was already completely swollen shut. At a Berlin train station, waiting for the trains that would take you to the various port cities, I fell asleep in my pain.

A strong shove in the stomach woke me up: a huge German gendarme stood over me and shoved me in the side and stomach with the tip of his boot: "Get up, you little Jew!" he shouted at my body, which was writhing in pain. German men and women stood by and laughed.

The German gendarme lifted me up by the collar with brutality, pushed me and threw me onto the platform where a train was standing.

[Page 292]

The closer the train came to Antwerp, the more I was paralyzed by the fear that they would not let me go to America because of my eyes. I moved into a corner and cried. A young fellow took pity on me. He lifted my eyelid and cleaned it with the tip of his tongue. By the time we arrived in Antwerp, the eye was almost healthy.

How the immigrants were sorted into the Antwerp hotels, I don't know. I only remember being led along the streets with other people. Everything spun and blurred before my eyes; the noise, the harsh lighting, and the roar of the streetcars. Each of us was tired and exhausted and just wanted to rest.

However, it was not granted to me to come to rest; not even in the strange, distant city and the unknown country. When we arrived in Antwerp, a vicious Jew with only one eye took over our leadership, speaking in a kind of Jewish German.

His first task was to instruct the immigrants in the use of the "privy" so that everyone would remember to keep the "privy" clean and not to place themselves in front of it (in an unsanitary manner). He illustrated this by grabbing my cap and wiping the seat with it.

I snatched my cap out of his hands and started brushing it over his face. He threw a tantrum and started hitting me. It became a scandal. Several young boys stood by me, and this had such an effect that the first night in Antwerp ended with brawls.

The owner came running, the fracas was stopped; but during the week in Antwerp there was really no shortage of trouble for me.

What is time? When something becomes unnecessary and a burden and you want to run away from it, time can become a great punishment and torment.

The week in Antwerp kept me in anxiety and impatience. A young fellow, who had been staying in the Antwerp hotel for some time due to not being allowed on the ship because he first had to cure his trachoma (Chlamydia trachomatis), accompanied me for the week. He led me to the shipping company to get my ship's ticket and became my guide in general.

[Page 293]

Antwerp, however, terrified me and choked me with fear. Those huge horses and the dogs harnessed to the wagons did not let me rest.

When I saw a "Negro" for the first time in my life, I panicked.

On an Antwerp street, a black figure suddenly appeared in front of my face. I was startled; for it was coming right toward me. In contrast to its blackness, a white shirt stood out, a white collar and a white tie. I began to scream. The figure laughed it off, and from its mouth flashed teeth as white as sugar.

Our ship packed itself on a Shabbat morning full of noise, crying, with women, children, elders and a bustling youth. We got the ship moving with our singing, our joy and our excitement. Only when the shore was already no longer visible to us did we begin to settle into our floating home.

The passengers of the tween deck were divided on both sides of the ship. On one side were the women with their children and on the other side the men. The two divided crowds were not allowed to visit each other. If you wanted to cross over to the other side of the deck, where the women were, you either had to bribe a sailor or sneak over.

Passengers of the same sex were quartered in one cabin each. This was a huge cellar right next to the cargo hold. The only furniture in the cellar were iron beds, forged together in length and height. Three beds were placed on top of each other, and the more able and skilled people took the very top beds.

They had an advantage because those on the lower beds had to endure a lot from their upper neighbors as soon as they became seasick. The stone floor made the feet freeze, even through the shoes.

Both the toilet and the water were on the deck, and so the sick used to fill teapots with water and keep them beside them. Food was served on a huge wooden table, around which were long wooden benches attached to iron pipes.

Food was procured in a feeding trough, just as for animals. A sailor brought the trough and threw the food (on tin plates) with a big wooden cooking spoon. Every day there was the same food:

[Page 294]

A piece of herring in dirty soup, mashed potatoes, and sometimes a piece of black meat that looked like it had been rolled in mud.

The sailors were truly vicious men. They treated the passengers as if they were arrested or prisoners from an enemy country.

One sailor even committed murder.

A woman from Warsaw, who was traveling with her two children to join her husband in New York, had fallen ill. She sat down on the stairs leading down to the cabin. The sailor came running, but instead of asking her to let him pass, he gave her a shove with his foot. She hit and suffered a fractured skull.

The sea became her grave.

I was among the tiny minority of passengers who did not suffer from seasickness. I went around the sick and served them. My willingness to help everyone in the cabin brought me close to a Jew from Odessa who was traveling with his son to (his other) children. This Jew was a very daring man and stood up against all injustice.

Once he stood up for me, almost causing a panic.

I had asked for a little more food, whereupon the sailor poured out a whole spoonful of hot food on me. I began to throw my tinware at him. He chased off to catch me, but the Jew from Odessa stopped him. There was a brawl and a commotion. Fortunately, an older man came along and stopped the turmoil.

Twenty-three days the steerage passengers suffered in this prison. When we saw the shore of America, our joy was not only to have arrived in the new land, but also to know that we would now be delivered from this ship.

Each of us was now filled with deep seriousness; each was absorbed in his own thoughts. We arrived to stand before a court.

Would we meet with favor? Would everything go smoothly? Everyone knew that the "Kesl Gardn"[1] was known as "the island of tears".

[Page 295]

Under the heavy burden of silence everyone dragged himself with his bundle to the avenues of "Kesl Gardn". Employees stood quietly and gave instructions in dozens of languages. People lined up one after the other. People in white coats and jackets opened eyelids and drew a sign with chalk on the jackets of the dispatched.

I walk behind the Jew from Odessa and his boy; I see how they paint the sign on him and he looks at me full of concern. I want to go to him.

An employee blocks my way and tells me to go upstairs. The stairs lead me into a cage made of coarse wire.

A fat man with a shiny face holds a young girl and tortures her with questions. She wrestles with him. He says sharply to her, "you are telling lies!"

An aged, tired person with a gray face calls out my name. He asks calmly, exhausted, "will you recognize your father?"

"Yes, there he is!"

Across the street I see Dad, he's in a "wire cage" too. "Go ahead, hug your dad!"

I bend down to the basket; the girl is still wrestling with the fat man. Suddenly he lets go of her, she rushes out screaming, grabs her head and falls down.

"What about her?" "She was detained, she told lies," says from the side the tired voice of a tormented person.

Dad is already holding my basket. He leads me to the asphalt paths of the avenues; I am chased by the screaming of the girl, she lies stretched out, her face becomes more and more yellow and sunken.

Joy pulsates around me and beside me, people hold each other, nestle together, talk with understanding and love. The buildings Papa has led me out of are moving farther and farther away.

"The ship," Dad says to me, "is about to take us to New York!"

Translator's footnote:

1.   kesl gardn= the Yiddish pronunciation of Castle Garden in New York, at the southern tip of Manhattan, which served to house immigrants until about 1891. In fact, however, Yosl Cohen arrived at Ellis Island on the ship "Finland" on 1 December 1911.

LAST NAME INDEX

APPENDICES

Name Glossary

Note from Beate and Susan:

In the late 19th and early 20th centuries, it was common among the Jewish population in Krynki to call people by their first names or Yiddish nick-names, the spellings of which varied. The surname often played a lesser role, and could be changed, or could also be spelled differently at different times. Often, instead of a surname, a nickname was given, which was "passed down," so to speak; or the child was named after the name of his father, or someone he had been raised by, e.g. "Khayim-Osher's." Marriages not infrequently took place within the kinship.

At some point, one can get the impression that "in Krynki everyone was a little bit related to everyone else!"

A

Abe (Aba) Yudel	son of Yankel Bunim
Adotshke	a crazy woman
Afroitshik	son of Yosl Moyshe the Cobbler
Ah(a)ron Velvel	eldest son of Yankel Bunim
Akhim (Okhim)	"the brothers," a gang in Kavkaz
Akiva (Ekiva) Eyger	a very famous Rabbi (1761-1838)
Aleksander	a gentile who kept the "fire house" in order
Alte	Nokhem Anshel's daughter
Alter Khales	a Krinker's nickname
Alter Mukhalop	had a daughter, Perl
Anshel Avreml the Blacksmith's	Meyshke's friend
Avrohem Shmuel of the Kugelekh	a teacher
Avrohem Shmuel	Abraham Shmuel Zuts, son of Moyshe Ah(a)ron the Katsev (Butcher)
Avrohem Yitskhok der Vilner	the leader of Krynki's anarchists, from Vilne (Vilnius)
Ayzik (Eyshik) "Zhuk" (Beetle)	son of Yisroel Toivye
Ayzikl	a visitor in the Kavkazer Bes-Medresh
Azhorer, Shmuel	a Krinker from Azhor
Azhiraner	a teacher

B

Barishe Family	a famous Bialystoker family, possibly Sime Feygl's maiden name
Baylke	daughter of the Ladies' Tailor
Bebelakh	a family nickname
Berl	the second man in the photo with two soldiers
Berl	son of Nokhem Anshel, factory owner
Berl Fishke's	eldest son of Fishke the Kalik'n, main "gabe"

Bertshekovitsh, Bertsokovitsh, Itke	a grocer; she distributed the mail
Bezdush/Bezdesh, Mordekhay and his wife Blumke	water carriers and beggars with beautiful daughters
Bitner, Dr.	a doctor in Shishlevitsh/Svisloch
Bobe Rive	Yosl's Grandma, married to Khayim-Osher Pruzhanski
Borekh Hersh	son of Khaye-Sore and Zundel Prilamer
Borekh Khokhem	one of the main gayboyem in the Kavkazer Bes-Medresh
Borekh Mair (Meyer)	son of Yosl Tsherebukh
Bovshover	Jewish author
Brash	Grodner governor
Breyne	younger daughter of Itshe Lya
Burnt ("Farbrenter")	(The Burnt), a nickname for the son of the carpenter

C

Cohen, Yosl, born Krinker	the author

D

Derushke (Doroshke), Fyodor	a later traitor and informer
Dinezon, Yakev	Yiddish author
Dodye, der Beker (the Baker)	Bobe Rive's son-in-law, from the So(y)fer family
Dovid	son of a bricklayer
Dovid Moreyn (Marein), aka "Todreses, Dovid"	a rich man
Dovid Reb Papa	"Bundist" agitator
Dovid Shloyme	a village tailor
Dovid the Damskn-Shnayder	Dovid the Ladies' Tailor; had a son, Yankel
Dratsh	a family nickname
Dubrover, Tsalke aka Tsalke with the goatee	a teacher
Dubrover, Shloyme	Dodye's friend, a joker
Dubrover, Shloyme	teacher Levenson's nickname
Dzhitkovski	gentile Polish doctor

E

Ebelakh	a family nickname
Edelshtat, Dovid	Yiddish poet
Eiger, Rabbi Ekiva (Akiva)	the preeminent Talmudic authority
Eliya the Mason	his daughter had studied obstetrics in Vilnius
Etel	Abe Yudel's wife

| Einshtein, Eynshteyn | a Hebrew teacher; his wife was Yosl's relative |
| Eyshik "Zhuk" (Beetle) | son of Yisroel Toivye |

F

Farbrenter (Burnt)	a nickname
Feygele	daughter of Yente Avremtshik
Feyve der Royfe	a healer
Feyvel "Schnants"	son of Perets
Fishke der Kaliker (the Cripple)	brother of Mair Yonah's wife Henye
Fishke, the Kalik'ns (the Kalik'n)	factory owner, son-in-law of Yankel Bunim's uncle
Flekhtl	a family nickname
Fridman, Nyomke	great hero of Krynki
Frumke	from the "Maravikher" family; Yosl's "girlfriend"

G

Gabeytshik's daughter	agitator in Krynki
Gamliel	founded a firefighting squad
Ganovim	"thieves," nickname of the Krinkers
Gapon	Georgy Appollonovitsh Gapon, Russian Orthodox preist
Garvi, P.	Social Democrat
Gendler, Avrohem Elye	a relative from Grodno
Gendler's family	relatives of the Tsherebukh family in Grodno
Gendler, Khaye (Chaia)	wife of Avrohem Elye Gendler, mother-in-law of the author Karlin
Gets, Fishl	a Bundist
Gimzhelakh	a family nickname
Grodski, Mordekhay Shimen	brother-in-law of Berl Fishke's
Goland	Goland's wine store
Goldberg, Dr., "Lupatsh"	Jewish doctor in Krynki
Goldfaden, Avrom	famous Jewish writer and composer
Grodner, Itshe	Krinker agitator
Grosmann, Hershl	factory owner in Krynki
Grusenberg, Oskar	a famous lawyer in St. Petersburg

H

Halpern, Yente and Osher	mentioned in the book's dedication
Halpern, Yosl Ayzik	Krinker agitator
Harkovitsher, Leyzer and his sister, Bashke the Blond	Bialystoker socialists
Henye	elder daughter of Yankel Bunim
Henye	Mair Yonah's wife
Henye Tabatshnik	mother of Roshke, wife of Shmuel Tabatshnik
Hershel Boyte	a boy of the Kavkaz "Zhabe Alley gang"
Hershel Pinke(s) the Shames's	agitator in Krynki
Hertske, Yisroel	factory owner, husband of Sheynke (Tabatshnik)
Hode	Roshe's sister

I/Y

Ilyodor, the Black Monk	aka Sergei M. Trufanov
Itke and Mashe	daughters of Pinke, son of the Shames
Itke-Kitke	a nickname
Itshe Lye (Lya)	son of Yosl the Yishevnik
Itshe Malekh-Hamoves	Itshe, the angel of death (nickname)
Itshe the Kaliker (the Cripple)	opened a barber shop
Itshke di Meydl	Itshke the Girl, a nickname
Itshke Kugelekh	a crazy man
Itshke Lavende	Yosl's name when smuggling across the border
Yakhe Feygl	wife of Khayim Shloyme
Yakev	a chimney sweep
Yakev Dineson	Yiddish author
Yampele	a nickname
Yankel the Blond	his son Dovid was involved in the attack on Nokhem Anshel
Yankel Bunim	Yosl's Grandpa (paternal side)
Yankel Motl	a healer
Yankel "Professor"	the author Yakev Krepliak
Yankel, son of Dovid the Ladies' Tailor	one of Yosl's friends
Yankel "Tsheyni" (Tshorny)	anarchist, agitator in Krynki
Yankel Yehuda	a blacksmith
Yanke Katyut	leader of the Kavkaz boys' gang of "Zhabe Alley;" his brother died of chickenpox; his father was a poor teacher.
Yente	daughter of Perets

Yente Avremtshik	mother of Feygele, a relative of Yosl
Yente Khayim- (Chaim)-Osher's	daughter of Khayim-Osher and Rive
Yente	a strong woman who owned many courtyards and two distilleries (see *Pinkas Krynki*), the namesake for Yente's Wood
Yente Kleyn-Kepele	Yente Little Head, a girl's nickname
Yiroel "der Grosse" (the Great)	son of Shoshke
Yisroel Hertske	Sheynke's husband
Yisroel-Iser the Shoykhet's	son of the kosher slaughterer
Yisroeltshke the Klezmer	father of Hershl "Boyte"
Yisroel-Toivye (Israel Tuvia)	son of Yosl Tsherebukh
Yisroel Khayim (Israel Chaim) Osher's	son of Khayim-Osher and Rive
Yisroel-Moyshe (Sofer)	son of Dodye and Dvoyre
Yoshke	son of Yisroel-Toivye
Yoshke Khatskel	a Krinker
Yosele	Reb Yosele, famous Rabbi in Krynki
Yosl Cohen	the author
Yosl	son of Itshe Lye/Lya
Yosl from the Parofke	Yosl's friend from the Mill-Street, called "big Yosl"
Yosl (the) Yishevnik	second son of Yudel, Yankel Bunim's grandfather
Yosl "Tsherebukh"	See under "Tsherebukh"
Yospe	daughter of Itshe Lye/Lya
Yudel	Yankel Bunim's grandfather, richest landowner in the whole Grodno County
Yudel (see Abe/Aba Yudel)	son of Yankel Bunim and Sime Feygl

K

Kadishevitsh	Yankel Bunim's original family name, the family came from Semyatitsh (Siemiatycze)
Kahan, Eyb aka David Bernshtein	famous writer, founder of the Yiddish newspaper *Der Forverts/The Forward*
Kalamnovitsh	Dodye's friend, a klezmer musician
Kanevski	a teacher
Katshandre	informant in Krynki
Khane (Chana)	daughter of Yisroel Toivye
Kapitses	a Kavkaz family
Katshkes	a family nickname
Khatskel	eldest son of Perets
Khatskel the She(y)nker	He ran a tavern in Krynki, where wedding celebrations took place
Khayim (Chaim) Gershon	eldest son of Yisroel Toivye
Khayim (Chaim) Hershl	son-in-law of Ayzik Krushenaner

Khayim (Chaim)-Leyzer	Yonah the Stolyer's (carpenter's) son
Khayim (Chaim)-Osher Pruzhanski	Yosl's grandfather; son of Yosl "Tsherebukh;" Rive's husband
Khayim (Chaim) Shloyme (later Heyman Cohen)	youngest son of Yankel Bunim
Kharif (Kharef), Reb Avromtshik/Avremtshik/ Abraham, the astute one	former Rabbi in Krynki
Khaye (Chaia)	wife of Perets
Khaye-Sore (Chaia-Sara)	eldest daughter of Yisroel Toivye
Khaye-Sore (Chaia-Sara)	daughter of Mair Yonah
Khaykel Muts (Chaikel)	anarchist and martyr, friend of Mair, Yankel Bunim's son
Kirbises, Dobe	sister of Zeydke Kirbises
Kirbises, Shloym(k)e	brother of Zeydke Kirbises
Kirbises, Zeydke	one of the "Zhabe Alley gang," Yosl's friend
Kishkel, Aleksander	a Christian, active in the "Bund"
Kohn/Cohen	Khayim Shloyme, who brought his whole family to America, was the first to change his name "Krinker" to Kohn/Cohen.
Kolner, Nokhem	factory owner
Kopl's, Eliya	a relative of Gamliel
Kopl Zalkin	son of Eliya Kopl, leather factory owner
Kotiel	a man who became psychically sick
Kreplyak, Kreplak, Yankel "Professor"	Yiddish author and political activist
Kreynes, Moyshe	leader of a music band, played the violin
Krinker	Yankel Bunim's family name after he moved to Krynki
Kronheym, Yudel	a relative in Horodok
Krupnik	teacher on a Russian school
Krushenaner, Ayzik	Khayim-Osher's nephew from Krushenan
Krushenaner, Rokhel	daughter of Ayzik Krushenaner, married Khayim Hershl
Kugelekh	a family nickname
Kugelekh, Avrohem Shmuel of the Kugelekh	a teacher

L

Lafonts with the Bells	a nickname
Lapinitser	the Lapinitser, he came from Lapinits
Lavski, Reb Borekh	former Rabbi in Krynki
Leyzer Drales	a Krinker's nickname
Leyzer Hersh	third son of Yankel Bunim; Yosl's father
Levenson	was also called Shloyme Dubrover, Russian teacher
Levin	grocer and librarian

Levin, Yente and Yankel	mentioned in the book's dedication
Levitan, Reb Avrohem Yakev	the old Krinker Maggid, follower of the Dubner Maggid
Lipe	Yankel Yehuda's son
"Lupatsh," Dr. Goldberg	Jewish doctor in Krynki

M

Machno, Nestor	Ukrainian anarchist
Makarov	vice-admiral Stepan Osipovich Makarov
Malatesta, Errico	Italian anarchist
Malke	daughter of Bobe Rive and Khayim-Osher
Malke from Krynki and her husband Yanek	she converted to Christianity; he was a Jew-hater
Mair (Meier)	from the Pruzhanski famliy, brother of Yosl Cohen
Mair (Meier)	son of Yankel Bunim; Yosl's uncle
Mair (Meier) Yonah	Yosl's great grandfather, third son of Yudel
Mair (Meier) Tsitsun	a crazy man
Mair (Meier)	son of Berl Fishke's
Maravikh(er)	a family name in connection with Kavkaz
Maril	a Polish Christian with two daughters
Mashe Khayim (Chaim) Osher's	daughter of Khayim-Osher and Rive and Yosl's mother
Mastavlyanski	The changed surname of Yosl Yishevnik
Matshes, Leybe	teacher, a Kotsker Hasid
Mayrem	a crazy man
Mayrem (Meyrem) Tsinges	an informant
Mayte	a crazy woman with a doll
Mazel	shames in the Kavkazer synagogue
Menakhem, Motl Arye's	socialist in Krynki
Mere	daughter of Yisroel Toivye
Meri	daughter of Yosl the Yishevnik
Meyshke (Moyshke)	son of Khayim-Osher and Rive; brother of Mashe
Meri	from the Tsherebukh family
Merke	a teacher, daughter of Moyshe Pinkes
Mezhi	daughter of Sheynke
Milb (Mite)	a family nickname
Milb(n), Alter	Apartment renters in Kavkaz
Miryam Reyzl	Jewish midwife, daughter of Moyshe the Khazn
Mirtshe	Aharon Velvel's girlfriend and wife
Motl Arye's, Menakhem	one of the first socialists in Krynki
Motl der Royfe	a healer
Motke (Motki)	a mad man
Mordekhay Shimen	brother-in-law of Berl Fishke's

Motsh-Potsh	family nickname
Moyshe Aharon the Katsev (Butcher)	father of Avrohem Shmuel Zuts
Moyshe Berl	son of Yankel Bunim
Moyshe Pinkes	had a daughter, Merke
Moyshe Yosl	son of Perets
Moyshe the Khazn	cantor in Krynki
Moyshke the Shenker (the Innkeeper)	Bobe Rive's father
Moyshe Velvel	son of Yisroel Toivye
Moyshe Zev Margolies	very famous Bialystoker Rabbi, R' Velvele, the "Mar'ot haTzov-ot"
Muts, Khaykel	anarchist and martyr
Mukhalap	a nickname

N

Nikolai I (Nikolaj, Nikolaus, Nikolas)	Tsar of Russia, King of Poland, Grand Duke of Finland
Nisl	Hode's husband
Nogi	General Nogi Maruseke
Noskes, Leybke aka Louis Sheyn	was involved in the attack on Nokhem Anshel, became an important member of the Krinker "Branch 389" in America
Nyomke	boyfriend of Mirtshe
Nyomke, Yonah the Stolyer's	brother of Sore'ke, son of Yonah the carpenter
Nyomke, Hershl the Kretsikn's, Nyomke Fridman	a great hero of Krynki

O

Orland, Khaykel, "the Pig"	husband of Meri

P

Paltyel	owned a leather factory
Palyuk der Stumme (The Mute)	helped in Dodye's bacery
Partse, Avrohem	Krinker agitator
Perets (der Toker, the Turner)	first son of Bobe Rive
Perl	Yosl's only sister
Perl	Alter Mukhalop's daughter
Peshe	Gendler's eldest daughter, wife of author A. Karlin
Pet, Khayim (Chaim)	Yiddish author
Peye	wife of Rabbi Shmuel Tentser

Peyshke der Sherer	a healer
Pines	famous ophthalmologist in Bialystok
Pinke the Shames	the caller to synagogue (Possibly a punctuation mark is missing and this is the son of the Shames.)
Pinke the Shames's son	his two daughters were Itke and Mashe
Pinski, Dovid	author of agitation booklets
Pontes, Yosl	a locksmith, one of the the Tsherebukh family
Poyzner, Rabbi Shloyme Zalmen	famous Rabbi in Warsaw
Prilamer, Zundel	son-in-law of Mair Yonah
Pruzhanski, Meyshke	youngest son of Khayim-Osher and Rive
Pruzhanski, Khaye Sore (Chaia Sara)	mentioned in the book's dedication
Pruzhanski, Fanye and Sheynke	mentioned in the book's dedication
Pruzhanski, Khayim (Chaim)	mentioned in the book's dedication
Pruzhanski, Fayv(e)l	mentioned in the book's dedication
Pruzhanski, Khane (Chana)	mentioned in the book's dedication
Pumpkin (Kirbes)	family nickname
Pushkin, Alexander	famous Russian author
Pyaves, Avrohem Mair (Meier)	a healer

R

Roshke, Rashke, Rokhe	daughter of Yisroel Toivye
Rashbam	the maiden name of Gendler's wife who descended from the famous Rabbi "Rashbam"
Reyne Gitl	youngest daughter of the famous Rabbi R' Moyshe Zev Margolies (Reb Velvele). Great-grandmother (paternal) of Yosl Cohen, the author.
Reyzen, Avrom	Yiddish author
Roshke	Nokhem-Anshel Kinishinski's wife, niece of Khayim-Osher
Rozenfeld	Yiddish author

S, Sch, Sh

Sasha and Helena	children of Aharon Velvel Krinker and Mirtshe
Semyon	a gentile boy
Sender	Rive's son-in-law
Sender, Rabbi Zalmen	Krinker Rabbi who loved the poor ones
Sforim, Mendele Moykher	famous Yiddish author

Shakhnes, Itshe and his wife	Itshe rented an apartment to Yosl's family. Yosl called the couple "Grandpa" and "Grandma." Itshe's son was a famous carver.
Shamshonovitsh	son-in-law of Nokhem Anshel, owner of a leather factory
Shamush	a family nickname
Shapiro	famous Rabbi in Krynki
Shaye Leyb the Kalike (Cripple)	a teacher
Sheyne	wife of Yosl Tshernebukh
Sheyne-Blume	daughter of Malke, Rive's eldest daughter
Sheynke (Tabatshnik)	daughter of Yisroel Toivye, sister-in-law of Nokhem Anshel
Shimen	son of Perets
Shimen a "Zhonki" (a "woman")	a crazy man
Shimen Ber der Royfe	a healer
Shimen der Meshuggene	a nickname
Slabets	a family nickname
Shloymeke	partner of Berl Fishke's, son of Alter dem Khoyker's
Shmulik	son of Perets, grandson of Khayim-Osher and Rive
Shmulikl	Rabbi Shmuel Weinberg of Slonim
Shmuel "Amerikaner"	factory owner in Krynki
Shmuel Avreml from Alinke	a teacher
Shmuel-Khonen	a hot-headed Hasid, prayed together with Khayim-Osher
Sholem	son of Avrohem Moyshe the Shpigelfaltser
Sholem-Aleykhem	very famous Yiddish author
Sholem (Simkhe's)	son of Simkhe the Feldsher
Shoshke	daughter of Yosl Tsherebukh
Shpigelfaltser (Mirror-Folder), Avrohem Moyshe	had a son, Sholem
Sime Feygl	wife of Yankel Bunim; Yosl's grandmother (paternal side); daughter of the famous Barishe family; grand-daughter of Rabbi R' Moyshe Zev Margolies (Reb Velvele)
Simkhe	a feldsher (medic)
Simkhe	son of Rokhel Matshke (Motshke), nephew of Yankel Bunim
Skreytshik	a family nickname
Sofer/Soyfer/Soifer, Dvoyre (Deborah)	daughter of Khayim-Osher and Rive
Sofer/Soyfer/Soifer, Yisroel (Israel) Moyshe	son of Dodye and Dvoyre

Sore	youngest daughter of Yankel Bunim
Sore'ke, Yone dem Stolyer's	daughter of Yone (Yonah) the Carpenter/ Joiner
Spadviler, Motl	lived in Kavkaz; he rented an apartment to Yosl's family
Stößel/Stoessel	General Anatoly Mikhaylovich Stoessel
Stolarski, Yisroel	Poyale Tsien Zionist activist
Sidrer, Dovid	the real name of Shloyme Dubrover
Sidrer, Meyshke	an anarchist
Stavski, Rabbi Borekh	Krinker Rabbi, possibly a spelling mistake (Rabbi Lavski?)
Stefanovtshekhe	Polish woman obstetrician

T

Tabatshnik, Sheynke	daughter of Yisroel Toivye, sister-in-law of Nokhem Anshel, sister of his wife Roshe
Tabatshnik, Shmuel	tobacconist, father of Roshke, Nokhem Anshel's wife
Tkatsh	a teacher's nickname
Tanye	Nokhem Anshel's granddaughter
Tentser, Rabbi Shmuel	first kheyder (cheder) teacher of Yosl
Teplov	socialist revolutionary
Tevl Vatshul	a beggar
The Little One	nickname of an uradnik (police prefect)
Todreses, Dovid aka Dovid Mareyn (Moreyn)	a rich man
Tsalel, Yankel	a baker and innocent victim
Tsales, Yankel	Bialystoker socialist
Tseroshke	daughter of Berl, the second man on the photograph with two soldiers
Tsharni (Charny), Daniel	brother of "Vladek," a poet
Tshaykovski, Nikolay	Russian revolutionary
Tsherebukh, Yosl	Wealthy merchant who had the "dub" (bark) trade in Krynki and surround-ing area. Yosl built the Kavkazer Bes-Hamedresh and was the father of Khayim-Osher. It is likely that his last name was Pruzhanski; his later name Tsherebukh is dertived from his place of origin.
Tshekhonovtser	a teacher
Tsholne(s), Motl	father of Aunty Sore's boyfriend, Yosl's father rented a basement room there

V/W

Velvel	third brother of Yosl Cohen
Vigder	factory owner, son of Rabbi Lavski
Virnyen, Virion, Viryon, and others	Jan de Virion, the namesake for Virion's Pond, land baron, Polish aristocrat
Volozhiner, Khayim (Chaim)	Chaim of Volozhin, very famous Rabbi (1749-1821)

Z

Zamkow	famous doctor in Grodno
Zeliks, Ayzik-Benyamin	a "good Jew"
Zeydke the Locksmith	a strong Jew in Krynki
Zundl	a boy from the Mill Street, son of a leather factory owner
Zuts, Avrohem (Abraham) Shmuel	famous blind Bundist, "The Eternal Light"

Picture Gallery

1.

2.

3.

4.

5.

6.

7.

8.

9.

1. *Aba Yudel Krinker, c.1900, possibly at his wedding.* Courtesy of Emily Kern.

2. *Aba Yudel Krinker and his family, c.1915.* Courtesy of Susan Pasquariella.

3. *Aba Yudel Krinker and his family, c.1907.* Courtesy of Susan Pasquariella.

4. *Mirtshe Shakhnes, first wife of Aharon Velvel Krinker.* Courtesy of Dr. Fran Krieger-Lowitz.

5. *Sime Feygl Krinker, 1933.* Courtesy of Dr. Fran Krieger-Lowitz.

6. *Helena, daughter of Aharon Velvel Krinker, and family, c.1937.* Courtesy of Liz Ozol.

7. *Yosl's parents, Leyzer Hersh Cohen and Mashe Cohen, before 1929.* Courtesy of Barbara LaBelle.

8. *Velvel, Yosl (seated), Reuven, and Mair Cohen, c.1931.* Courtesy of Barbara LaBelle.

9. *Cohen family, c.1931.* From left, Maxie, Paul, Yosl (seated), Velvel, Mashe, Mair, Leyzer Hersh, Reuven, Ida (Yosl's first wife), Benny, Perl, and Davie. Maxie, Benny and Davie are Yosl and Ida's sons. Paul, Yosl, Velvel, Mair, Reuven and Perl are Leyzer Hersh and Mashe's children. Courtesy of Barbara LaBelle.

10. *19th-century Kiddush cups that belonged to Yankel Bunim Krinker's son Aba Yudel.* Courtesy of Susan Pasquariella.

11. *Yosl Cohen, c.1975, Hallandale, Florida.* Courtesy of Barbara LaBelle.

12. *Leyzer Hersh and Mashe Cohen, probably in Newark, New Jersey, c.1940.* Courtesy of Barbara LaBelle.

13. *Headstone of Yosl Cohen, Clifton, New Jersey.* In Yiddish: "Yosef, Son of Leyzer Hersh." Courtesy of Susan Pasquariella.

Family Trees

Yosl Cohen Family Tree (Pruzhanski/Tsherebukh Side, maternal)

According to *Vi Nekhtn Geshen* with selective additions ▲
(Not in original book)

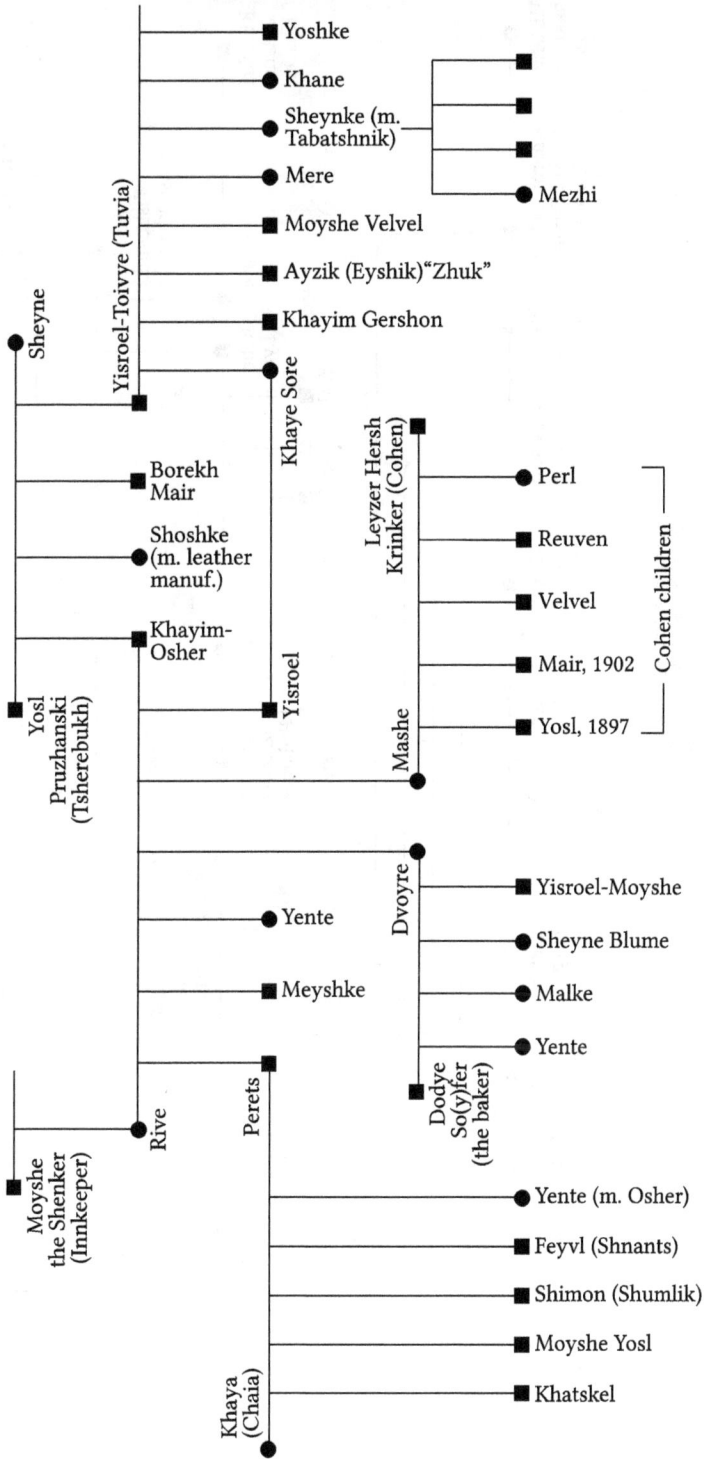

Yoshke

Khane

Sheynke (m. Tabatshnik)

Mere

Mezhi

Moyshe Velvel

Ayzik (Eyshik) "Zhuk"

Khayim Gershon

Yisroel-Toivye (Tuvia)

Khaye Sore

Sheyne

Borekh Mair

Shoshke (m. leather manuf.)

Khayim-Osher

Yisroel

Leyzer Hersh Krinker (Cohen)

Perl

Reuven

Velvel

Mair, 1902

Yosl, 1897

Cohen children

Mashe

Yosl Pruzhanski (Tsherebukh)

Dvoyre

Yisroel-Moyshe

Sheyne Blume

Malke

Yente

Yente

Meyshke

Dodye So(y)fer (the baker)

Rive

Perets

Moyshe the Shenker (Innkeeper)

Yente (m. Osher)

Feyvl (Shnants)

Shimon (Shumlik)

Moyshe Yosl

Khatskel

Khaya (Chaia)

Yosl Cohen Family Tree (Krinker Side, paternal)

According to *Vi Nekhtn Geshen* with selective additions

(Not in original book)

▲

Yudel Kadishevitsh

Rabbi Eliezer of Hlusk
(desc. from Judah Loew Ben Bezalel,
the Maharal of Prague)

Rabbi Moshe Zev Velvele Margolies
of Bialystok (the Mar'ot haTzov-ot)

Khaykel Orland ("Khazer")

Yosl (the Yishevnik) Mastavlyanski

(12 children)

Meri

Itshe (Lya)

Mair Yonah Kadishevitsh

Yosl   Yospe   Breyne

Khaye Sore

Avrohen Zundel Prilamer

Borekh Hersh

Henye

Rabbi from Volpe

Reyne Gitl

Yaakov (Yankel Bunim) (Kadishevitsh) Krinker, 1850

Sime Feygl Barishe, 1857

Mirtshe Shakhnes 1879

Aharon Velvel Yankel Bunim Krinker 1873

Etel Rotbart 1877

Aba Yudel Krinker 1877

Moyshe Beri Cohen 1881

Leyzer Hersh Cohen 1882

Mashe Khayim-Osher's 1882

Yakhe Feygl

Khaim Shlomye Cohen 1883

Mair Krinker 1886

Henye Krinker 1891

Sore (Sarah) Krinker c.1893

(2 children, Sasha and Helena)

(4 children)

Yosl Cohen and his siblings
(see preceding page)

(Translation from the original pages continues)

A second part of Yosl Cohen's autobiography is in progress.

Those who wish to facilitate the publication of this important and interesting work may send their contribution or subscription to:

Yosl Cohen
2950 Ocean Avenue
Brooklyn 35, N.Y.

*

Books by Yosl Cohen:
Shtot (poems), New York, 1926
Fun Yener Zayt Yam, (poems), Moskow, 1931
Krume Vegn (poems), New York, 1936
Der Morgn iz Eybik (poems and poetry), New York, 1948

Ready for printing:
The second part of the autobiographical work.
A volume of poems and poetry

**Many thanks to the group of Trade Union Leaders
who made the publication of this book possible:**

Charles Kreindler, Abraham Miller, Abraham Shneider, Misha Falikman, Louis Heimen, Izidor Sarkin, Jack Spitzer, Martin L. Kahn, Louis Riss, Daniel Nisnevitch, Louis Dvarkin, Chaim Beker, Rabbi Chaim Yehuda Horovitz, Herold Lipel, Yosef Belski, Gadalia Lederman, Philip Boris, Izidor Lef, Benny Levin, William Wolfert, Morris Horn, N. Chanin, Benjamin Gebiner, Morris Goldowski, Mike Kuperman, Morri(s) Kalker, Louis Langer, A. Mendelson, Max Gaft, Paphavitz, Moshe Blumenreich, Joe Gold, H. Burakof, Neiten Erlich, Harris Horovitz, Harris Rubinski, Sam Zeldin, Ruven Tzukerman, Sam Burger, Abraham Hershkovitch, Saul Zaler, Jack Wiezelberg.

The Jews (sic):
Benny Troy, Louis Goldspiner, Benjamin Shiller, Eizik (Isaak) Hemlin, Israel Stolarski, Mr. and Mrs.Yosef Sachs, Louis Shein (Leybke Noskes), I. Fogel, Harry Morgenshtern

Afterword

As it happened yesterday...
A Relative's Reflections on Finding Family

My search for family began as a curiosity several years ago, and ultimately turned into an obsession and a mitsve. I was ill-equipped for the genealogical journey. I knew almost nothing about my family, Eastern European history or Jewish culture, and I knew no Yiddish other than those phrases that are part of New York City patois. But I was lucky. I found a relative, Yosl Cohen, who had been a Yiddish writer and poet and who, among his final works, published a memoir *(Vi Nekhtn Geshen/ As It Happened Yesterday)* and a book of poems *(A Funk in Tunkl/ A Spark in the Dark)* that are memorial tributes to his family and their shtetl, Krynki. Together these works have provided a much-needed guide.

This English translation of *Vi Nekhtn Geshen* has been lovingly done by Beate Schützmann-Krebs. It is hoped that the translation will demystify family history for my relatives and enable a wider audience to read Yosl's remarkable narrative and the contextual and contemporary historical material Beate has translated and added.

My special thanks go to those who have helped me along on my journey: to Bernie and Nick for their patience, and to George Kaye, Emily Kern, Michael Ozol, Fran Krieger-Lowitz, Debbie Kaye Roberts, Barbara Labelle, Eugene Kern, Jerome Kern, Meyer Kern, John Anton, Sam Krieger and Cecylia Bach-Szczawińska, for sharing their recollections; to Leo Greenbaum for his perseverance, and to Odeda Zlotnik and others on JewishGen Viewmate for their translations. My deepest gratitude goes to Joanna Czaban and Tomek Wisniewski for providing photographs of Krynki, and to Tomek also for providing historical background, photographs, postcards and even films.

Finally, I will be forever grateful to Beate for this translation—this precious gift. She has gone beyond the role of a translator and has provided historical context in the form of concurrent newspaper accounts and relevant scholarly articles. All the while, Beate patiently answered my questions and helped me to understand what I was reading. Thank you, my friend.

With everlasting love to Velvel and Minna.
Yosl, I see everything more clearly now... as it happened yesterday.

Susan Kingsley Pasquariella

For Yiddish Readers:
These Yosl Cohen books can be read online:

Shtot (City), Poems, ©1926 by Yosl Cohen.
https://archive.org/details/nybc209697

Krume Vegn (Twisted Roads), Poems, ©1936 by Yosl Cohen.
https://www.yiddishbookcenter.org/collections/yiddish-books/
spb-nybc209696/cohen-yosl-krume-vegn

Der Morgn iz Eybik (The Morrow is Eternal), Poems and Poetry,
©1948 by Yosl Cohen.
https://www.yiddishbookcenter.org/collections/yiddish-books/
spb-nybc209688/cohen-yosl-der-morgn-iz-eybik

Note: Web addresses may change over time.